900 Miles on the Butterfield Trail

A. C. GREENE

900 Miles on the Butterfield Trail

A. C. GREENE

University of North Texas Press

Denton, Texas

10 9 8 7 6 5 4 3 2

Requests for permission to reproduce material from this
work should be sent to
Permissions
University of North Texas Press
Post Office Box 13856
Denton, Texas 76203–3856

The paper used in this book meets the minimum requirements of the American National Standard for Permanence of Paper for Printed Library materials, Z39.48.1984. Binding materials have been chosen for durability.

Library of Congress Cataloging-in-Publication Data

Green, A.C., 1923-
900 miles on the Butterfield Trail / by A.C. Greene
    p.   cm.
Includes bibliographical references (p.) and index.
ISBN 0-929398-73-4
1. Butterfield Overland Trail. 2. Coaching–West (U.S.) –
History. 3. Overland journeys to the Pacific. 4. West (U.S.) –
Description and Travel. I. Title
F593.G8145 1994
917.804'2–dc20
                                                        94-20107
                                                           CIP

DESIGN BY W. THOMAS TAYLOR

ILLUSTRATIONS BY TERESA AVINI

The maps are from Roscoe and Margaret B. Conkling,
The Butterfield Overland Mail 1857-1869. 3 Volumes, 1947,
The Arthur H. Clark Co., Glendale, California,
and are used by permission.

Publication of this book was made possible in part by
support from the Summerlee Foundation.

Dedicatory

For Bob Green – Brother, not of flesh but of spirit.

Table of Contents

Acknowledgments

There are several persons who were most helpful in adding information for this book or were generous in spending time and effort on behalf of my wife and me. Lloyd A. Siewers, of Minnesota, President of the Butterfield Overland Mail Society, provided new material which was put to good use. Paul R. Thompson, Ranger-in-Charge of the Fort Bowie National Historic Site (Apache Pass), furnished insights that greatly enhanced our appreciation of that lovely, remote place, and Ranger Richard McCamant, of Guadalupe National Park, where the Butterfield Pinery station was located, first told me of the BOM Society. In addition to Jackie and John Means, whose hospitality is detailed in the story, we also thank Jim Morrow, manager of the Fort Chadbourne Ranch, and Cliff Teinert, manager of the Reynolds Long X Ranch. Cliff not only put up Jerrie and Fred Smith, Nancy and Bob Green and Judy and me for the night, he entertained us with voice and guitar. Don Koch, manager of the Kent Mercantile Co. that lonely (and welcome) oasis far out on Interstate 10, showed us the wagon and coach rebuilding project he and Cliff Teinert are undertaking there. Betty and Charlie Dean, at the Double V Ranch in New Mexico, made our modern Butterfield travelers welcome, fed us heartily and bedded us down beautifully. And Joe Peacock, of Bronte, steered Don Franks's report on "Head of Concho" my way. Our thanks to each and every one.

A New Look

Although much has been written about the Butterfield Overland Mail service, there are five eyewitness accounts on which a good part of the sum total has been based. The first, to which every subsequent western historian is indebted, is the account by Waterman Lily Ormsby, Jr.,[1] of his adventures as the only through passenger on the first Southern Overland Mail trip westward from Missouri to San Francisco in 1858. Butterfield was paying the fare for twenty-three-year-old Ormsby, a reporter for the New York *Herald*. His stories ran in that newspaper as he wrote them on the move and mailed them back east. He was not only a good writer—few reporters of any age have bettered his clear, humorous, style—but also a fine observer.[2] His eyewitness account of the journey and the country he traveled holds up almost point by point nearly 140 years later. As for accuracy and interpretation, the years have proved him also to be a good historian. Writing at a time when national tempers were on edge, when sectionalism was racing toward its disastrous Civil War climax, he is impartial and appreciative of human individuality—guilty of neither editorializing nor factionalism. In addition to his other virtues, he uses a modern tone, his prose free from the orotund verbiage and mawkishness of so much of that period's writing. His Butterfield Trail reports have been reprinted twice, but the best version of *The Butterfield Overland Mail* was edited by Lyle H. Wright and Josephine M. Bynum and published by the Huntington Library in 1955.

A second volume involving Ormsby's work, plus three more accounts written by Butterfield travelers, is Walter B. Lang's 1940 publication, *The First Overland Mail: Butterfield Trail*. Mr. Lang includes the reports of an early (October–November 1858) eastbound trip by

I

J. M. Farwell, of the *Daily Alta California* newspaper of San Francisco; the shorter, less detailed official report of Mr. G. (Goddard) Bailey, a special agent of the Post Office Department,[3] after an inspection of both the steamship mail service (via Isthmus of Panama) and overland mail service in October 1858; and the 1860 record of a trip by the Reverend William Tallack, returning from Australia to England eastward across the United States, by way of the Butterfield stage.

In September of 1859 another eastern newspaper correspondent, Albert D. Richardson, made the east-west Butterfield passage and wrote a reliable account of it in a book titled *Beyond the Mississippi*, which was published in 1867.

However, the work that stands out most magnificently in the study of the Butterfield Overland Mail is the three volume set by Roscoe P. and Margaret B. Conkling, titled with typical Conklingian simplicity, *The Butterfield Overland Mail 1857–1869; Its organization and operation over the Southern Route to 1861; subsequently over the Central Route to 1866; and under Wells, Fargo and Company in 1869.* Published in 1947, after twenty years of the Conklings' travels and investigations, its thoroughness (the husband and wife lived in El Paso, Texas, to be as near the center of the old route as possible) and the waving of time's eroding hand over the trail forfend the possibility of there ever being anything to match it. Attacking every recognized facet of interest in the Butterfield stage line, it gives a detailed biography of John Butterfield, briefer biographies of the officers of the company, a mile-by-mile study of the location and history of every station along the route—not just in Texas but from Missouri through California to San Francisco, and even dimensions of the various coaches and wagons used, as well as a condensed history of the coach makers.

Volume I takes you from Tipton, Missouri—where the Butterfield stagecoach started its westward run—to Franklin (now El Paso), Texas. Volume II carries the traveler over the second (1859) Davis Mountain route to El Paso, on to San Francisco, and Volume III includes maps, illustrations, and layouts of many stations. There are errors here and there, but niggly ones, most of which should have been caught by a proofreader—for example, Denison, Texas is misspelled *Dennison*; and there are a few details of Texas history that are not correct, but you can't come up with very many questions about the Butterfield operation for which the Conklings don't supply an answer.

Some ask, then, why write another book on the Butterfield Trail? Can anything new be said about the old Butterfield Overland Mail route? The question has been asked before. J. W. Williams began his 1957 *Southwestern Historical Quarterly* article, "The Butterfield Overland Mail Road Across Texas," with it. Williams felt justified in returning to the topic because he researched the location of the road itself by use of land records and surveyors' field notes which show, in most areas, specifically where the old roads, built by Butterfield engineers or used by the mail coaches, were encountered. The article is useful if you are attempting to place a monument along the old trail, but I find it frustrating: you can't find or get to three-fourths of the locations for which Williams gives surveyors' notes because they are on private lands or have been made inaccessible by nature or modern engineering.

But I am offering "another Butterfield book" because interesting historical points on the Texas route have come to light which were not noted in previous accounts. And while the Conklings were thorough, they made their various journeys and visits more than fifty years ago—sixty years in many instances—and the countryside has changed greatly, not just its geography, but the very feel of some regions. That is why my wife and I decided to drive, walk, or clamber over as many miles of the old road as possible, starting at the north bank of the Red River and going on to Arizona. We wanted to repeat, if possible, some of the quotidian jolts, jars, hungers, and thirsts (don't take that too literally) which those nineteenth-century passengers endured.

The landscape of history and (I admit) its sentimentality, arouse strong emotions in my heart when I visit the places or drive the old pathways, even those buried under cactus, concrete and asphalt. I

3

want to try and pass along some of those passions—history, to me, being the story of human intentions, decisions, feelings, dreams and emotions. What good does it do for us to know that the Butterfield Overland Mail traveled 732 miles across Texas if we know nothing about those miles: the countryside they traversed—the grass, the trees, the wildlife, the rocks and hills they skirted, the rivers they forded—not to mention the people who lived and drove and rode along them? Those things are, to me, history. Anything else is geometry.

An old frontiersman said to me when I was a boy, "You just should have been here," as though the emotion of the event were as important as the site or the event itself, for we were standing (at that moment) precisely where *his* history had taken place. There was a sense of loss, of finality in the face of inevitable change—change that was both brightly anticipated and sadly feared. I think it rather amazing how appreciative of their role were the old writers and pioneers during the late nineteenth century. They felt history. They knew their generation was experiencing an era that was soon to be lost and gone forever; they were anticipating the end of something that had motivated American life for three hundred years. It was not an "*apres moi le deluge*" attitude, it was one of awe and wonder that they had been so privileged; "history that will never be repeated," one writer titled his memoirs.[4] The so-called modern world was just over the horizon, its legions of change arriving on the steamboat and the locomotive, heralding its supremacy along the telegraph wires and in the headlines of the new daily newspapers. Suddenly there was so much to know, to understand, to foresee, and to accept.

But the heralded changes were not all mechanical. Even greater social and cultural changes were moving toward an inevitability that climaxed but didn't culminate in a Civil War. The phrase "out of date," once used most often for fashions in clothing, now encroached on the daily thinking of the nation. Things and concepts concrete for millenia were now open to question, if not radical revision.

Butterfield passenger Albert D. Richardson, in the epigraph to

4

his book, more than sensed this; he saw the prediction in a little-recognized quotation from Whittier:

Behind the squaw's light birch canoe,
The steamer rocks and raves;
And city lots are staked for sale
Above old Indian graves.

But even more significant is his prefatory comment:

I have sought to picture a fleeting phase of our national life; not omitting its grotesque, lawless features; not concealing my admiration for the adventurous pioneers who have founded great States from the Mississippi to the Pacific, and made a new geography for the American Union. . . . We seem on the destiny of a destiny higher and better than any nation has yet fulfilled. And the great West is to rule us.[5]

Notes

1. Born in New York City on December 8, 1834, Waterman Ormsby, Jr., was the son of a renowned engraver who was one of the founders of the Continental Banknote Company. When he made his famous overland journey, he was married and the father of nine-month-old Waterman Ormsby III.
2. For example: "The men [Pima Indians] are lazy and take good care to make the women do all the work. We saw numbers of sovereign lords walking along or riding, and making their squaws carry the loads—a spectacle which would give one of our women's rights women fits instanter." Waterman Lily Ormsby, Jr., *The Butterfield Overland Mail*, ed. Lyle H. Wright and Josephine M. Bynum (San Marino: Huntington Library, 1955), 98.
3. See "An Inspector's Report," p. 217.
4. Don Hampton Biggers, *History That Will Never Be Repeated* (Ennis, TX: Hi-Grade Printing Office, 1902).
5. Albert Deane Richardson, preface to *Beyond the Mississippi: From the Great River to the Great Ocean* . . . (New York: Bliss, 1867).

PART ONE

John Butterfield's "gamble worth making" Begins – from St. Louis to the Red River

Remember, boys, nothing on God's earth must stop the
United States mail!
  —John Butterfield's instruction to his drivers

S HORT as the life of John Butterfield's Southern Overland Mail
turned out to be (less than three years in its span), the saga
of the Butterfield Trail remains a romantic high point in the
westward movement, forming familiar elements in historical plots,
functioning as a vibrant backdrop against which mythic adventures,
western thrillers, movie serials, and television spectacles have raced:
the driver standing, lashing the teams furiously, the guard leaning
back across the top of the stage, firing at the pursuing Indians, one
or two gentlemanly pistols thrust out the coach's windows, terrified
women passengers, a lead horse shot and stumbling.

We want the myth and legend to be stronger than life. We want
John Wayne always to be aboard the stagecoach, telling the women
to stay calm; we want some hero to edge his way out among the frantic horses pulling the coach, cutting loose the injured animal, or
grabbing the "ribbons" when the driver is hit. As a matter of history,
a Butterfield stagecoach was attacked only once on the Southern
Overland Mail route. That was in Arizona, and no one on the coach
was killed.[1]

Today, more than a century and a third after the first Butterfield
coaches rolled, even with the decades of fictional enhancement, we
are hard put to imagine how awesome, how fearful the actual passage was. Two thousand miles of this southern route were across
country virtually unknown to the average American citizen, and what
was known was frightening. And as for the journey itself, there was
nothing leisurely or romantic about it. The overland traveler could,
at best, anticipate periods of thirst and hunger while accepting the
trials and discomforts that came with even the finest horse-drawn
transportation devices in use. At worst, he must travel under the

ominous possibility of death from many causes—Indian attacks being only one of them—or suffer excessively from the unpredictable natural elements, which might include blistering heat and a freezing norther during the same trip across Texas. This awesome prospect was so often the case that many of those travelers felt compelled to write about their fearsome passage after making it safely through.

A San Diego newspaper of the 1850s, addressing riders of the San Antonio-San Diego line (whose route for hundreds of miles was the same as the Butterfield's), recommended special equipment, revealing how chancy a trip by stage was viewed:

> One Sharp's [sic] rifle and a hundred cartridges; a Colts navy revolver and two pounds of balls; a knife and sheath; a pair of thick boots and woolen pants; half a dozen pairs of thick woolen socks; six undershirts; three woolen overshirts; a wide-awake hat[2]; a cheap sack coat; a soldier's overcoat; one pair of blankets in summer and two in winter; a piece of India rubber cloth for blankets; a pair of gauntlets, a small bag of needles, pins, a sponge, hair brush, comb, soap, etc., in an oil silk bag; two pairs of thick drawers, and three or four towels.[3]

Despite the dangers and discomforts of all western routes, the strident voice of the emergent Pacific Coast was raising an affluent cry for mail, news, and faster passenger service from the East. Half a million people in the State of California, the Oregon Territory, and the gold camps of Nevada demanded closer ties with "home." The original route to California around the southern tip of Cape Horn, 15,348 miles from New York to San Francisco, was time-consuming and extremely hazardous. Even after William Henry Aspinwall had completed the Panama Railroad across the Panamanian Isthmus in 1855—making this the fastest route to the gold fields—the trip remained dangerous and costly.

But more and more often, more and more of the world wanted through to the Golden West—and quicker and quicker. In answer to this demand for speed, mail, and news, a much debated overland mail bill was finally passed on March 3, 1857, mainly through the efforts of Senator Thomas J. Rusk of Texas, Senator W. M. Gwin of California, and Congressman John S. Phelps of Missouri—each of whom represented a state with potential to benefit from the bill.[4]

On April 20, 1857, the United States Post Office Department advertised for bids on a mail route across the deadly wastes of the "Great American Desert," as most of the Southwest was termed. It called for a contract "for the conveyance of the entire letter mail from such point on the Mississippi River as the contractors may select, to San Francisco . . . for six years at a cost not exceeding . . . $600,000 per annum for semi-weekly (service)."[5]

The contract required the service be performed "with good four-horse coaches or spring wagons, suitable for conveyance of passengers, as well as the safety and security of the mails." The contract winner had the right to pre-empt 320 acres "of any land not then disposed of or reserved, at each point necessary for a station, not to be nearer than ten miles from each other." Service was to be "performed within twenty-five days for each trip."[6]

Thus, the proposal for overland mail service was all business, with no hint of the adventure, the difficulty, and romance (as we see it) to be found in operating "the longest stagecoach ride in the world." But politics, as usual, entered the picture very shortly. Nine bids were submitted for "the Great Overland Mail Contract" (as some newspapers dramatically called it) and were opened "amidst great excitement" in June, 1857. Three of the bids were for semi-weekly mail service from St. Louis to San Francisco along the 35th Parallel by way of Oklahoma, the Texas Panhandle, and Albuquerque, New Mexico. These bids were submitted by John Butterfield and associates.[7]

The first of the three Butterfield bids for the 35th Parallel route was for $585,000 per year; a second bid, for a line starting at Memphis, Tennessee instead of St. Louis and going to San Francisco was for $595,000; and a third bid, for what Butterfield himself called "The

Bifurcated Route," was for a line which would start west simultaneously from St. Louis *and* Memphis, converge at a point "to be determined later," and then follow the 35th Parallel to the West Coast. Butterfield added to the bids that he and his group would be willing to alter "any portion of the route which the Postmaster General might decide best." That short phrase changed Texas history, for without it there would have been no Butterfield Trail across Texas.[8]

John Butterfield, President of the Overland Mail Company, was the greatest stager and freighter in American history. But he had seen the railroads gradually take over the eastern passenger business and the movement of mail; thus, in 1850, along with Wells & Company and Livingston & Fargo, he had formed the American Express Company, which was tied to railroads. By 1857 when the Overland Mail contract with the Post Office Department was signed, he had made his fortune and was a household name in the field of transportation.

Butterfield was generally considered an upright man, wealthy but not greedy, a man whose ambitions were toward deeds, not power and income. The Conklings give a human sidelight to his public image:

> He was scrupulous in his dress and appearance, his clothes being of the finest quality . . . always wearing high leather boots with his pantaloons drawn down over the tops. His appearance in a long yellow linen duster, and flat-crowned "wide-awake" hat, the attire he adopted on his western journeys, set a fashion for the young men in many of the large communities in Missouri and Arkansas, where the windows of every general merchandise store from Warsaw to Fort Smith, displayed the latest in Butterfield coats, hats and boots, and even Butterfield shirts and cravats.[9]

It isn't too fanciful a thought that for John Butterfield the Overland Mail was a final grand gesture. The days of the stagecoach, particularly the mail coach, were drawing to a close, and he knew it;

almost everything east of the Mississippi already was going by rail. Butterfield, at age fifty-six, was successful, famous, and well liked. He had shifted operations with the times: first the stage, then the packet boat on the canals, then the railroad which formed the basis for his flourishing American Express Company. But John Butterfield, who had learned the business the hard way, from the freight dock to the stagecoach box, saw a last glorious challenge in his contract for the overland mail route, the "impossible" stage ride. Only in the West was the stagecoach still offering the possibility of profit and adventure. That Butterfield was so proud of it and worked so hard to make that mail contract succeed can either be viewed as the "last hurrah" of an old stager or a final grab for business immortality.[10]

Although he didn't realize it, only in the West could the Butterfield stage, by undertaking to cross the uninhabited, little-known and Indian-inhabited Southwest, become a legend before it carried its first sack of mail or took aboard its first paying passenger. To Butterfield the whole enterprise was a gamble worth making, a victory even if a losing proposition—and there was no question that those long, lonely stretches of the road across Texas, New Mexico, and Arizona would lose him money. Only the lines in Missouri, Arkansas, and California might be profitable. Whatever the cost, the gamble paid off in fame, for today Butterfield's name is remembered, not for his various rail presidencies, his wealth, or his role in founding American Express—but for the Butterfield Trail.

The "Bifurcated Route," allowing westward mail to start simultaneously from St. Louis and Memphis, was proposed by Butterfield as a political expedient. He knew that southern congressmen were determined the eastern terminal should be Memphis or New Orleans, while powerful northern politicians were just as determined that St. Louis should mark the eastern end—adding that the route should be along the 35th Parallel, away from the heinous influence of the slaveholding states. The Butterfield group thought it had won the overland mail bid with a route along the 35th Parallel, but the members were "quite astonished to find that, though the act

13

read 'as the contractors may select,' they had no voice at all in selecting the route upon which their money was to be expended," according to Waterman L. Ormsby. Postmaster General Aaron Venable Brown, a former governor of Tennessee and a passionate southerner (remember, the sectional dispute was already beginning to boil), wouldn't accede to the 35th, or "northern," route. It was too far north—although Brown never *officially* voiced this sentiment.

Having made that voluntary compliance paragraph part of their successful bid (foreseeing only minor route changes and compromises), the Butterfield group was forced to accept a fourth version of the routing. Both St. Louis and Memphis would become eastern *termini*, ordered Postmaster General Brown, from which letter mail would leave on the same day at the same hour, converging at Little Rock, Arkansas, "thence, via Preston, Texas,[11] or as nearly so as may be found advisable, along the 32nd Parallel to the best point of crossing the Rio Grande, above El Paso [Franklin] to Tucson, etc."[12]

When the contract's routing terms were announced, the northern press cried foul. This southern line was condemned by the Chicago *Tribune* as "one of the greatest swindles ever perpetrated upon the country by the slave-holders."[13] Expert testimony was hurriedly assembled to prove that the northern route contained not only never-failing supplies of water and abundant grass, but that the climate, year around, was pleasant and mild, in contrast to the 32nd Parallel route, where hot sands and waterless deserts characterized virtually every southwestern mile. And although he had successfully operated stage lines in the North and East for years, Butterfield's foes jeered that this eastern stager would never be able to establish stations across that wild desert country, much less keep twenty-eight hundred miles of line supplied with food, feed, horses, mules, and rolling stock—and make a twice-weekly schedule.

The opposition never let up the entire time the Southern Overland Mail ran. But reporter Ormsby, preparing to board the first Butterfield stage in 1858, announced:

14

Your humble servant feels so confident that the men engaged in this work will not belie their reputation, and that the mail to California, overland, will reach its destination, that he risks the success of the enterprise, and . . . will go through with the first mail bag.[14]

The Overland Mail Company, once it began operation, was commonly referred to as "the Butterfield line" by people along the route. In Missouri it was often called "The Great Southern Overland," although an 1859 passenger noted that in southwest Missouri, where the Ozark Mountains make the trip extremely jolting, it was sometimes sarcastically referred to as the "Underland." In California it was called the "California Overland Express." Newspapers, even in more eastern portions of the route such as Fort Smith, Arkansas, frequently mentioned the "California mail" or "Pacific mail" when the Butterfield Overland Mail was meant. Actually, with a great deal of justification, the operation could have been termed "The Wells, Fargo Overland Mail," since in California, and eventually in its entirety, the Overland Mail Company was controlled by Wells, Fargo & Company, which had advanced all the money for building and maintaining the Rio Grande to San Francisco section of the route and had a majority of directors on the Overland Mail Company board.[15]

After getting Postmaster General Brown to change the point of convergence in Arkansas from Little Rock to Fort Smith, Butterfield and his partners pushed a marvelous engineering chain across the continent—a truly astonishing chapter of the Butterfield legend and a chapter little researched and less reported upon. According to Ralph Moody in *Stage Coach West*, Postmaster General Brown ordered that the mail road should proceed "through the best passes and along the best valleys for safe and expeditious staging to San Francisco and back." Within one year the employees—surveyors, engineers, pick-and-shovel men and superintendents—working in the shadow of Indian attack, had set up stations every twenty miles, located fords, cut down banks at river crossings, constructed roads "through the best passes and along the best valleys," dug wells and dammed tanks, and built bridges and culverts so that the vehicles might have year-round footing. By the standards of the day, the Butterfield Overland Mail route was a road. A clue to how it really looked can be found in a description of the similar San Antonio-El Paso road, which was "nothing more than a set of rough wheel tracks with chutes cut in the steepest stream banks and rock-walled mountain passes hacked wide enough to let a wagon through."[16]

Historians are vague about just how much of the route John Butterfield actually traveled. Moody says John Butterfield made an inspection trip "in midsummer [of 1858] over the line, gathered his men at the various way stations, and gave them their final instructions."[17] However, Roscoe and Margaret Conkling report he "made Fort Smith his headquarters during the investigation of the routes in the summer of 1858. Although he never traveled on his own route beyond Fort Smith, he had in some way made himself familiar with every mile of it from that point on to San Francisco."[18]

Of horses, mules, and material, there were sufficient numbers so as "to have one [horse or mule] for every two miles, and a wagon or coach for every thirty miles."[19] After the mail contract was won by Butterfield, specifications for 250 coaches, freight and tank wagons were issued; and drivers, conductors, station-keepers, blacksmiths, mechanics, helpers, hostlers and herders were employed. In all there were more than 2,000 men and women and 200 stations along the 3,134 miles of the line, including the 322 miles from Memphis to Fort Smith.

A small steamer, the "Jennie Whipple," was purchased for $7,000 by the Butterfield company in December, 1858, to carry Memphis passengers and mail on the Arkansas River to and from Little Rock and Fort Smith, but Ormsby wrote "because of the low stage of the river, the attempt to carry the mail by water between these two points had to be abandoned."[20] However, the Conklings, with later information, state, "This river service developed into a regular mail, passenger, and baggage service operating on a semi-weekly schedule, and was well patronized."[21]

The equipment was the finest available, and included nine-passenger Concord coaches,[22] weighing 3,000 pounds, as well as a specially developed lighter wagon for Butterfield frontier service called a "celerity wagon."[23] The heavy coaches were supplied by such famous coachmakers as J. S. Abbott & Sons of Concord, New Hampshire (later Abbott, Downing & Company), Eaton, Gilbert & Company, of Troy, New York, and James Goold, of Albany, New York (maker of the first westbound coach used by Butterfield's Overland Mail). Goold also made the first one hundred "celerity wagons" ordered by Butterfield. One-third of the Butterfield's larger coaches were made by Eaton, Gilbert, & Company, whose "Troy coaches" were noted for heavy duty ruggedness. James B. Hill & Sons, of Concord, made the heavy four- and six-team harnesses.

Butterfield coaches had russet leather interiors with cushions and side curtains of the same material. Many had an original oil painting in the lower panel of the door. Some of the coach bodies were red, others a dark bottle green; all under-carriages were yellow, striped in black or brown. Two candle lamps were located inside the cabin, and two carriage lamps were attached to the top front of the coach behind the driver, who sat up some six feet from the ground. All stock and equipment was marked "Overland Mail Company," or "OMC." Latter-day illustrations of coaches lettered "Butterfield Overland Mail" or "Southern Overland Mail" are mistaken; these were never official terms.

Butterfield's heavy coaches could carry a 4,000-pound load. Woodwork was choice hickory, and all the metal, except for brass trim, was steel, including the axles. The spindles, around which the big dished and canted wheels spun, were two-and-one-half inches thick and fourteen inches long. For more efficient use of power, especially in sand or soft terrain, Butterfield ordered his coach tires to be four inches wide, as on freight wagons, rather than the two-and-one-half inch tires usually found on coaches.[24] The coach body swung on three-and-one-half inch wide leather thoroughbraces of the style introduced by James Goold—heavy straps woven through steel stanchions lifting the body above the axles. This gave it a hammocky swing which cushioned the human form so that the ride was reasonably pleasant unless the coach was tilting or bouncing down a rough, rocky decline. The driver's seat (unlike those on European coaches, which were attached to the undercarriage), was also attached to the thoroughbraced body, allowing him an easier ride.

Inside the coach were three wide seats, forward, middle, and rear, which reached from side to side of the coach and were quite close together. The middle and rear seats faced forward while the front seat faced backward. Passengers in the front and center seats often had to "dovetail" their legs, as the process was termed. The middle seat could be lowered to form a bed. Each seat nominally held three people, but as the Reverend Mr. Tallack, an English Quaker divine who wrote about his 1860 Butterfield trip, commented, "An American vehicle is never 'full' there is always room for 'one more.'"[25] The cushions were built with coiled steel springs, padded with horse hair. The roof, which was covered with the very heaviest of painted, waterproof ducking, held extra baggage, and when the occasion demanded, as many extra passengers as could find room there.[26] The Troy coach, in particular, had a seat behind and above the driver's box where as many as three passengers could ride, and some coaches had a rear seat or "dickey" for the conductor, which could also be used by two or three passengers facing rearward. Thus equipped, on occasion as many as two dozen passengers could be hauled on a Troy coach—if not in comfort, at least effectively.[27]

The men employed by the Butterfield company were not all westerners; many were old stage drivers from Butterfield's New York lines, including some Canadians. While not so true of the Texas part of the trail, many stationkeepers were also from the East. According to Ormsby, all "men and drivers were uniformly courteous."[28]

The conductor, who most often rode to the left of the driver, was captain of the ship, having charge of the mails, passenger tickets, and general operation of the coach. The Butterfield conductor was also the person who called "All aboard!" and blew a stubby brass bugle to start the coach and to notify stations from as far as two miles out that the mail coach was near. The Butterfield bugle call, while not unique in coaching, attracted the comment of many riders. The Reverend William Tallack remarked, "Throughout our Overland journey our approach to a station, whether previous to a relay [changing horses only] or a meal, was announced at a distance by a long blast from the conductor's horn, often heard far away in the silence of the wilds, and serving to economize time by enabling the station-keepers to prepare the requirements both of the hungry passengers and the jaded mules."[29] Another overland passenger wrote in the *New York Post*: "The blast of the stage horn as it rolls through the valleys and over the prairies of the West, cheers and gladdens the heart of the pioneer. . . . He knows that it brings tidings from the hearts and homes he left behind him; it binds him stronger and firmer to his beloved country."[30]

The "whip," as the driver was called (the reins were called ribbons), drove from the right-hand side of the box, where the tall, powerful foot brake was provided. If trouble was expected, an armed guard rode beside the driver, typically packing a pair of six-guns and a sawed-off shotgun loaded with buckshot.

Under the driver's box was a compartment for safekeeping of small costly items or items of company business. However, because of highwaymen, one of the operating rules of the Overland Mail Company was that no gold, silver, or bullion would be carried "under any circumstances." (It was ordinarily sent by ocean vessels.) A leather-covered boot for valuables and smaller baggage was at the driver's feet, while at the rear of the coach was a hinged leather- or chain-supported platform and a leather- or canvas-hooded boot for heavier luggage. Forty pounds of luggage were allowed each passenger, which seems a liberal amount in our time of lightweight luggage, but the restriction drew complaints from some passengers who had to ship excess baggage via Panama, "the rates of which," asserted the Reverend Tallack, "were extortionate enough . . . upward of five pounds per cwt."[31]

Approximate costs of the various heavy-duty coaches can be discerned from an 1870 price list by Abbott, Downing & Company, which offered a fully equipped heavy coach to seat nine inside for $975. A rear deck seat was an additional $20, packing (or padding) for the full coach was another $20, and plush lining added $25 to the cost, for a total figure of $1,040. But such handsome vehicles proved inconvenient for the rugged southwestern sections of the Butterfield trail. Besides the greater burden for the animals pulling them, these heavy Concord-type coaches were too liable to upset to be of use for frontier travel. The Concord coaches were seldom used from the Indian Nations through to Los Angeles, California. Instead, the Butterfield company ordered 100 of Goold's celerity wagons, the lighter, boxier version of the Concord coach, utilizing the same undercarriage but with smaller wheels and lighter wood for the body, while roof, side curtains, and doors were of canvas rather than leather.[32] The roof would have caved in under the weight of much more than a man. In fact, one of the more frequent passenger complaints came from having to share the interior of the coach with mail bags and luggage when mail sacks were carried in large numbers.

The normal interior capacity of the celerity wagon was almost the same as that of the Concord coach, but because of the canvas roof, the outside capacity was limited. Albert D. Richardson, whose 1859 Butterfield Trail journey was in a celerity wagon, wrote:

> It is covered with duck or canvas, the driver sitting in front, at a slight elevation above the passengers. Bearing no weight upon the roof, it is less top heavy than the old-fashioned stagecoach for mudholes and mountain-slides, where to preserve the center of gravity becomes, with Falstaff's instinct, "a great matter." . . . [I]t does best under a heavy load. Empty, it jolts and pitches like a ship in a raging sea; filled with passengers and balanced by a proper distribution of baggage in the "boot"

behind, and under the driver's feet before, its motion is easy and elastic.[33]

The seats of the celerity wagon also made a bed, which, in the amused words of passenger Ormsby, "was capable of accommodating from four to ten people, according to their size and how they lie."[34] A newspaper account of a trip by Mr. George S. Dana quotes him as saying, "Sleep is shy at first, but after that the passengers get used to the thing [celerity wagon] and could sleep if the coach were tumbling a precipice."[35]

Horses were used to pull the stages from Missouri to Fort Belknap in Young County, Texas. From that point, teams of four mules pulled the wagons generally to Tucson, Arizona, but sometimes all the way to Fort Yuma, on the Arizona-California border. There were exceptions to this policy, as various contemporary writers pointed out. Ormsby, frequently annoyed by the difficulties inherent in the use of wild mules, noted thankfully that from Tucson to San Francisco, "The line is exceedingly well stocked and but few mules are used."[36]

Driving a four- or six-horse hitch called for a high degree of experience and skill. The lead team was the most critical pair. A good driver was said to watch the ears of the lead pair for movement and a kind of advance signal. The lead horses had to be agile and able to move sideways quickly. The swing team in the middle of a six-horse hitch had to be steady yet responsive, not turning too quickly. The wheel horses, hitched directly to the tongue, had to be strong and durable, as well as accustomed to pulling to the rear on command. (They were the only horses equipped to back up and were harnessed differently.) In a four-horse hitch, the wheel and lead teams remain the same. A single animal added in front of the lead team was called a "wildcat" or "spike" team; this was true of both four- and six-horse hitches.[37]

John Butterfield himself signed the list of special instructions given "To Conductors, Agents, Drivers & Employees." The first is full of urgency and exhortation:

Have teams harnessed in ample time, and ready to proceed without delay or confusion. Where the coaches are changed, have the teams hitched to them in time. Teams should be hitched together and led to or from the stable to the coach, so that no delay can occur by their running away. All employees will assist the Driver in watering and changing teams in all cases, to save time.[38]

Conductors were also ordered to report to the Superintendent "in all cases if Drivers abuse or mis-manage their teams."[39]

The coaches averaged five miles per hour over the entire St. Louis-San Francisco distance, reaching a maximum speed of twelve miles per hour on smooth, level portions of the road, but sometimes, as in heavy sand, hours were spent going only three or four miles. All in all, however, the Butterfield mail was late remarkably few times, and never by more than a few hours at the terminals. Most of the time the trip was made in twenty-three days and a few hours. The quickest passage ever was twenty-one days, and within a year the 1858 times of twenty-four days and several hours had been trimmed considerably. A U.S. senator, using figures supplied by the San Francisco postmaster, told his Senate colleagues that the average time for trips made during the six months from October, 1859, to April, 1860, was twenty-one days and fifteen hours.[40]

It was also important to realize that maximum time in a station, except for meals, was set at ten minutes.[41] At the time of the first journey in 1858, some Butterfield stations, still under construction, were mere tents, so passengers could expect very little in the way of amenities. By the time the Butterfield stage ceased operations in 1861, travelers could expect a good deal more comfort in most cases. Still, by today's standards, conditions remained near primitive. "I know what hell is like. I've had twenty-four days of it," said one passenger completing a journey to San Francisco by Butterfield stage.

H. D. Burrows, a fellow passenger, wrote that it "possesses a wonderful charm, especially in remembrance."[42] A later historian, describing western stage travel in general, wrote:

> At the stage station you would find a stationmaster in charge, a handful of hostlers to care for the animals, and perhaps a rough eating house or restaurant. The buildings would be of logs, whipsawed lumber, sod, or adobe, depending on location. There'd probably be a tin basin on a bench beside the door where you could wash up, aided by some soft soap in a side dish—soap that would curl the hide off a hippo. A roller towel that had seen better days and a more or less toothless comb, detained by a rawhide string, would help you complete your toilette. Inside there'd be a big fireplace, acrid, sputtering tallow candles. . . . Your meal would be the inevitable hog and hominy or beef and beans of the frontier.[43]

Despite the romantic notions of film and television, wherein a beautiful damsel (usually in distress) was always aboard the coach when trouble was encountered, not many women were carried on the Overland Mail stages, especially through the reaches of West Texas, New Mexico, and Arizona. Thus, without women, such considerations as modesty and manners seldom had to be observed. When the passengers were all male, a "comfort station" was no farther than the nearest bush, if that. When women were along, the sexes divided, one side of the coach used by men, the other side by the women. A story is told about a stage driver whose teams, having had a hard pull up a hill, were given a minute or two to rest. He discreetly inquired whether those aboard needed to take advantage of the halt. Many did. "Ladies first," the driver ordered, and helping two females from the coach he directed them to some brush nearby. Then he noticed the men passengers who had climbed out were letting their gaze wander too much to suit him. "Eyes this way, boys," he ordered gently, "the ladies is pick'n daisies."[44]

There were some realistic suggestions for stage travel outside the list of regulations given by the company. One such sheet tells the passenger that the best seat inside the stage is the one closest to the driver, and even if the traveler has a tendency to motion sickness when riding backward,[45] "you will get over it and will get less jolts and jostling. Do not let any sly elf trade you his mid-seat." It is further suggested: "When the driver asks you to get off and walk, do so without grumbling." Also, if the team runs away, "sit still and take your chances. If you jump, nine shots out of ten you will get hurt."[46]

Other items hint that the passenger "not growl at the food," not smoke a strong pipe inside the coach, and "spit on the leeward [downwind] side." Neighborliness is emphasized: "If you have anything to drink, pass it around . . . do not lop over neighbors when sleeping . . . do not lag at the wash basin," and finally, "Do not point out where murders have been committed, especially if there are women passengers."[47]

A popular ballad of the stagecoach period, "The California Stage Company," reveals some of the less pleasant aspects of stage travel.

There's no respect for youth or age
On board the California stage,
But pull and haul about the seats
As bedbugs do about the sheets.

The ladies are compelled to sit
With dresses in tobacco spit;
The gentlemen don't seem to care,
But talk on politics and swear.
The drivers, when they feel inclined,
Will have you walking on behind,
And on your shoulders lug a pole
To help them out some muddy hole.

They promise when your fare you pay,
"You'll have to walk but half the way";

24

Then add aside, with cunning laugh,
"You'll have to push the other half."[48]

A summary of the outrageous discomforts that could attend all
stage travel (not to mention the outrageous disregard for passengers)
is contained in "Notes of Travel" published January 4, 1859, by the
San Francisco *Evening Bulletin* from "Our Special Overland Correspondent":

> When we reached Dardinelles [Dardanelle, Arkansas] it was
> late at night, and raining in an old-fashioned way. . . . We were
> most unceremoniously turned out of the coach by the driver
> and delivered into the charge of the ferryman, who took the
> mail-bags on his shoulder, and, his lantern in hand, told us to
> follow him to his boat at the ferry landing, about one mile dis-
> tant up the river. There was no remedy for this unexpected
> tramp; so, placing our blankets on our backs, and valise in
> hand, the passengers proceeded to accompany him, through
> a torrent of rain, up the river bank and across the stream to his
> small boat. It was well for the coachman [a leased stage, not
> Butterfield's] that he could not be found when we started on
> after the ferryman; he certainly would have been roughly han-
> dled, as it was his duty to have carried us to the ferry. We all
> got soaking wet by the time we reached the coach on the op-
> posite bank, and three of our party were considerably used up,
> next day, from the effects of the drenching.[49]

The fare for the terminal-to-terminal trip on the Overland Mail
stage was originally $200 westbound and $100 eastbound, but when
cries of "unfair!" were heard, in a few months both were reset to $150
and remained there till the end of service. Fares "in way" were ten
cents a mile—and many times there were so many of these passengers that the through ones, who felt they should be given preferen-
tial treatment, complained of being crowded by the newcomers. The

through ticket was a simple handwritten document. In addition to the date and the signature of the clerk, an eastbound ticket, for example, bore the words, "Good for the passage of the bearer by the Overland Stage from San Francisco to the terminus of the Pacific Railroad [in Missouri]."[50]

The postal rate for U. S. mail was ten cents per one-half ounce. The Butterfield mail coaches also carried British mail for British Columbia and the Canadian Pacific coast. The letter rate for this type of mail was twenty-four cents.[51] The mails were more precious than the passengers, it would seem. The Conductor was told, "You will be particular to see that the mails are protected from the wet, and kept safe from injury of every kind . . . and you will be held personally responsible for the safe delivery at the end of your route . . . of all mails and other property in your charge." In other words, The Mail Must Go Through! Conductors were never to lose sight of the mails "for a moment, or leave them, except in charge of the driver or some other employee of the Company." As was the case with gold, silver and bullion, no money, jewelry, bank notes, or valuables "of any nature," were allowed to be carried "under any circumstances whatever."[52]

Reporter Ormsby was so impressed with the efficiency of the Butterfield Company, that at the end of his transcontinental trip he predicted Butterfield would be able to establish a *daily* mail to San Francisco within a year. He also wrote: "The journey has been by no means as fatiguing to me as might be expected by a continuous ride of such duration, for I feel almost fresh enough to undertake it again."[53] However, he returned from California to New York by boat.

The San Francisco *Daily Evening Bulletin* of December 16, 1858, carried a November 19 letter from Washington, D.C., charging Ormsby was employed by the Butterfield Company. There is no question his way was paid by Butterfield or that Ormsby's dispatches show good humored tolerance of trying circumstances, but they are not uncritical of the Butterfield operation. The real complaint of his critics seems to be that he argued for the 32nd Parallel route over that of the 35th Parallel—a position some eastern writers and politicians never accepted, even after it worked.

Notes

1. See "Tragedy at Apache Pass," p. 251.

2. A low-crown, wide-brim, soft felt hat worn by men. It had become so popular by the 1860 elections that one group of young Republicans adopting it as their symbol became known as the "Wide-Awakes." Some 20,000 of them marched in a single parade in New York City that year. "Wide Awake," *Grolier Encyclopedia*, Vol. 10, 1951.

3. Leroy Hafen, *The Overland Mail, 1849–1869* (Glendale: Arthur Clark Co., 1926), 98.

4. Senator Rusk did not live to see Texas benefit; he committed suicide July 29, 1857.

5. Waterman Lily Ormsby, Jr., *The Butterfield Overland Mail*, ed. Lyle H. Wright and Josephine M. Bynum (San Marino: Huntington Library, 1955), 141. In addition to sending back feature stories to the New York *Herald* on his journey, Ormsby was to supply a background report on the overland mail contract and the Butterfield company operation.

6. Hafen, 99. The Butterfield Mail arrived late at San Francisco or St. Louis only three times in the nearly three years it ran.

7. Butterfield's associates were William B. Dinsmore, William G. Fargo, James V. P. Gardner, Hamilton Spencer, Alexander Holland (Butterfield's son-in-law), and Marcus L. Kinyon, who later became Superintendent of the Tucson to San Francisco section of the line.

8. Roscoe P. and Margaret B. Conkling, *The Butterfield Overland Mail 1857–1869*, Vol. I (Glendale: Arthur H. Clark, Co., 1947), 114.

9. Conkling, Vol. I, 35.

10. John Butterfield's three sons were active in the first Butterfield Overland Mail operation. John Jay Butterfield drove the first westbound Butterfield Mail stage out of Tipton, Missouri, his excited father taking a hand with everything from unloading mail to catching and harnessing the horses and driving the coach. Eldest son Charles E. Butterfield was in charge of the Overland Mail Co. agency and the Butterfield hotel at Fayetteville, Arkansas for some time. Daniel Butterfield, an 1849 graduate of Union College, prepared the first OMC timetables, which were scrupulously adhered to throughout the Butter-

field Overland operation. Later Daniel was superintendent of the New York City office of the American Express. During the Civil War he entered the Union army as a colonel, was active in several major campaigns, was wounded twice, and was brevetted a Major General; but he is most famous for being the composer of the bugle call "Taps." Allen Johnson and Dumas Malone, ed. *Dictionary of American Biography*, Vol. 3 (New York: Charles Scribner's Sons, 1946), 373.

11. In the early 1850s Preston was more important than Dallas or recently established (in 1849) Fort Worth. A major gateway to Texas, it was located at the northern end of the Preston Trail to Austin via Dallas and Waco. That road is still a major thoroughfare (now Preston Road) leading north out of Dallas. John Neely Bryan, that city's founder, had ridden down the trail in 1841 from Coffee's trading post, to plant the seeds for his city. Even after the Overland Mail route was established, U.S. Army movements to the Texas frontier forts ordinarily crossed the Red River at Preston. The town lost its significance when the cattle trails moved west in the 1860s and then in 1872 the railroads bypassed it. Preston disappeared beneath the waters of Lake Texoma in 1944.

12. Conkling, Vol. I, 115.

13. Conkling, Vol. I, 121.

14. Ormsby, 134.

15. W. Turrentine Jackson, "A New Look at Wells Fargo, Stagecoaches and the Pony Express," *California Historical Society Quarterly*, December 1966, 295–300.

16. Ralph Moody, *Stagecoach West* (New York: Thomas Y. Crowell, 1967), 79.

17. Moody, 108.

18. Conkling, Vol. I, 37.

19. Ormsby, 139.

20. Ormsby, 168.

21. Conkling, Vol. I, 216.

22. Later in the nineteenth century there was a tendency to refer to all heavy stages as "Concord coaches," so that it became a style of coach rather than a trademarked name. The original Concord, named for the New Hampshire city, was made by Abbott & Sons. Hereafter, all heavier type stagecoaches will be referred to as "Concord" coaches.

23. Following the Civil War, this vehicle was further adapted into the famous western "mud wagon." G. C. (Tom) Tompkins, *A Compendium of The Overland Mail Company On the South Route 1858–1861 and the Period Surrounding It* (El Paso: G. T. Co., 1985), 195.

24. For specifications of coach weight and construction see August

Santleben, *A Texas Pioneer, Early Staging and Overland Freighting Days on the Frontiers of Texas and Mexico* (Waco: W. M. Morrison, 1967), 63–64; for extra width of Butterfield coach tires, Tompkins, 203. The fame of the American coachmakers had spread far afield. Not only did they supply vehicles to countries around the globe, but they also built the first coachlike railroad passenger cars in the United States. Goold Company and Eaton, Gilbert Company both built railroad cars and streetcars by the thousands. Goold once made a steam-driven passenger road coach with engine and boiler in front and the passenger and baggage compartments in the rear. In 1859, Goold got an order from the Russian government for a steam-driven six-coach sleigh train; steam engine and boiler mounted on runners propelled with an endless chain device similar to that used in today's snowmobiles.

25. Walter B. Lang, *The First Overland Mail: Butterfield Trail* (Washington, D.C.: n.p., 1940), 131.

26. "The coach was manufactured (1867) by Abbott, Downing & Co., and it was imported by Mr. A. Staacke [of San Antonio], their agent for such vehicles and Concord buggies in west Texas. . . . We paid Mr. Staacke nine hundred dollars for the first coach . . . and later $1250, without the harness. The set of harness that was made for it was intended for six horses, to weigh about twelve hundred pounds, but it was useless because our animals were much smaller. We drove six animals to the coach in Texas, and in Mexico eight, on account of the heavy traffic. The seat on the hind end of the coach, above the boot . . . had a top attached to it like those used on buggies, that could be raised or lowered." (Santleben, 64-65) Buffalo Bill Cody's famous Deadwood stage, used in his show to carry many of the crowned heads of Europe, was an Abbott, Downing coach built in 1873. It is now in the Smithsonian Institution.

27. Charles Veazie, of Troy, originated the "dickey" or "rumble" seat, also the 24-inch iron baggage railing around the roof of the coach which all the stagecoach makers sooner or later adopted. The rear appendage was called "the rumble" because it was positioned over the back wheels and was noisy. The term was preserved in the automobile age.

28. Ormsby, 99.

29. Tallack, coming from Australia, had to wait ten days to get aboard an eastbound Overland Mail stage at San Francisco, enroute to his home in England. Lang, 130.

30. Hafen, 99.

31. Lang, 132.

32. Although one contemporary illustration depicts the celerity wagon riding on elliptic springs, Ormsby specifically speaks of the celerity wagon being "set on leather straps instead of springs." Ormsby, 18.

33. Albert Deane Richardson, *Beyond the Mississippi: From the Great River to the Great Ocean* . . . (New York: Bliss, 1867), 159. Though born of an old Massachusetts family, Richardson (1833–1869) early became fascinated by the west, moving to Pittsburgh at age 18, then to Cincinnati a year later where he married Mary Louise Pearce in 1855. In 1857 he moved his family to Kansas and served for short periods as adjutant-general of the Territory and secretary of the legislature. Already a well read journalist, he gained national fame in 1859 when he accompanied Horace Greeley and Henry Villard on their trip to Colorado, reporting for Greeley's paper *The New York Tribune*. A short time later Richardson made a trip west via the Butterfield Overland Mail, writing the classic *Beyond the Mississippi*, published in 1867. During the Civil War, as a war correspondent for the *Tribune*, he was captured by the Confederates and held prisoner for 18 months before escaping. While he was a prisoner, his wife, and an infant daughter he had never seen, died. In 1869, on the eve of his marriage to Addy Sage McFarland, he was mortally wounded at his desk at the *Tribune* by Dan McFarland, Addy's alcoholic and psychotic former husband. On Richardson's deathbed, he and Addy were married by Henry Ward Beecher. Several books about the murder and the subsequent trial in which McFarland was acquitted, have been written, the most recent *Lost Love*, by George Cooper in 1994.

34. Ormsby, 18.

35. Lang, 128.

36. Ormsby, 101.

37. Tompkins, 215-20. Tompkins was a commissioned Army officer "who spent most of the time in the field with six-horse teams and carriages."

38. Ormsby, frontispiece.

39. Ibid.

40. Hafen, 98.

41. Conkling, Vol. I, 124.

42. Captain William Banning and George Hugh Banning, *Six Horses* (New York: The Century Co., 1930), 115–29. For a more detailed (and hilarious) description than this one of the pains and perils of western stagecoach travel see *Six Horses*.

43. Foster-Harris, *The Look of the Old West* (New York: Viking Press, 1955), 172.

44. Tompkins, 140.

45. "The fastidious [Raphael] Pumpelly's trip [on the Butterfield Overland route] was made all the more unpleasant by the fact that a frontier family shared his seat and that across from him. The man was a 'border bully,' the woman dipped snuff, and their two daughters for several days were overcome by

motion sickness and in this had 'no regard for the clothes of their neighbors.'" Marilyn McAdams Sibley, *Travelers in Texas 1761–1860* (Austin: University of Texas Press, 1967), 31.

46. Displayed in Wells, Fargo Bank history room in San Francisco.

47. Ibid.

48. John A. Lomax, *Cowboy Songs and Other Frontier Ballads* (New York: Macmillan Co., 1936), 411.

49. The Memphis-Fort Smith section was initially a leased operation and Butterfield was not involved. But great outcry was raised about the poor service and poorer facilities of this section and the Butterfield Company took over and improved both, according to a Van Buren (Arkansas) newspaper of August 3, 1860, when it reported "The stages of the California Overland Mail Co. now carry the Memphis mail on the north side of the Arkansas."

50. Lang, 130.

51. Tompkins, 154.

52. Ormsby, tipped-in Special Instructions.

53. Ormsby, 58.

PART TWO

The Long and Dangerous Days – The First
Overland Mail Trip & Stations
Along the Route

T HE first Butterfield Overland Mail trip westward started on time from St. Louis at 8 A.M., September 16, 1858. It didn't start by stagecoach, it began by steam train, going from the St. Louis station via Pacific Railroad to the end of the rail line at the new town of Tipton, Missouri, which the Pacific Railroad had created. John Butterfield and Waterman L. Ormsby accompanied the two small pouches of mail from St. Louis. Ormsby tells us that the mail pouches were prepared for their transcontinental adventure by means of a simple branded stick:

> San Francisco, California
> Per Overland Mail
> St. Louis, Sept. 16, 1858
> Return Label by Express[1]

It was an historic moment. Ormsby sensed the importance of the Butterfield experiment and was perplexed, even annoyed, that so few others attached the same significance to the event, as he wrote for the readers:

> Although some of the St. Louis papers noticed that this important enterprise was to be commenced today, but little attention appeared to be paid it, except by the personal friends of the contractors and a few others. Indeed, I have been somewhat surprised to find that in the West—which, above all other sections of the country, is to be benefitted—so little attention is paid to the great overland mail.[2]

"I looked forward in my imagination," he wrote that first morning, "to the time when . . . instead of having to wait over forty days for an answer from San Francisco, a delay of as many minutes will be looked upon as a gross imposition, and of as many seconds as 'doing from fair to middling.'"[3]

Turning south from Tipton, the stage reached Springfield, Missouri. Once during this portion of the ride, Butterfield actually shared the reins with his son, "Young" John, the regular driver. The mail road crossed northwestern Arkansas and reached Fort Smith, where the westbound mail from Memphis was taken aboard and the elder Butterfield apparently disembarked. Although the line would pass through higher mountains before reaching San Francisco, the "steep and rugged hills which surround the Ozark range in this section of Arkansas"[4] remained fearful to cross, according to later travelers.

From Fort Smith the path led directly into Indian Territory—fording the Poteau River—and through the Choctaw Nation, then a semi-independent province. Most of the stations within the Choctaw Nation were owned and operated by members of the Choctaw tribe, as land ownership in the area, under Choctaw law, was forbidden to anyone not a tribal member.[5]

The first Butterfield station southwest of Fort Smith was Walker's, kept by tribal Governor George Tandy Walker. Then came Trahern's station (the Conklings spell it "Trayhern"), called the Council House, operated by Judge James N. Trahern, of the Choctaw courts. Continuing the road toward the Red River, William Holloway's station was at the entrance to a gentle pass called "The Narrows" where Holloway, with a charter from the Choctaw Nation, operated a toll gate. John Riddle's station, in present-day Lamar County, was next. It had a coal mine that provided blacksmith coal to several other stations. The stage then encountered a small relay station called Mountain Station before reaching Silas Pusley's station, which has the historical misfortune of being spelled three or four dozen different ways in various historical accounts (Pursley, Pulsey, Pusey, etc.). Casper Blackburn's station, a little further to the southwest, was located in the fairly sizable community of Brush Settlement, while the station at Waddell was first called "Old Beale" and later named J. Colbert's after the Butterfield stopped running.[6]

A. W. Geary's station (later Well's and Roger's), had a tollbridge over the North Boggy River, and Old Boggy Depot, the next station, was at a well-traveled crossroads of the old Texas Road and the military road west to Fort Washita and Fort Arbuckle. Boggy was the busiest and most important Butterfield station between Fort Smith, Arkansas, and Sherman, Texas.[7]

At J. H. Nail's station on the Blue River, also called Nail's Crossing, Waterman Ormsby was amazed and delighted to discover that Nail was a subscriber to Ormsby's own newspaper, the New York *Herald*. The next station, Fisher's, was called Carriage Point, both before and after it was a Butterfield station. When the stage finally reached the Red River, it arrived at Colbert's Ferry,[8] by way of which it crossed the river to the Lone Star State.

Initially the convergence point for the St. Louis-Memphis mail on the Bifurcated Route was to have been Preston, Texas on the Red River, with the southern run continuing to Big Spring. When Fort Smith, Arkansas, was designated as the place the two branches would come together, the resulting trail excluded both Preston and Big Spring. Nevertheless, travelers and historians have mistakenly cited Preston as a Butterfield site ever since. Albert Richardson's 1860 account records, "At Preston we crossed the Red River into Texas," but adds that "the first Texas town was Sherman."[9] Had the stage actually crossed at Preston, Sherman would not have been on the route at all. Richardson wrote eight years after his travels, so his memory may have misled him. Some later historians who have placed the crossing at Preston were probably misled by the wording of the original contract, which listed Preston as the entry point.[10]

Ormsby's impression of the actual crossing place at Colbert's Ferry was recorded on Monday, September 20, 1858. He says,

> We now arrived at Colbert's Ferry on the Red River, about eight miles below Preston, on the Texas border. . . . Mr. Colbert, the

owner of the station and of the ferry, is a half-breed Indian of great sagacity and business tact. [He] evinces some enterprise in carrying the stages of the company across his ferry free of charge. . . . His boat is simply a sort of raft, pushed across the shallow stream by the aid of poles in the hands of sturdy slaves. The fare for a four-horse team is a dollar and a quarter."[11]

After crossing the river on the ferry, Ormsby noted that a number of Colbert's slaves were "busily engaged in lowering the present steep grade of the banks." On its thirteen-mile run from the Red River to Sherman, the Butterfield route traversed the future site of Denison (1872), crossed Duck Creek on a new bridge, passed by the already-famous Sand Springs with its Inscription Rock, and possibly paused at Cooke Springs.[12] Ormsby recorded seeing "several large gullies, or beds of creeks" before he reached the next station, all of which were "being bridged at the expense of Grayson County."[13]

The next station was on the public square in the village of Sherman, county seat of Grayson county. The largest town in Texas to be served by the Butterfield Overland Mail Company, Sherman was described by Ormsby as "a pleasant little village of about six hundred inhabitants," whose energetic citizens were responsible for the "many improvements on the road" in Grayson county.[14]

Sherman's inhabitants had been foresighted enough to discern that the Butterfield stage would bring new money and new citizens, so when Preston was initially designated "port of entry" for Texas, they expended great effort to persuade the Butterfield engineers that their town would make a better station. First, they promised that passage on Colbert's Ferry would always be free for Butterfield vehicles. Then they promised to pay for the new road from the ferry landing to Sherman, with Ben Colbert's aid. Finally, when the Butterfield locating team came to Sherman, they (along with Colbert) invited the officials to join them in what legend has termed "a sumptuous champagne dinner" which, incidentally, lead to an amusing local episode.

John Butterfield himself is said to have been the major guest—

although most authorities say that Butterfield never traveled west of Fort Smith. The flowing wine created an air of good fellowship, but led to an argument among the Shermanites as to whether or not an old gray duck—some say goose—had built a nest under the courthouse. About midnight, much wine had been drunk and many bets had been placed. The crowd marched to the frame courthouse and in the midst of high festivities proceeded to take it apart, a plank at a time. While the demolition was in progress, a member of the crowd supposedly sat on the hitching rail and played the banjo.

One version has it the old gray duck's nest was found; another states that no one remembers—which might better fit the occasion. The next morning when the sheriff came to post legal notices on the door of the courthouse, he had to drag the door from under the wreckage, nail the documents to it, and lean it against a tree. But regardless of whether there was an old gray duck, and whether or not this caused the courthouse to be dismantled, in 1858 the Grayson County commissioners advertised for bids for the construction of a new brick courthouse on the square. It must be admitted, whatever you believe really happened, that the old gray duck story has a definite Texas touch to it.[15]

In 1859 Sherman was to become one of the most important towns on the Butterfield route, being made a distribution point through which other Texas towns and settlements dispatched mail and received it by way of Overland Mail delivery. El Paso was the only other such point in Texas. Westbound mail was due in Sherman on Sundays and Wednesdays at 12:30 A.M.; eastbound mail on Friday and Tuesday at 8 P.M. Dale Babcock was the only agent for the Butterfield line in Sherman. When the Civil War broke out he left Sherman and joined the Union army while his brother Charlie, also a Butterfield employee, enlisted in the Confederate army, taking a lot of the company stock with him.[16]

Passenger traffic, like mail traffic, was also heavy in Sherman. S. H. West, in his memoirs, claimed that on January 19, 1859, there were two hundred men at the Butterfield station "all clamoring to get on the stage. They all heard of the Gila River mines in Arizona, which created great excitement in that locality. They quarreled for half an hour before they could agree who would go."[17]

On the first Butterfield Overland Mail trip through Sherman, Ormsby reported that departure was delayed because District Superintendent Henry Bates "objected to a heavy load of ammunition which was in our wagon, as too much of an incumbrance for the mail,"[18] and another wagon was rolled out to share the load. This incident indicates how dangerous and primitive the West Texas frontier was. There were so few Army posts to guard the nearly 700-mile stretch across the Lone Star State, that the Butterfield Company, for protection of its remote stations and stands, had to furnish arms and ammunition for the personnel.

From Sherman the newly built stage road went directly west. Superintendent Bates used a rider (Ormsby calls him "our express") to precede the coach so that things would be in readiness for its arrival at the next station. Ormsby wrote, "our course lay across a fine rolling prairie, covered with fine grass, but with no trees and scarcely a shrub for eighteen miles."[19]

A later historian wrote:

> Actually, the citizenry of this whole area of Texas from Red River to Belknap prepared the way for the incoming stage coaches as if they were unrolling a carpet for the footpath of a bride. Cooke County appointed an overseer exclusively for the Overland Mail road, and Jack County rushed at the job like a runner out of breath and opened thirty miles of road less than two weeks ahead of the first stagecoaches. The Young County commissioners appropriated $150—a sizable sum in 1858—to cut the new road through both timber and prairie eastward from Belknap.[20]

The first station after Sherman, at a distance of twenty miles, was Diamond's (or Diamond's Ranch), located a mile west of the present town of Whitesboro. (The post office at Whitesboro was not established until March 12, 1860.) A curiously worded historical marker on the old town well on Whitesboro's Main Street says, "Settlers moved to this site after Ambrose B. White merely camped here on his way west from Illinois in 1848. His inn here was on the Butterfield Stage Route after 1858." This seems to imply that White continued west, but he didn't. The town promoter, he was its first postmaster and first mayor. His Westview Inn of a later date became a landmark. There is no mention made of an inn at this place in Butterfield schedules or by Butterfield passengers.

At Diamond's, Ormsby witnessed "the operation of harnessing a wild mule." He estimated it took thirty minutes per mule (four were used), and he remarked, "I was much amused with the process, but it seemed a little behind the age for the mail to wait for it."[21] Diamond's station was kept by John R. Diamond, whose home was already there when the new road came through. John R. was one of six Diamond brothers who had come to Texas from Georgia a few years before. He and the Butterfield operation later figured prominently in that Civil War massacre known as The Great Gainesville Hanging (see p. 219).[22]

Ormsby, on that first westward trip, called Gainesville, "another flourishing little town." The Butterfield station and stables were located at 101 California Street, still a main traffic artery in town. The street was named for the hopeful forty-niners who envisioned California just across every river and just over every hill on the way west, scattering the California designation among half a dozen landmarks, natural and manmade, through West Texas. Gainesville, at the time the second largest Texas city on the Butterfield, was a meal and team-change station. Of his time there on that first trip, Ormsby writes, "after hastily swallowing supper and changing horses, we were off again and made our next station in the woods [Davidson's] fifteen miles distant, in two hours and fifteen minutes." Ormsby, writing to New York *Herald* readers, pointed out, "We travel night and day, and only stop long enough to change teams and eat."[23]

Soon after leaving Gainesville, Ormsby noted, "we strike the

Lower Cross Timbers . . . the trees grow wide apart, and are mainly of post oak. The open spaces, absence of underbrush, and clean looking grass gave the entire wood the appearance of a vast orchard, and I could not get rid of the impression that there was plenty of fruit at hand."[24]

At Davidson's Station, operated by Dr. J. F. Davidson, Ormsby reported that Superintendent Bates was annoyed because "nothing was in readiness." The explanation was rather vexatious: the express rider, who was to ride ahead of the coach to alert the station, had lost his way, this being a new road. Also, as Ormsby commented wryly, "some detention was experienced in harnessing more wild mules."[25] (We may sympathize with the express rider who missed the way. He was unfamiliar with that stretch of country between Gainesville and Jacksborough—later shortened to Jacksboro—and was looking for a brand new road that had been accepted by the Jack County commissioners only a few days before the first Butterfield coach rolled over it.)

Twenty miles farther (three miles southeast of the present town of Sunset) the stage arrived at a station listed on the schedule as Conolly's, the name of which Ormsby didn't mention. The Conklings decided the stationkeeper might have been J. J. Conelly, as that was the only similar sounding name they could find in Wise County.[26] Here the travelers had, in Ormsby's words, "the first of a series of rough meals which lasted for most of the remaining journey." The arrival of the Butterfield coach was unexpected, and "there was some bustle getting both breakfast and the team ready." We also find in this entry an example of the reporter's sense of humor. The station house, he wrote, "was of rough logs laid together roughly. . . . forming one room . . . occupied by two men keeping bachelors' hall, as might well be judged from the condition of things, of which the reader may imagine."[27]

Accommodations were amusingly minimal: "The breakfast was served on the bottom of a candle box, and such as sat down were perched on inverted pails or nature's chair." There were only four tin cups for the travelers, so "those not lucky enough to get a first cup [of black coffee] had to wait for the second table." Breakfast was a one-dish meal: "a kind of short cake, baked on the coals, each man breaking off his 'chunk' and plastering on butter with his pocket knife." The host, putting the meal on the table, yelled, "Hurry up before the chickens eat it," a suggestion more than rhetorical, as chickens were evidently mealtime contenders. Ormsby comments that after the warning the travelers hurried, "to the no little discomfiture of the chickens."[28]

The stage made good time over the eleven-day-old road to Joseph B. Earhart's station at Hog Eye Prairie (as the area was called) just inside Jack County. Earhart's house was a large one, some sixty by twenty-seven feet (he had seven children), surrounded by a palisade of upright timbers. Captain Earhart was a relative old timer to the region. He had been an Indian trader with Holland Coffee's trading post at Preston Bend in 1845 and operated a ferry at Colbert's station in Choctaw Nation (now Oklahoma) until 1850. In 1856, after he had operated a steam mill in Grayson County for two years, he moved to Hog Eye Prairie at age forty-four.

Earhart's daughter, Jo Ellen, was such a beauty she was known across the state as "The Wild Rose of Texas," and "Queen of the Prairie." The eldest Earhart son, Eliphalet "Lif" Penn was born in 1845 at Rock Bluff (on the Red River at Preston Bend). As an old man he described the Earhart station and how he helped his father build the nearby section of the Butterfield road. Apparently Superintendent Bates, who had a glass eye, slept on the floor at the station. The twelve-year-old boy was sure the eye stayed awake all night, "filling [his] heart with uncanny fear."[29]

Ormsby, on that first westbound journey, rode directly from Earhart's to Jacksborough, fording the West Fork of the Trinity River about halfway between the two stations. In December, 1858, a small station was established at this West Fork crossing because frequent flooding often caused the river to be too high to ford, so passengers and mail needed shelter until the water went down. Albert D.

Richardson, on September 28, 1859, arrived on the westbound stage at 1 A.M. and "found the West Trinity too much swollen for fording. The little station was full; so we slept refreshingly upon corn-husks in the barn." Next morning passengers crossed the river on "a slippery log" while the drivers, conductor and station men carried the heavy mail bags over the same way. Another coach was waiting on the far bank to continue the trip.[30]

At Jacksborough, eight miles west from the West Fork station, Ormsby reported that the plain on which the town was located "looked like a passive lake, so even and level was its surface."[31] Jacksborough, although the county seat, was only one year old at the time and had only two hundred residents. The Butterfield Overland Mail station was on the north bank of Lost Creek, on the east side of the town.[32] Here fresh mules were hitched to the stage, but on the road they proved to be stubborn and lazy, "and required the most constant urging to keep them on a respectable trot," Ormsby reported disgustedly. He wonders why horses wouldn't be more economical "in both time and labor" on this and other portions of the route. Thanks to the recalcitrant mules, the stage arrived at the next station four hours behind the time "in which [they] should have made it"—but overall the stage was still a full day ahead of schedule.[33]

Albert Richardson, visiting Jacksborough a year after Ormsby, found the station owner ("the landlord" he called him) bragging about being under bail of three thousand dollars for killing a Butterfield employee three weeks earlier, a sum Richardson felt was too low for murder. A stage driver commented sourly, "If you want to gain distinction in this country, kill somebody!"[34]

From Jacksborough the Butterfield went sixteen miles almost due west to Murphy's Spring, where Irishman Dennis J. Murphy's station (which Ormsby does not mention, possibly because he was asleep when passing) was located some four miles south of today's little town of Loving.

Sixteen miles west of Murphy's was a major Butterfield station at Belknap, the town adjacent to the military post of Fort Belknap, and at the time, county seat of Young County. This was a timetable station; that is, mail from the east was due on Mondays and Thursdays at 9 A.M., and mail from the west on Mondays and Thursdays at 11:30 A.M. The company had erected a building and a stone corral for this station. Ormsby described the town at Fort Belknap as having about one hundred fifty inhabitants, with houses "most of them" looking neat. As was true of most Texas military outposts, Fort Belknap was not a strong, walled installation, but merely a collection of stone and log structures built around a parade ground. "The fort is not very formidable," Ormsby noted, obviously disappointed at seeing his first frontier fort and finding no ramparts and redoubts.[35] Reverend Tallack saw Fort Belknap from the opposite point of view. Since he was traveling west to east, it represented not the beginning of the frontier fort system, but the end of it. On reaching the segment east of Fort Belknap he gives a sigh of relief, writing:

> With the uninhabited solitudes of the desert and prairie we have also left behind us the rough and often villainous station-keepers and their coarse fare. The stations hereabouts and henceforward are kept by persons . . . whose accommodation and manners are a decided improvement on what we have hitherto met with.[36]

Fort Belknap was also supposedly the point at which mules were substituted for horses going west, and vice versa going east. However, as we discover from Ormsby, mules were used during the first trip between Sherman and Fort Belknap, and they continued to be used on this stretch of the route more often than horses. Horses furnished too great an attraction to raiding parties, even with Fort Belknap astride the road.[37]

The Butterfield stage forded the Brazos River just west of Fort Belknap, and the dirty red water was said by Ormsby to be "not deeper than an ordinary New York sewer." He acknowledged the river was very low at the time and that it often reached a depth of as much as sixteen feet. The company contemplated establishing a ferry at this point, he said.[38] No ferry was ever used, so far as Butterfield documents tell us. At the river crossing, seams of coal were easily descried (and stick out even today from cuts and grades). The soldiers of Fort Belknap mined coal here for their use, and the Butterfield blacksmiths along the Texas route may also have been supplied with coal from the Bridgeport-Fort Belknap area. In later times several large mining companies shipped coal from both Bridgeport and Newcastle, just north of Belknap.

In 1858, the Brazos River was considered the eastern boundary of civilization. There was then, and still is today, a change in the terrain and the atmosphere "beyond the Brazos." Richardson said he felt it was "the jumping-off place" and noted, "We were soon on the plains where Indians claim exclusive domain, and every traveler is a moving arsenal."[39]

In the twenty miles or so from the Brazos River to Franz's station, Ormsby was bored, "with hardly a house or field to beguile the dreary spectacle." The only objects of interest passed on the road from Fort Belknap, he said, were a train of government mules, herds of cattle "taking care of themselves," and a Comanche Indian woman "riding 'straddle,'"[40] an unthinkable act for a many-petticoated Anglo woman.

Franz's station, as Butterfield records spelled the name, was located just north of the present town of Woodson, in Throckmorton County. It was in the home of James Madison "Uncle Mat" Franz (or France or Frans as the name was spelled by the family).[41] Speaking with the Conklings nearly seventy-five years later, Mrs. Elizabeth F. Tharp of Throckmorton, a daughter of the France (as she wrote it) family, remembered Superintendent Bates. As was the case with twelve-year-old Lif Earhart, Bates's glass eye made a deep impression on the young girl at a similar age. She also recalled her mother cooking all meals, for family and Butterfield passengers alike, in the open fireplace. The family sometimes got up in the night to prepare passengers' meals. When this happened, nobody in the family was allowed to go back to bed until the dishes had been washed.[42]

In 1860, Uncle Mat France moved his family thirteen miles farther west and operated the Clear Fork Station for Butterfield.[43] John Chadbourne Irwin, the venerable memorist born in 1855 who spent his entire life in central West Texas, told the Conklings his father (John G. Irwin) and T. E. Jackson were associated with the Clear Fork station at some period in 1859. Regardless of who eventually ran the Clear Fork station, when Ormsby visited it on that first trip the station keeper's log house was just being erected. The intrepid New York reporter states that the Clear Fork of the Brazos, despite its name, was not very clear, "but even its muddy waters were a grateful boon for a bath while our horses were being changed. . . . Dr. Birch, the Mail Agent, had everything in readiness, so that I had to finish dressing in the wagon, so short was the delay."[44] The Reverend Mr. Tallack was rather horrified at the bathing habits of some of his fellow passengers. Noting that he carried towels and a sponge with him so as to take quick advantage of a hasty bath when possible, he added, "Many passengers go through the entire route without once changing their linen, and sometimes without the barest apology for [not] washing."[45]

From the Clear Fork the Butterfield Trail went southwest along the north bank of Lambshead Creek, today within historic Matthews-Lambshead Ranch. On the ride, passing around and over the low hills of southwestern Throckmorton County, Ormsby noticed two bluffs "whose position reminded me forcibly of East and West Rock as seen on entering New Haven harbor." The stage road also weaved its way between the cavalry post at Camp Cooper (1856-1861) and the hilltop site that would become Fort Griffin in 1867. Entering Shackelford County, the road crossed what is today the J. H. Nail ranch, continuing southwestward to Smith's station. No house had been built there by September 1858, and those at the station were living in tents, cooking on an outdoor fire. "Our supper," Ormsby wrote, "consisted of cake cooked in the coals, clear coffee, and some dried beef cooked in Mrs. Smith's best style . . . we swallowed supper in double quick time and were soon on our way again." Ormsby recognized that the rolling plains were "covered with good grass" (it is still fine ranch country), but he found it "a sorry landscape, I assure you." The sorry landscape, however, was much enlivened by "Big Dick," the driver "who amused us with accounts of how he was three days on the [Erie] canal and never saw land because he was drunk in the hold."[46]

The name of Chimney Creek, on whose east bank Smith's station was located, was named for the chimney of the Butterfield station. The Conklings state that the name was not applied to the little watercourse until later in the 1860s. Still, some romantics are convinced the name has a mysterious history; that the stream was called Chimney Creek before the Butterfield people started operations there. If this were the case, some surveyor may have fancied he saw a chimney in a rock formation, but nothing in the way of such a natural formation can be found today. When the Butterfield road party under command of Colonel James B. Leach passed through the country in 1857, it camped at a spring where Smith's station was later located. Leach, in his diary, makes no mention of a chimney.[47] However, when Captain Randolph Marcy passed through the area in 1849, he noted that flat limestone rock is abundant along the creek banks, already cubed "as if prepared by some great Natural Mason."[48] Shackelford County historians find no evidence that any settler preceded Smith's station on Chimney Creek, but one longs to fantasize that some mysterious mason—a Spaniard from Coronado's 1541 wanderings?—found a way to survive, making friends with the tribal rulers.

Continuing southwest, the old mail road crossed Deadman Creek, named for James Moorehead, a Missouri soldier buried on its banks, who froze to death in a blizzard on November 11, 1851, when he wandered from camp. His unit was on its way to establish Fort Phantom Hill, the next Butterfield station on the westward journey. Ormsby doesn't have much to say about the intervening countryside, there being no unusual geological features on the surface. Later there was, for a few years, a little town of Rising Sun, across whose future site the Butterfield trail ran. But despite Rising Sun's optimistic name, its day was short—so short that its very existence is questioned by landowners in that region who look across the field where the town was supposed to grow and see nothing but furrows.

Fort Phantom Hill station, located about twelve miles north of present-day Abilene, utilized three of the stone houses left standing by the military when the fort was abandoned in 1854. The magazine, a tightly built rock structure, was taken by Dr. Birch, the mail agent, as a company storehouse, and one of the houses with extant walls became the station. "Altogether, Phantom Hill is the cheapest and best new station on the route," Ormsby said. He praised Mr. Burlington and wife, the stationkeepers, "all alone here hundreds of miles from any settlement, bravely stopping at their post, fearless of the attacks of blood-thirsty Indians—as brave a man as ever settled on a frontier and a monument of shame to the cowardly soldiers who burned the post."[49]

Ormsby seldom preached during his Overland Mail trip, but he took the occasion of visiting Fort Phantom Hill to do a little sermonizing.

The station is directly in the trail of the northern Comanches as they run down into Texas on their marauding expeditions. To leave this and other stations on the route so exposed is trifling with human life, and inviting an attack on the helpless defenders of the mail. As I have already said, there will be designing white men as well as Indians whose cupidity must be overawed by adequate military protection.[50]

The name of this fort has mystified several generations, and a number of myths have tried to explain it in ghostly terms. For example, Albert Richardson wrote, "Daylight found us at Phantom Hill, named for the white, ghostly chimnies [sic] of a burned fort."[51]

The fact is, the fort sat on a small rise and from a distance (partic-ularly from the east, the direction so much early travel came from), this rise looks to be a true hill. But on arrival there, the hill has dis-appeared—a phantom hill. There is a good reason for us to accept this as the origin of the name: this is the explanation given by Cap-tain Marcy in 1849, two years before the fort was erected there on his recommendation.

Most of the ghostly myths about the Phantom Hill name concern incidents told by the soldiers who came at a later time.[52] For instance, in 1854 when the troops abandoned Fort Phantom Hill (which was officially named "Post on the Clear Fork of the Brazos"), legend says the officer in charge remarked he wished nobody would ever have to serve in that hell-hole again, and two men of his command, over-hearing him and feeling it was almost a direct order, rode back and fired the entire set-up. (There is also a version stating that Co-manches fired the fort.) Although most of the buildings were jacal, or upright posts, several were of stone (and nearly every building had a rock chimney), so the destruction was not total. Ormsby, who had heard this story, was quite disapproving of the alleged military ac-tion. "Over half a million dollars' worth of property was destroyed . . . yet after a pretended investigation no conclusion was arrived at as to the cause of the diabolical deed."[53]

On Ormsby's visit, there were no fresh mules awaiting at Fort Phantom, so the coach proceeded with the "already jaded animals [that had] brought us already thirty-four miles at a good pace, but we had to go fifteen miles further, or half way to Abercrombie Peak, before we met another team."[54] Abercrombie Peak—indeed, the en-tire range—was named by Lieutenant Colonel J. J. Abercrombie, the first commander of Fort Phantom Hill, who rode over West Texas naming things for himself, a practice he seemed to enjoy, continu-ing the custom with Fort Abercrombie in North Dakota five years later.[55]

The station at Mountain Pass (or Abercrombie Pass, as Ormsby calls it) served the coach breakfast "which consisted of the standard—coffee, tough beef, and butterless short cake, prepared by an old Negro woman, who, if cleanliness is next to godliness, would stand but little chance of heaven."[56] According to a St. Louis newspaper, a Negro cook—not believed the one whose uncleanliness was mentioned by Ormsby—was killed in a February 1, 1859, raid by the Comanches on Mountain Pass station shortly before the Butterfield stage arrived. That same week at Phantom Hill, a passenger told the newspaper that twenty-eight mules got stampeded by the Comanches just at the moment the stage was driving up to the station. The Mountain Pass site was to see further Indian troubles in future decades. On August 22, 1867, a troop of U.S. Army soldiers was ambushed at the pass by Comanches and two troopers were killed. They were buried by the trail until their bodies were later removed to San Antonio's military cemetery.

On New Year's Day, 1871, eighteen cowboys and Texas Rangers led by Captain James Swisher and rancher Sam Gholson overtook a small Comanche raiding party moving stolen horses from Coleman County, and forced the raiders to retreat hurriedly into the hills on the west side of the pass. A day-long battle ensued, with the Indians slipping away after nightfall but leaving behind the stolen stock. J. M. Elkins, a member of the Texas party, states that one Indian was killed and one cowboy was wounded.[57]

Emma Johnson Elkins, who spent most of her life in West Texas, wrote several stories about events there in the nineteenth century, many of which were reprinted in her husband's 1929 publication, *Indian Fighting on the Texas Frontier*. Her historical accuracy is indifferent, subject to memory and hearsay, but it has a certain eyewitness charm and most of the errors are easily recognized. For example, Mrs. Elkins writes, "The overland mail route was terribly harassed by the Indians, who on several occasions attacked stages on the road, giving them some lively races." This is an overstatement, as the Butterfield stage experience in Texas was nearly free of Indian "harassment." She also writes, "The station at Mountain Pass was attacked one evening just at sunset and the keeper and two of his employees killed and scalped, the horses turned out of the corral and driven away. A Mexican sheep herder was also killed."[58] There may be a taint of truth to this little insertion, possibly the attack mentioned by the Conklings, but the losses don't appear to have been as drastic as Mrs. Elkins presents.

The Mountain Pass station and the Valley Creek station, the next one on the line, were both kept by men named Lambshead. Ormsby remarks that the Valley Creek stationkeeper "was appropriately named for he had a drove of 300 sheep grazing, growing, and increasing without expense to him."[59] Fifty-three-year-old Thomas Lambshead was from Devon, England. He and his wife had come to Texas prior to 1848 as part of the Texas Emigration and Land Company project (the Peters Colony) in North Texas which covered all or part of twenty-six modern counties. Generous grants (640 acres) were given to married or widowed colonists; most located in such settled counties as Dallas, Collin, Denton and Cooke. But Thomas Lambshead's grant was in Throckmorton County, reportedly "next to the outside grant" on the western border of the colony, far beyond white civilization. The east boundary of the Peters Colony began along the eastern edge of Dallas County, some 200 miles away. Lambshead Creek, mentioned as being along the Butterfield pathway, was named for Thomas, and the famed Lambshead Ranch grew from his original acreage. The other Lambshead noted by Ormsby may have been a brother named John; Ormsby is the only Butterfield passenger to mention him.[60]

Riding through the section after Valley Creek, Waterman Ormsby makes a sensible suggestion, one that was followed up seven or eight decades later. He noted that the stage line could save some 200 miles if it went directly west at Fort Chadbourne, the next station. Instead, it cut a full degree south to avoid "the much dreaded [waterless] Llano Estacado." He remarks that all of this troublesome routing "might have been saved had the money which has been expended in trying to sink artesian wells on the Staked Plains been applied to building plain tanks to catch the water when it falls, as it often does in copious quantities." Ormsby is referring to the unrewarding efforts of Captain John Pope who had drilled artesian wells in Far West Texas and New Mexico since 1855, but had failed to find adequate water supplies. As Ormsby suggested, by mid-twentieth century, man-made lakes large and small dotted that "much dreaded" region.[61]

The next station after Valley Creek was Fort Chadbourne, in the northwest corner of Coke County. Ormsby, confusing Oak Creek on which it is situated with "the little Colorado," reached Fort Chadbourne on Thursday afternoon "the 23rd of September, nearly twenty-four hours ahead of time table, having traversed 955 miles of our journey without accident and but little delay." It is a historically significant post, and, unlike many ante-bellum West Texas forts which were often of log or *jacal* construction, Fort Chadbourne had been carefully crafted by German stonecutters and masons brought up from San Antonio in 1852. Ormsby noticed this, remarking that "some of the buildings look unusually neat for this section of the country." The large station itself, on the north side, separate from the fort, was also built of stone, one of the more substantial Butterfield structures on the entire Texas run. One spacious room, twenty-eight by eighteen feet, had a big fireplace, probably used for cooking. Ormsby also notes that Chadbourne "is almost surrounded by a sort of barricade which was built a few years since in anticipation of a sweeping attack by the Indians—which did not come off."[62]

Chadbourne was a time table station. Westbound mail was due on Tuesdays and Fridays at 3:15 P.M. and eastbound mail on Wednesdays and Sundays at 5:15 A.M. It is easily assumed that the arrival of the Butterfield coach was a major event, bringing news and national gossip to parts of the world where cities and towns were nonexistent. Some historians have asserted that the stage line also brought greatly increased population along its route. But in Texas, once beyond the Brazos, this doesn't seem to have been the case. However, a few civilian "towns" grew up around some of the forts, and some soldiers who were married (most were not) brought their families west to live with them. Frontier storyteller Emma Elkins's father was a sergeant at Fort Phantom Hill where she was a baby, and John Chadbourne Irwin (born 1855), was the first child born at Fort Chadbourne, where his father was First Sergeant—hence his middle name.

The Reverend Mr. Tallack seemed ambivalent about the conditions in the Fort Chadbourne station when he wrote, "Today we reached Fort Chadbourne and breakfasted at the first inclosed farm we have seen since leaving California, and at the same time met with the first appearance of slavery in our route, as a regular institution." And you can almost see the scowl on his face as he remembers, "Our table and food were black with clustering flies, which crowded even into our tea, and had to be spooned out by wholesale."[63] The English divine, inspired, perhaps, by nature's West Texas absolutes like flies and heat, recorded some interesting, if questionable (to modern readers), food ideas, such as the following. Before reaching Fort Chadbourne he noted, "We passed crops of maize, wheat sugarcane, and sunflowers—the latter cultivated on account of their leaves, from which a kind of 'tea' is extracted by decoction."[64]

Sitting as it did on the edge of the West Texas frontier, Fort Chadbourne was the "jumping off place" for emigrants headed for California by way of the upper road through the Guadalupe Mountains. In 1861 hundreds who left Texas for the loyal territories of the West Coast moved out through the Fort Chadbourne area. Noah Smithwick, who in April, 1861, sold his holdings near Austin and started west with a wagon train, wrote: "At Fort Chadbourne we encountered the first visible effects of impending war in the absence of the American flag from the fort where it had fanned the breeze for so long."[65]

As the Civil War was beginning, Fort Chadbourne had two of what may be termed "final" visits from the Butterfield Stage. The final westbound U.S. Mail is reported to have left Fort Smith, Arkansas, early in April, 1861, but to have gotten only as far as Fort Chadbourne.[66] Anson Mills was aboard the last eastbound Butterfield stage, which arrived at Fort Chadbourne on March 12, 1861, after the fort had been taken over by Texas troops of the Committee on Public Safety.[67] Mills wrote in his autobiography,

> The secessionists had organized several companies of state troops commanded by the McCullough [McCulloch] brothers and others. We met part of this force under the younger McCullough [Henry E.], near Fort Chadbourne, and we were all excitement to know what they would do, as it was rumored they would seize the mail company horses for cavalry. Marching in columns of two, they separated, one column to the right and the other to the left of the stage coach. We told the driver to drive fast and to say that we were carrying the United States mail. The soldiers laughed at this, and four of them taking hold of the right hand wheels and four of the left, the driver could not, with the greatest whipping, induce the horses to proceed. They [the secessionists] laughed again and called out: "Is Horace Greeley aboard?" Horace Greeley had been lecturing in California, and had announced his return by the Butterfield route. The soldiers were familiar with his picture and, after examining us, allowed us to proceed.[68]

Horace Greeley, a vehement foe of slavery, would have been easily recognized, with his "mild, pink face, fringed by throat whiskers, his broad-brimmed hat, white overcoat, crooked cravat, his shambling gait and absent-minded manner."[69] After Horace Greeley's trip west, instead of returning via Overland Mail, he returned to the east via steamship. His change of plans was not cowardly. Albert Richardson, who had traveled with the famous editor to Denver, explained that by the time Greeley arrived in California "he was visited with the traditional annoyance of plains travelers—boils which covered his body, compelling him to return home by steamer instead of the Butterfield overland route."[70] Boils are an infection (staphylococci) which can be spread by drainage; cleanliness, not always possible on the frontier, is a factor.[71]

Departing Fort Chadbourne, Ormsby recorded that the station handlers encountered the wild mule problem again. Ormsby wrote,

Mr. J. B. Nichols . . . was to drive and Mr. Mather . . . was to proceed on horseback, point out the road, and maintain a general supervision. Whether from the inefficiency of Mr. Nichols' driving, or because Mr. Mather's furious riding frightened the mules, or because the mules were wild, or that the boys had been having a jolly good time on the occasion of the arrival of the first stage, or by a special dispensation of Providence—or from a combination of all these causes—I will not pretend to say, but certainly, some unforeseen and vexatious cause, we here suffered a detention of some hours.

The mules reared, pitched, twisted, whirled, wheeled, ran, stood still, and cut up all sorts of capers. The wagon performed so many evolutions that I, in fear of my life, abandoned it and took to my heels. . . . Mr. Lee, sutler at the fort, who . . . had come out on horseback to see us [the coach] start, kindly offered to take me up behind him—to which, though not much of an equestrian, I acceded with the view of having a little better sight of the sport from a safe distance.[72]

The affair ended up with mules and harness tangled, the exit of both lead mules "into the woods, and the complete demolition of the top of the [celerity] wagon," while the handlers flopped on the grass, tired out and disgusted. "For my part," Ormsby said sourly, "I thought it the most ludicrous scene I ever witnessed." But despite this short spurt of ill-humor, even at this point, Ormsby's good nature took over:

Both of the leading mules having escaped, and Mr. Mather having become completely anxious that everyone should go to the d—l, and understand he did not care a d—n for anyone, I thought the progress of the mail, for that night at least, was stopped; but Nichols averred that the mail should go on if he went alone with the two wheel-mules; and sure enough, he started off after getting the harness once more disentangled, and kept the road in fine style.[73]

Seeing wagon and driver going on without him, Ormsby reports, "I rode up to him [on Mr. Lee's mount], and, finding persuasion to no avail, overcame my strong objections" and boarded the coach, "though," he added, "if I had had any property I certainly should have made a hasty will."[74]

By now it was dark. Mr. Mather's profane announcement that every one should go to the d—l and that he was going home, meant there was no guide, only an outrider who accompanied the stage to take back the two-mule team pulling it. In addition to the condition of stage and team, the Butterfield road here crossed a major Comanche war trail. In view of the other problems, it seems inconsequential to add that the coach, with its top ripped off, had no lanterns. But pretty soon Ormsby seems to have recovered his composure and records an amusing bit of dialogue:

"How far is it to the next station?" [Ormsby asked.]

"I believe it is thirty miles." [Nichols said.]

"Do you know the road?"

"No."

"How do you expect to get there?"

"There's only one road; we can't miss it."

"Have you any arms?"

"No, I don't want any; there's no danger."[75]

Despite wishing he could have started under other circumstances, Ormsby felt he was "bound to go with the mail." Fortunately, the night was clear and bright and the "course was a clear and straight one, leading across an apparently boundless prairie, with not a tree or shrub to be seen." The single team of mules was willing and the moon came out, making it easier to finish this leg of the journey. Ormsby alternately drove while Nichols slept, or slept while Nichols drove, or rode horseback with the outrider. But about 2 A.M. the wayfarers came to a steep and stony hill "right in our path and impossible of avoidance." Ormsby reports,

One mule could neither be coaxed or driven up, so we had to camp until morning, when, after much difficulty, we ascended the hill and discovered the station . . . a speck among the trees [and] soon reached it. The station men had seen the coach coming and were herding the mules as we drove up.[76]

This was Grape Creek station located on what Ormsby terms "a fine stream" and completely enclosed by a fence of upright timber five feet high. He seems deliberately to compliment Mr. Henry Roylan, the agent in charge, for having things ready—understandable after the debacle at Fort Chadbourne. Mr. Roylan himself took the reins over the rolling prairies for the next leg.

Farwell's *Alta Californian* report, made a few weeks later, was more sinister: "Here [Grape Creek], upon our arrival, the keeper of the station informed us that on the day previous . . . the Indians had been in and 'stampeded' seven mules and one horse. These animals were outside the corral, and the Indians came in one day and drove them off, the three men at the station looking on unable to prevent it."[77]

Mrs. Emma Elkins tells an interesting story about the final days of the Grape Creek station—a story which has become part of West Texas frontier lore. The station keeper at that time (1861) was named Joel Pennington, who lived there with his wife, his brother-in-law Charles Cox, and hostler Elijah Helms. Mrs. Elkins writes that in February of 1861, the Grape Creek station was besieged by a band of thirty Comanches who took all the stock and held station personnel at gunpoint. The Comanche chief, looking over the take, complained that the stock was quite inferior. He told Pennington that he and his band would return in a month and if Pennington couldn't furnish better stock, they would all be killed. Grabbing a blanket off Mrs. Pennington's bed and tossing it over one shoulder, this bold chieftain strode out the station door and rode away.[78]

Meanwhile, the Butterfield stage made its last trips, and the Penningtons and other employees were preparing to leave the station when the same chief appeared. There was nothing left but a wagon team and one or two ponies, and so he attempted to fulfill his threat.

Fortunately, the station house was made of split logs and was virtually bulletproof, but the Indians set fire to the place and the occupants had to fight their way out. Pennington, running from the burning house, ran close to the palisade fence and received a shotgun blast which tore away part of his face. Helms and Cox drove off the Indians and carried the wounded Pennington a few miles and hid him in some bushes. Leaving Mrs. Pennington and Cox to guard, Helms rode to Fort Chadbourne for aid. An ambulance brought Pennington to the fort hospital where, Mrs. Elkins wrote, "In company with my mother, I visited Pennington . . . and must say this was the most terrible sight I ever witnessed. Contrary to the expectations of all who saw him, this man recovered and was sent under escort to his home at Fort Mason."[79]

After leaving Grape Creek station, Ormsby either did not make himself clear as to his next stop or his words were garbled in transmission from his penned report to the printed page. The newspaper report states,

A few miles from Grape Creek we crossed the Concho, and then, leaving the old road, which follows its winding course, we took a new road, across the country, which has been made under the supervision of the company—a ride of about thirty miles, again at a station about twenty-five miles from Chadbourne, after following the Concho to its source on the borders of the dreaded Staked Plain, where we arrived about 2:30 A.M. of Saturday, the 25th of September.[80]

The Butterfield station he barely mentioned was at the mouth of Rocky Creek, less than a mile south of the site of old Arden in Irion County. The station (on the Middle Concho River) was referred to by Goddard Bailey (see "An Inspectors Report," p. 217) and on the first schedule simply as "Concho."[81] Within a few months this station would be moved some four miles west to the site of the former Camp Joseph E. Johnston, established by the Army in 1852 and named for Colonel Johnston who had explored the region in 1849 and 1851 and was Chief Topographical Engineer of the Department of Texas from 1848 to 1853.[82]

Between the Middle Concho and the Head of Concho station, the Butterfield route lay across a plot that would become, in April, 1868, Camp Charlotte, a picket post of Fort Concho, which had been established the year before. Camp Charlotte was installed to protect the mail road, which remained in use long after the Butterfield stages stopped using it. While seldom listed as a separate military post, Camp Charlotte came closer to most people's idea of a western fort than did the majority of Texas military centers. It had a very large stockade within which were the mess hall, stables, quarters and various housing for cook, tailor, blacksmith, saddle maker, and stable hands. Guard posts were built at the four corners and there was a big front gate, just like in the movies.[83]

Beyond the future Camp Charlotte site was the Head of Concho station, built by the Butterfield company. It had eleven-foot high stone and adobe walls with a gate tall enough to admit a coach and team, the walls creating a corral with rooms opening inside along the walls. The Conklings said a chain of twenty-five stations of similar plan had been built from Head of Concho at strategic points into Arizona. The station was in the northwest corner of what is now Irion County. Ormsby, many hours after departing the unnamed station [Middle Concho] back at Rocky Creek, wrote:

> We reached the head of the Concha [Concho] River early on the morning of Saturday, the 25th of September, and found there a most comfortable camp. . . . Our arrival was unexpected, and all haste was immediately made to get us something to eat and start us again on our journey. The good natured Dutchman who officiated as cook quickly arranged the tin cups and plates and got us some broiled bacon, shortcake, and coffee, which was considered quite an aristocratic meal for so early a settlement, and which our long ride certainly made acceptable, however different from New York fare.[84]

Once again, however, the wild mule problem arose and an hour was lost getting the beasts in harness, but eventually the wagon, well supplied with canteens of water, was "on [its] way to the great Staked Plain."[85] In reflecting on the waterless quality of the upcoming terrain, Ormsby admits,

> It was, then, with no little fear that I approached this, what I deemed the most dangerous part of the journey, where for a distance of seventy-five miles . . . not a drop of water could be procured for all the wealth of the world. Indeed, I was so carried away with the horrors of the trip that it was some time before it occurred to me that we might carry some water in the wagons—which reflection finally consoled me not a little.[86]

Ormsby mentions encountering only the Mustang Springs (where "we let our mules drink their fill"), but most early maps show other waterholes on the route to the Pecos River, even though (to the sorrow of those using the maps) such were usually dry or were saline. For example, on the 1857 Bureau of Topographical Engineers map, between "Head Springs of Concho" and the Horsehead Crossing of the Pecos River, there are "Mustang Ponds," "Flat Rock Ponds," and "Wild China Ponds" along the 1849 route of Lieutenant F. T. Bryan and the 1851 trail of Lieutenant Colonel Joseph E. Johnston.[87]

These "ponds" of water, though shown on maps, were notorious for their unreliability. Oscar Call, Burnet County surveyor, was working near Horsehead Crossing in July and August of 1858 and kept a diary of what he called an "Exploring Trip to the Ojo de los Santos of the Pecos." One entry states, "We found a little water standing in a hole . . . but did not stop to replenish our canteens, thinking that we would find water in the Flat Rock Ponds, but were sweetly deceived by 'Young & Co. Map Makers'. . . . [Then] at midnight passed the celebrated 'wild China ponds' but found not a drop of water for our suffering horses."[88]

Major Robert Neighbors, passing through in 1849, had been more optimistic, but possibly too optimistic, since subsequent accounts nearly all contradict his findings:

> There is no portion of the route [to El Paso] I cannot represent as possessing an adequate supply of water at all seasons except it be from the head of the Concho to the Pecos . . . and there are four water holes known to be upon it with water enough for all purposes: should these fail in the hot summer months, the difficulty can be easily obviated by sinking wells in the valley of the wild China Water hole, and the pass of the Castle Mountain [Castle Gap], at which points water can be reached within a few feet of the surface.[89]

After leaving the Head of Concho, the Butterfield line crossed another future military site which would eventually be known as "Centralia" or "Central Station," a second picket post from Camp Charlotte. It is named for Centralia Draw (or vice versa?), which is a "central" prong of the Concho River. A. M. (Gus) Gildea, a cowboy quoted in *Trail Drivers of Texas*, said that in September, 1876, "At Centralia, which was a stage station on the high plains guarded by Negro troops, we left the stage road and followed the old Butterfield route to Horsehead Crossing."[90] J. W. Williams says that Centralia was built as a way station on Ben Ficklin's mail road. His opinion differs a bit from Gildea's, as Williams claims that "all visible evidence indicates that his road was the same as the road used by Butterfield interests."[91]

Ormsby, rolling across the country between Head of Concho and Horsehead Crossing, which even today remains remote and little visited, wrote, "I was agreeably surprised to see, instead of a tedious sea of parched sand, a variety of curious though weird vegetation." He also remarked on what he termed "the most curious plant . . . called the Spanish dagger. In the twilight they may easily be transformed into imaginary Indians by the timid. I often mistook them for men as we passed along."[92] Large droves of antelope were frequently seen, along with "quail, snipe, and other specimens of the feathered tribe." Ormsby remarks that "dog towns" were innumerable and that "they [prairie dogs] seem to be a cross between a squirrel and a rat terrier."[93] The Reverend Mr. Tallack, on his summer of 1860 ride, also noted the little animals, reporting "we have travelled through many 'dog towns,' or districts full of the burrows of the prairie marmot." Tallack, observing the "dog towns," points out the presence of numerous rattlesnakes and owls "that are popularly said to form a vast 'happy family' with the marmots; but the probability is . . . that the little prairie dogs and their young not only afford lodgings but board also."[94]

Although Ormsby doesn't report on nature *per se* as does Reverend Tallack, he noted, at the end of his ride, "The route is prolific in interest to the naturalist, the mineralogist, and all who love to contemplate nature in her wildest varieties and throughout the whole 2,700 miles the interest in new objects is not allowed to flag."[95] Farwell, traveling eastward, seems to have been similarly impressed: "From the reports which we had obtained, I had imagined that this was a barren and sterile waste. Nothing is more erroneous. It is one of the pleasantest features of the whole journey. The road across it— a distance of eighty miles—cannot be excelled. . . . This plain abounds in game—antelope, deer, hare, pinnated grouse, quail, etc."[96] Tallack tells of seeing herds of antelope, several red deer, a wild turkey "and several muleared hares." Writing for an English audience, he relates,

After sundown one of the passengers exclaimed, "Lightning bugs!" and, on turning to see what these were, we found them to be fire-flies, a number of which were gliding in beautiful curves across a stream like silent floating stars of bright green fire amongst the deepening shades of the surrounding foliage . . . and from hence we observed fire-flies almost every evening. . . . They are one of the principal ornaments of an American landscape after dark.[97]

It was a rugged existence, even for its time. Richardson, writing about this long stretch, says, "We journeyed for eighty miles across a corner of the desert, passing two or three mail stations, the most desolate and lonely of all human habitations." Richardson was obviously repeating something he had been told when he offered this little myth of natural history: ". . . in ancient lake beds, our coach wheels crushed rattlesnakes lying lazily in the road. They seldom bite *except in August*, when they are said to be blind and snap indiscriminately at every living thing."[98]

Nature's grimmer images were recorded by Ormsby also. Originally riding through this area along with a delightful breeze and saying, "I could not realize that I was in a desert," he soon found deadly evidence of that fact "strewn along the road and far as the eye could reach along the plain—decayed and decaying animals, the bones of cattle and sometimes of men (the hide drying on the skin in the arid atmosphere), all [telling] a fearful story of anguish and terrific death from the pangs of thirst . . . silent witnesses of the eternal laws of nature."[99] Although Ormsby has proved to be a reliable reporter, we might be entitled to question that he saw "sometimes the bones of men . . . hide drying on the skin." Perhaps, as noted before, his copy was misinterpreted or mis-edited, a typo was made, or a stick of type was "pied" back in New York. In any case, when someone died along the old trails they were usually buried nearby. In 1883 a surveyor found this inscription on the gravestone of one such child:

> Where are the ones who loved so dear
> the little one buried here?
> Have they forgotten that their child
> still sleeps in Western Texas wild?[100]

During the long passage from Head of Concho station to Horsehead Crossing, the Butterfield stage on its first westward journey passed through Castle Gap, a noted landmark in early days. It is situated about nine miles southeast of the present-day town of Crane, and some markers refer to the area as Castle Mountain. One local legend recorded on a historical marker involves the "treasure" of Emperor Maximilian said "to have been buried in the vicinity by his aides in the 1860s." Another marker in the nearby town of Rankin notes that the ranch of Dr. George Washington Elliott, built in 1886, "near the old Butterfield Stage Road, [in Upton County] had to haul water from Head of Concho, fifty miles."

On the long dry stretch to the Pecos River, Ormsby's driver was a New Yorker named Jones, "of Herculean frame, from which he has been surnamed the 'baby'." At one point, Baby Jones captured a rattlesnake and gave the rattles to Ormsby who, after exalting in the freshness of the Great Staked Plain, by then had pronounced riding on the plain a bore.[101] The Pecos was reached at Horsehead Crossing, but the stage did not actually cross the river at this point. Ormsby records that there were "no trees nor any unusual luxuriance of foliage on the banks at the point where we struck it . . . [so] if our driver had not been on the lookout we might have been wallowing in its muddy depth."[102] Farwell had this to say about the famous river: "The Pejos [sic] is almost red in appearance, and hardly drinkable. Capt. Skillman, who has for many years resided in Texas, informed me that it was supposed to flow over beds of copper ore, gypsum and saltpetre. It is considered healthy in its effects."[103]

Horsehead Crossing was named for the lines of horse skulls found by some early explorers, who believed they were used by the Comanches to mark one of the few rock-bottomed passages on the upper stretch of the Texas Pecos. According to John S. (Rip) Ford,

The Indian explanation was simple and plausible. The crossing being on the main trail to and from Chihuahua was a favorite camping place both going and coming. The first waterhole southwest of the crossing was sixty miles distant. Indians returning from Mexico, with stolen horses, would drive them hard to reach water. The loose animals, on reaching the Pecos, would plunge into the stream to quench their thirst, and drink until they became sick, and would die soon.[104]

Albert Richardson's 1859 description of this major crossing of the dread Comanche war trail used by raiding parties on the way to and from Mexico is of deeply worn, separate paths where warriors rode as many as eight abreast.[105]

Horsehead Crossing station was a timetable station, the westbound mail arriving on Thursdays and Sundays at 3:45 A.M. and the eastbound mail on Mondays and Fridays at 4:45 A.M. Division superintendent James Glover, pushing supplemental stock for the desolate stretch of upcoming road, had arrived at the station a few hours before the stage carrying Ormsby. Ormsby surveyed the attendants with scorn: "A more miserable looking set of fellows I never saw. They stood shivering over the fire, and had to be fairly driven off to get the things in readiness for our immediate departure." To make matters worse, the usual hullabaloo harnessing the wild mules was undergone here, as in several past stations.[106]

The original Butterfield mail road continued along the east bank of the Pecos, passing by both Horsehead Crossing and Emigrants Crossing, and going through Skillman and Pope's Camp before crossing over. This was the trail laid in 1855 by Captain John Pope, taking boilers and drills northward on his artesian well expedition on the Llano Estacado. The Butterfield company called it "Capt. Pope's new road," but Ormsby's evaluation of it was quite low: "It was full of stumps and bunches of weeds which made it by no means pleasant riding in the . . . wagons, for the jolting was almost interminable and insufferable, and I frequently wished that Captain Pope could experience *my* ride over his road."[107] On August 1, 1859, the Butterfield company abandoned this path, changing to what became known as the "lower route," crossing the Pecos at Horsehead Crossing and going south through Fort Stockton, and to Fort Davis, up the Rio Grande to El Paso. (This 1859 route is discussed in Part III.)

The east bank road was hard on everybody, including the stock. Ormsby wrote: "We started with four mules to the wagon and eighteen in the *cavellado* [*caballada*, or *remuda*]; but the latter dwindled down in numbers as one by one the animals gave out. Most of them tired out before they started. The prospect seemed pretty dreary for us . . . as we had 113 miles to travel before we could get any fresh stock." Fortunately for the travelers, after riding sixteen miles on "Capt. Pope's new road," the stage met a train of wagons belonging to a Mr. McHenry, a freighter who was en route from San Francisco to San Antonio with a load of grain for the Butterfield stations along the way. Ormsby relates,

By his invitation we stopped and breakfasted with him, giving our mules a chance to eat, drink, and rest. On hitching up we had another exhibition of the efficiency of the wild mule system, losing another half hour for the amusements of the Mexicans, who dexterously larrietted the animals, threw and harnessed them, and considered it wano [bueno] (good).[108]

The road got no better, and neither did Ormsby's temper, as he complained of "thumping and bumping at a rate which threatened not to leave a whole bone in my body." In addition, the passengers were still riding in the celerity wagon that, as Ormsby put it, "was so unceremoniously uncovered at Chadbourne," with the heat, the sun and the dust "pouring directly on [their] heads." Muddy as that river was, he wrote, "[I] readily availed myself of the opportunity to plunge into the Pecos."[109]

Ormsby's driver after Horsehead Crossing station was the redoubtable Captain Henry Skillman, who had started the first mail run in 1850 between San Antonio and El Paso. The New York reporter calls him "an old frontier man who was the first to run the San Antonio and Santa Fe mail at a time when a fight with the Indians, every trip, was considered in the contract." Skillman was about forty-five years of age at the time and Ormsby describes his appearance as "much resembling the portraits of the Wandering Jew, with the exception that he carries several revolvers and bowie knives, dresses in buckskin, and has a sandy head of hair and beard. He loves hard work and adventures, and hates 'Injuns' and knows the

67

country about here pretty well."[110] Skillman certainly proved that he loved hard work. He kept the reins of that first westbound stage from Horsehead Crossing all the way into El Paso, spending four days on the box without a break, behind four wild mules over 306 miles of the most twisted, nearly waterless, rock-strewn, narrow passages on the entire Butterfield trail—an almost superhuman feat of stage-driving.[111]

At the Emigrant Crossing station, which was located some eleven miles west-northwest of the modern town of Grand Falls, the three Americans and half a dozen Mexicans at the station had built what Ormsby called "a very fine 'adobe' corral and had started a house of the same material."[112] Adobe was good protection against bullets and arrows and the Emigrant Crossing men claimed they could defend the stock against "a whole tribe of Indians." Although the station had been unmolested at that date, this was in Apache lands and the Apache tribe was characterized as "a very numerous and troublesome body in this section of the country."[113]

After Emigrant Crossing station,[114] the road got neither easier nor more comfortable: "we continued our weary and dusty road . . . inhaling constant clouds of dust and jolting along almost at snail's pace," wrote Ormsby. Several of the mules gave out and had to be left on the road, "and by the time we reached Pope's Camp at least half a dozen had been disposed of this way." As the stage approached Pope's Camp, near the New Mexico border, Ormsby said the bright moonlight showed the Guadalupe Mountains, sixty miles distant on the other side of the river, "standing in bold relief against the clear sky, like the walls of some ancient fortress covered with towers and embattlements."[115]

Pope's Camp had been established by Captain John Pope as the base of operations for his government sponsored well drilling project. Ormsby noted, "The buildings . . . are built of adobe in a substantial manner, and form quite a little town."[116] The camp had been abandoned by government troops in July, 1858, although Pope's well drilling experiment continued at other sites until 1859. Superintendent Glover's Butterfield men occupied the camp later in August. The camp was rather extensive; the Conklings' drawing of the plan of Camp Pope shows a system of stone and adobe walls forming an irregular pattern some 200 feet by 150 feet by 200 feet, embracing all sorts of permanent structures within an oddly shaped rampart which resembled a large and irregular five point star.[117]

Alton Hughes wrote a later view of the camp in 1978, "[Pope] established a good sized camp, sometime called Pope's fort. . . . The camp consisted of some ten limestone and rock houses, a guard house and some tents. Each house had a fireplace and the floors were paved with flat stones. These structures were in rather good condition until late 1930 when vandals invaded the place and pretty well demolished things in their search for relics and treasure."[118] Hughes also notes that Barney Gallagher, a noted outlaw in the nineteenth century, established a camp a short distance up the river from Pope's Crossing and often made life exciting and perilous for campers. Gus Gildea (in 1876) records Gallagher's death:

When we arrived at South Spring, the headquarters ranch of John S. Chisum, we camped on the ground where the Slaughter outfit had camped a few days before and saw where a Texas cowboy had been shot from his horse by one of Slaughter's men as he rode into their camp, his congealed blood lying in a pool on the ground where he fell and died. His name was Barney Gallagher, and I knew him at Carrizo Springs. . . . He was generally known as "Buckshot," a typical cowboy character of those frontier days.[119]

At the time of Ormsby's trip, crossing the Pecos was perilous, the coach being pulled by only four mules and "the stream being quite rapid and nearly covering the hubs of our wagon." After safely gaining the western shore, the stage ran about thirty miles. Ormsby wrote, "we camped at sunrise near the head of Delaware Creek, cooked our breakfast with a fire of buffalo 'chips' . . . and our breakfast was quite acceptable to me, notwithstanding the buffalo 'chips,' which struck me as rather a novel and at first distasteful idea."[120] This was one of the few times the first coach passengers had to camp and prepare food. There may have been a station underway, but Ormsby doesn't mention one. Goddard Bailey, the post office investigator who visited only a few weeks after Ormsby's stay, recorded a station at Delaware Springs, which he said was forty miles from Pope's Camp. However, he found the stationkeeper and helpers still living in tents, so there may have been no cooking facilities at the time of either his or Ormsby's visit.[121] The Conklings, inspecting the ruins in 1930, believed the station was built sometime in October or November of 1858. The springs had been visited in 1849 by Captain Marcy on his return from Doña Ana to Fort Smith. He said of one spring, "it's [sic] flow as pure, sweet water as I ever drank." The Conklings, on the other hand, pronounced the water "far from pleasant to the taste."[122]

On the road past Delaware Springs, Ormsby wrote that Guadalupe Peak "loomed up before us all day in the most aggravating manner. It fairly seemed to be further off the more we travelled." Ormsby was viewing the highest elevation in Texas (at 8,751 feet). On the advice of Captain Skillman, the stage stopped at Independence Spring, although it was only five miles to the next station, the Pinery. Skillman, who had been driving stages through far West Texas for more than six years, predicted that without a stop the animals couldn't finish the climb. And even after the rest Ormsby reported, "We were obliged actually to beat our mules with rocks to make them go the remaining five miles to the station."[123]

Pinery Station, at the foot of the Guadalupe Mountains, had a keeper named Henry Ramstein who, according to the Conklings, "was connected with the El Paso district surveyor's office in 1855."[124] It had a corral built of "heavy pine timber," which Ormsby found notable.[125] And as a matter of fact, the Guadalupes are the only place in Texas where the ponderosa pine may be found. The station was located near Pine Spring, which was later used by many ranches.

The Conklings called Pinery Station "one of the most favorably situated stations on the route. . . . The scenic beauty of the region is on a grand scale."[126] For years after the Butterfield stage began using the lower route through the Davis Mountains, the Pinery remained in use by emigrants, freighters, soldiers, Indians—and renegades. The trail through the Guadalupes, in fact, gained a hard reputation among travelers, who preferred to travel it only in larger groups.

Ormsby's stop at the Pinery was brief, but he noted that the trip from this point turned spectacular:

After getting another stereotype meal, with the addition of some venison pie and baked beans, we started for a sixty mile ride to the Carnudas [Cornudas] mountains through the Guadalupe Canon. The wild grandeur of the scene in the canon is beyond description. . . . The road winds over some of the steepest and stoniest hills I had yet seen, studded with inextricable rocks, each one of which seems ready to jolt the wagon into the abyss below. . . . [T]hink what havoc one mischievous man could make with an emigrant train passing through the canon.[127]

On a later trip, Farwell described two graves he found in Guadalupe Pass. One was that of a famous Mexican guide for Captain Longstreet's 8th Infantry.

He was sent forward to look for water, and when in the narrowest position of the pass, he was shot full of arrows by some Apache Indians . . . his head stone reading "Jose Maria Polancio, Guide; killed Feb. 1st, 1855, by Indians." It is said, that after he was found by the soldiers, the Indians stole seven blankets from the corpse which had been spread over it successively. The second [grave] is that of an American who was killed by another in a quarrel.[128]

71

The Butterfield stage carrying Ormsby got through the canyon about sunset and he became poetic describing the sensation: "I never shall forget the gorgeous appearance of the clouds: tinged by the setting sun above those jagged peaks, changing like a rapid panorama, they assumed all sorts of fantastic shapes, from frantic maidens with dishevelled hair to huge monsters of fierce demeanor, chasing one another through the realms of space."[129] But the poetic was suddenly replaced by the portentous.

> We had hardly passed through before the sound of voices and the gleaming of a light denoted that there was a party ahead of us. The awe inspiring scenery and the impressive sunset had almost set me dreaming as I lay listlessly in the wagon; but the possibility of meeting foes, perhaps a band of murderous Indians, in this wild and lonely spot filled me for a time with fears; but I had great faith in the captain's [Skillman] prowess, and felt somewhat easier when he declared it to be his opinion that the party was an American one.[130]

It was, in fact, the first eastbound Butterfield coach, which had left San Francisco on September 15 with five through passengers—and now (September 28) eight hours ahead of time. "After exchanging congratulations and telling bits of news, both parties passed on," the eastbound coach now carrying Ormsby's dispatch to the New York Herald.[131] Actually, one thinks, the occasion should have been marked by champagne.

Farwell, going in the opposite direction from Ormsby, tells of his similar experience a few weeks later at the Hueco Tanks station:

> As we [left] the station house, we . . . could see at a distance the camp fires of the Apaches. It was about nine o'clock as we commenced the ascent of a canon leading to the steep portion of the road. It was very dark, the only light being that shed by the coach lamps, and being in the narrow part of the canon,

the "side rider" who had ridden ahead called out: "Stop! Stop! here they are!" The driver and conductor both jumped up, pulled out their pistols, as did the passengers, every one expecting that the canon was full of Indians, and for which we had been on the look-out; an instant more, and, by the lights, we discovered the heads of two horses approaching, and the front of one of the mail coaches. Mr. Glover, the superintendent and manager of this part of the road, was a passenger, and after exchanging news, we separated, each on his way, our nerves much relieved from apprehensions of further surprise by Indians.[132]

The Butterfield trail led out of Guadalupe pass and then turned northwest just above the old post office of Ables, across the desolate Salt Basins, through the site of present-day Dell City to Crow Flat or Crow Springs (Ojo del Cuervo). The Conklings describe this part of the road in terms worthy of Ormsby at his most poetic:

And as the road descends from the rugged pass and emerges on the playa of Crow Flat, one has the impression of leaving the rock and pebble-strewn strand of a towering continental land mass and venturing out over a trackless frozen sea. . . . The road [leading] around and among white and glistening dunes of decomposed gypsum, and across flats of glistening crystalline salts that in the dazzling glare and quivering heat of mid-day, sometimes appear like alluring pools of blue transparent water. . . . Under a full moon the aspect of this silent white land is even more fantastic, ghastly and unnatural, conveying something of the impression of an ideal lunar landscape.[133]

Ormsby called the camping place Crow Spring, and pronounced the waters "sulphur but palatable enough when one is thirsty."[134] Sometime after the first months of the Butterfield operation a relay

73

station was built here, of adobe and gypsum blocks. Perhaps this building literally dissolved after the upper road was abandoned by Butterfield, because Williams says a surveyor map dated 1859 omits it.[135]

A contemporary state historical marker on U.S. Highway 180 at the tiny modern-day community of Salt Flat tells the spring's sorrowful story in an almost poetic manner:

> Crow Springs (15 miles north). Named for birds habitually there in abundance. Crow Springs was an oasis for Indians for centuries. The Butterfield Overland Mail in 1858 built a relay station at the springs, but used it less than a year before shifting the route south. . . . During the Apache Wars of the early 1880s, Texas Rangers and the U.S. 10th Cavalry camped at Crow Springs occasionally, to prevent Indians in New Mexico from joining the war leaders, Victorio and Nana, in Mexico. Today the springs are dry, the station has fallen to dust, and the crows have disappeared.

From Crow Springs it was only a mile to the New Mexico border, as the Butterfield stage went, and Williams says the trail "passed out of Texas between two monuments erected on the state line by the joint Texas-U.S. Boundary Commission in 1859."[136] The Conklings report it passed near the deserted settlement of Orange, New Mexico, "a discouraging reminder of a comparatively recent unsuccessful citrus fruit growing venture."[137] The next station, Cornudas de los Alamos, was in Otero County, New Mexico. Ormsby said, "There is quite a large station here, and we procured a fresh team and a side driver and set out for Waco Tanks [Hueco, meaning "hollow" or "trough" in Spanish], thirty-six miles distant [and back in Texas]."[138] The Conklings wrote that the Cornudas station "was located about two hundred fifty feet south from the entrance into the cavern leading to Thorne's Well in the southern face of Cornuda mountain."[139] Ormsby, admiring the mountains, wrote, "The rocks or boulders are of red sandstone, and on the principal peak are of an oblong character, set with such remarkable regularity as to appear to be a work

74

of art." Although he does not name the Thorne's Well, he adds, "The water collects in natural basins from the rain and stands the year round. As yet they have furnished a sufficient supply of water . . . and can be easily enlarged."[140] Gillett, twenty years later, also found the mountains fascinating: "This Cornudas is a strange conglomeration of dark granite rocks shot high in the air in the midst of the plains by some eruption of the earth in ages past."[141]

Concerning Thorne's Well, Lieutenant F. T. Bryan of the U.S. Topographical Engineers, in his exploration trek across West Texas, had reported on July 26, 1849: "Inside the mountains, in a cavern, there is a fine large well of pure water; this is full to overflowing."[142] And six weeks later Captain Randolph Marcy found the "arched entrance into a large cavern which is lighted from above, and in this we found a well fifteen feet deep, filled to the top with beautifully pure water."[143] However, the water was not always there. Certain accounts remark, for instance, that the well "was perfectly dry . . . and inside the cavern were several recently excavated holes, evidently made by a former emigrant party in a frantic search for water."[144] The Conklings say the well "is believed to have been named for one Thorne of the firm of Thomson and Thorne of San Antonio, who freighted over this route in the latter part of 1849." The Conklings call Thorne's Well and Cornuda mountain "one of the most fascinating points of interest on the route . . . although the well is filled up."[145]

About sixteen miles farther on the road, according to Ormsby, the stage passed Ojos de los Alamos, "which are springs in a mountain about half a mile from the road."[146] The station there, built later in 1858, was large and well built of stone and adobe, among the best protected on the entire route, with inner and outer walls. Some histories refer to this station as "Cottonwood Springs" (*alamos* means cottonwood trees in Spanish), and the Conklings still found an isolated grove of cottonwood trees growing there when they visited in 1931.

Between Ojos de los Alamos and Hueco Tanks, according to Ormsby, "the road all way is excellent, being a rolling plain with the exception of a very steep hill near the Sierra Alto, down which I much feared we could not descend in safety; but our driver [the redoubtable Capt. Skillman] seemed to know every stone and we whirled along on the very brink of the precipices with perfect safety, though the night was quite dark."[147]

Although the Hueco Tanks were famed for centuries for their water supply held in natural cisterns among the rocks and rock caves, the first Butterfield riders discovered things could be otherwise. Ormsby wrote:

> On reaching the Waco Tanks we found an excellent corral and cabin built; but to our consternation the station keeper pointed to two eight gallon kegs, saying, "that is all the water we have left for a dozen men and as many head of cattle." The Waco Tanks have been reported to be inexhaustible, but the unusual droughts had drained them, and a most rigorous search through the mountain did not bring to light any more. [148]

Farwell arrived at the Hueco Mountains (which he heard as "Sierra Gueco") and the Hueco Tanks station on October 27 and had time to inspect what he called "remarkable caves." An excellent supper was awaiting the stage and,

> After partaking of which and having a few moments to spare, I went . . . to visit some caves in the rocks nearby. Our guide had brought with him a light by which we were enabled to see numerous heroglyphics, both cut and painted, upon the face of the rock. There was painted a rattlesnake, some 30 feet in length, darting at what is supposed to be an enemy of the Comanches. Another was a horse, caparisoned for battle, animals of various kinds, a representation of the dwellings of several tribes . . . [and] three Comanche warriors, mounted, with lances in rest, rushing upon their foes, and one figure, which particularly attracted my attention, represented an altar, with

burning lights upon it, as though prepared for some ceremony. Time would not permit a stay of but a very few moments, and I reluctantly left.[149]

The area is now part of Hueco Tanks State Park. Many of the petroglyphs described by various travelers can still be seen, but modern spray-paint vandals have destroyed many others.

After changing horses and eating supper, Ormsby reported, the Butterfield stage left Hueco Tanks. He continued:

[A] few hours' ride brought us to Franklin City [now El Paso, Texas] on the Rio Grande river, opposite the ancient town of El Paso [del Norte]. As we neared the river the delightful aroma of the fruit and herbs was most grateful after so long and dreary a ride over the desert, and at that moment I could have endorsed all the encomiums on "the fertile valley of the Rio Grande." We passed many vineyards and comfortable ranches built of adobe and looking extremely neat. About two miles from Franklin is Fort Bliss, now occupied by a small garrison of United States troops. The fort is built of adobe.[150]

C. L. Sonnichsen, writing 110 years later, noted of this part of the Butterfield Route, "Traces of [Butterfield's] stage stations east of El Paso can still be seen—Pinery, Ojo del Cuervo, Thorne's Well, Alamo Springs, Hueco Tanks."[151]

The first westbound Butterfield stage, with Henry Skillman still on the box, arrived at Franklin (El Paso) at 5 P.M., Thursday, September 30, 1858. The first eastbound Butterfield stage had arrived at 1:15 P.M. on September 27, 1858, driven by Brad Dailey. Ormsby, continuing to record his impressions, noted, "The city of Franklin, on the American side of the river, contains a few hundred inhabitants and is in the midst of a fine agricultural district. The onions as well as the grapes of this locality are of world-wide celebrity, and El Paso wines are universally appreciated."[152] At the time of the arrival of the first Butterfield stage, the Overland Mail station was the biggest building in Franklin and also the largest company-built station on the entire Butterfield line.

After leaving Franklin at 5:40 A.M. on September 30th, Ormsby records:

> To my great relief the mules were dispensed with for a while and a good team of California horses substituted, which spun the wagon over the ground at a rate which was quite new to me. About twenty-one miles from Franklin we changed horses at a station [Cottonwoods] in a pretty grove of cottonwood trees—the only habitation before reaching Fort Fillmore [New Mexico], eighteen miles further on.[53]

And thus did the Butterfield Overland Mail stage finish the first western trip through Texas with Waterman Ormsby aboard. At San Francisco the 2,800-mile run was finished successfully October 10, 1858, twenty-three days, twenty-three and a half hours from St. Louis. Within days others began making the same voyage, going west, coming east—but Ormsby's first reports have continued to furnish the backbone for all Butterfield Overland Mail history.

Notes

1. Waterman L. Ormsby, Jr., *The Butterfield Overland Mail*, ed. Lyle H. Wright and Josephine M. Bynum (San Marino: Huntington Library, 1955), 2.
2. Ormsby, 1.
3. Ormsby, 2.
4. Ormsby, 22.
5. Many non-Indians, however, had married into the tribe or were the products of mixed marriages.
Observers Ormsby and Richardson both commented on slavery among the

Choctaws. Ormsby said slave ownership was "quite common" and that the Choctaws in general were "more lenient than the white slaveholders, and appear to let them do pretty much as they please . . . [and] with whom, I am told, they often cohabit" (Ormsby, 26). Richardson also thought that Indian slaves were shown more leniency than were black slaves; in fact, he felt the Choctaw slaves ran things as much as the owners (Richardson, 224).

6. The name was possibly Ward because no Waddell can be found on any other record.

7. Several Choctaw governors and other notables are buried in the Old Boggy Depot cemetery, now within an Oklahoma State Park. When the railroad was built two miles to the south, the post office was moved to New Boggy Depot and Old Boggy was abandoned.

8. The Colbert family was prominent and wealthy. In addition to having its name on the Colbert Ferry and the present-day Oklahoma town of Colbert, there was Jim Colbert's stage stand on the Butterfield line as it passed through what is now Pittsburg County, Oklahoma, and Colbert Institute, near McAlester, all named for the family. Benjamin Franklin Colbert (1826-1893), a full-blood Chickasaw, was thirty-three at the time the Butterfield Mail began. Shortly after the first Butterfield stage passed, the Chickasaw Legislature authorized Colbert to keep a ferry at his residence "for the accommodation of travelers, emigrants and rovers," and to fence in the landing at the ferry on the Chickasaw [Oklahoma] side of the river with a good rail fence and put up a ferry gate. Travelers were to be accommodated "at all times," and Colbert was required to give a $500 bond "for the faithful performance of these requirements." Muriel Wright, "The Butterfield Overland Mail One Hundred Years Ago," *The Chronicles of Oklahoma*, 25, (1957): 1–12.

9. Albert Deane Richardson, *Beyond the Mississippi: From the Great River to the Great Ocean* . . . (New York: Bliss, 1867), 225.

10. Apparently some behind-the-scenes—and unrecorded—political maneuvering took place to get the entry point changed from Preston, which had a reputation as a wild and dangerous place. Or maybe it was a matter of sweet revenge on the part of Benjamin F. Colbert. In 1853, the Texas Supreme Court kept Colbert from building a ferry at Preston in competition with one already operated by George N. Butts, a U. S. Army major and third husband of the memorable Sophia Suttonfield Auginbaugh Coffee Butts Porter. After receiving the restraining order, Colbert selected a site eight miles below Preston for his ferry operation. Somehow, when the final determination of the Overland Mail route was announced, the Texas entry point had been moved to Colbert's ferry site.

11. Ormsby, 35.

12. An 1879 map of Texas shows Red River City on the Texas side of the Red River west of Colbert's Ferry. Railroad historian S. P. Reed explains that the Katy (Missouri-Kansas & Texas Railroad) had trouble getting its track from the Red River to Denison, a distance of six miles. The H&TC (Houston & Texas Central, now Southern Pacific) had reached Denison in March 1872, and had already graded its line to the Red River and laid out a town on its south bank called Red River City. Katy forces undertook to grade alongside the H&TC grade and on its right-of-way from the Red River to Denison, but were stopped by an injunction. An agreement was effected under which the H&TC abandoned Red River City, took up its tracks from Denison to Red River City and entered into a contract for a joint station at Denison. S. P. Reed, *A History of the Texas Railroads* (Houston: The St. Clair Publishing Co., 1941), 377.

In 1885 the *Texas State Gazeteer and Business Directory* said Red River City was a station on the Katy (at the time in Missouri Pacific ownership) and a post office. By 1900 Red River City had been taken over by Denison.

13. Ormsby, 35.

14. Ibid.

15. Mattie Davis Lucas and Mita Holsapple Hall, *A History of Grayson County, Texas* (Sherman: Scruggs Printing Co., 1936), 93.

16. Ocie Lea Swint and Howard Hudnall, *The History of Sherman and Grayson County, Texas (1846–1987)*, (Sherman: Sherman Public Library, 1983), 74.

17. S. H. West, "Life and Times of S. H. West." (unpublished manuscript in Sherman Public Library, Sherman, Texas), n.p.

18. Ormsby, 36.

19. Ormsby, 42.

20. J. W. Williams, "The Butterfield Overland Mail Road Across Texas," *Southwestern Historical Quarterly*, LXI (July 1957): 6–7.

21. Ormsby, 43.

22. See "The Great Gainesville Hanging of 1862," p. 219.

23. Ormsby, 43. William B. Parker, in his very readable commentary, written while he accompanied one of Captain Randolph Marcy's West Texas expeditions in 1854, tells of a tornado that had struck Gainesville in May of that year. "Two women were taken up and blown three-quarters of a mile, impinging three times against the ground in their terrific flight." Five persons were killed when the tornado hit the home of William Howeth, and Parker notes that Louise Howeth was one of the women swirled away. William B. Parker, *Notes Taken . . . Through Unexplored Texas in the Summer and Fall of 1854* (Austin: Texas State Historical Association, 1990), 85.

24. Ormsby, 44.

25. Ibid.

26. A memorial to Governor H. R. Runnels, dated September 18, 1858 at Decatur, Wise County, asking protection from the Indians, is signed by 61 men, including H. Connolly and J. W. Connolly. But some of the recognizable names are misspelled, so it is a difficult list to rely on. "Protection of the Frontier of Texas," House Ex. Doc. No. 27, 35th Congress, 2nd Session, 1859, 62.

27. Ormsby, 45.

28. Ibid.

29. Conkling, Vol. I, 302. The Conklings consistently misspell Earhart as "Earheart."

30. A. Richardson, 225. Later, the Butterfield Company used dugout canoes to ferry passengers and mail over this fork of the Trinity River. The inconvenience of all this had a great deal to do with the company's changing its route to take advantage of the new Bridgeport bridge over the same river.

31. Ormsby, 46.

32. The name of the town was spelled Jacksborough until 1899. It had originally been known as Lost Creek, then Mesquiteville.

33. Ormsby, 46. J. M. Farwell, writing for the *Daily Alta California* newspaper of San Francisco, made the eastward Butterfield trip starting in October, 1858, sending his paper stories similar to those Ormsby sent to the New York *Herald*. He told of an ingenious method of controlling mules used at an Arizona station: "While we were waiting . . . we heard the sound of a gong, thumped with a vigor and skill creditable to a Chinaman. Looking in the direction of the San Diego stage, we saw that they were just on the point of starting and that the mules that had been turned loose were hastily collecting about the stage. Subsequently I learned that the mules had been trained to collect round the stage for the purpose of being fed, at the sound of the gong." Included in Walter B. Lang, *The First Overland Mail: Butterfield Trail* (Washington, D.C.: n.p., 1940), 119. The wild mule problem led to some amusing consequences. Eyewitnesses said that when the coach reached Jacksborough often the drivers had to circle the courthouse square two or three times before the teams could be brought to a stop. Joseph C. McConnell, *The West Texas Frontier*. Jacksboro: Gazette Print, 1933, Vol. 1, 104.

34. Jacksborough became famous as site for the trial of the Kiowa chiefs who were charged with leading the attack in the Warren wagon train massacre of 1871. The trial was held in Jack County's first stone courthouse. Both the defendants were sentenced to hang, but neither did. This was the first time an Indian leader was put on trial under the civil process. (See "Later Tragedies: Warren Wagon Train Massacre, Elm Creek Raid, Turtle Hole," p. 234 for the story of the massacre in which seven freighters were ambushed and slain.)

35. Ormsby, 47. Fort Belknap was ordered abandoned February 23, 1859, greatly reducing Butterfield use.

36. Lang, 155.

37. In 1859 a tragic drama was played out along this section of the Butterfield trail, although the episodes did not involve the stage line. Five years earlier the Texas legislature had set aside several leagues of land for an Indian reservation (the Lower Reservation) along the Brazos River, a few miles below Fort Belknap. It was an area to which a number of minor tribes such as Caddo, Waco, Keechi, and Ioni had fled before the encroachment of the whites. In 1855 a smaller Upper Reservation on the Clear Fork of the Brazos River was instituted for the Penateka ("Honey-eaters") branch of the southern Comanches. Camp Cooper, within the reservation bounds, was established to protect the agency operation, as well as the resident Comanches, from their wild cousins. Although the reservations were generally a success, they were not accepted by certain white settlers within the area, and continual demands that the tribes be ousted grew along the frontier from Waco to Weatherford. In August of 1859, the federal government, for the safety of the tribal members, finally agreed to remove the reservation tribes beyond the Red River.

On September 14, 1859, Major Robert S. Neighbors, the government agent in charge of the two reservations, was assassinated on the streets of the town of Fort Belknap the day after he had returned from successfully escorting the tribes to new homes in Indian Territory. Neighbors, a well known explorer and frontiersman, was en route to San Antonio where his wife and children awaited him.

The reservation Indians had been forced to leave Texas because of the animosity (plus greed for reservation lands) of a group led by John R. Baylor, formerly the Comanche reservation agent. Baylor had been dismissed by Neighbors when Baylor's erratic personality formed a barrier to agency success. This act created an almost insane hatred in Baylor for both his former charges and his former boss. From that point on Baylor dedicated himself to eliminating both the reservation Indians and Neighbors. Even though successful with his first goal, Baylor was not satisfied because Neighbors remained alive. All 1,420 of the reservation inhabitants (who were not always guilty of the crimes and raids with which the whites charged them) had been delivered north of the Red River, but hostility to Neighbors remained strong. (He had also earned the hatred of hot-headed George T. Howard, the Indian Agent he had earlier replaced.) With so many enemies, Neighbors had been warned by friends against returning to Fort Belknap, even for a visit.

In the town, Neighbors, stepping out of a business house, was confronted by Butterfield driver Patrick Murphy, characterized as a ne'er-do-well, though he had been the first sheriff of Young County. Murphy pretended to challenge Neighbors over a comment he claimed Neighbors had made about the wanton murder of Choctaw Joe, an old Indian, and his wife by Baylor followers. While Neighbors was attempting to understand what Murphy was saying, the former agent was shotgunned in the back by Ed Cornett, a hired killer (and brother-in-law of Patrick Murphy), whom Neighbors may not have known. So fearful were townspeople that Neighbors's body lay in the street most of the day. Residents of the town of Fort Belknap had been so stirred up by Baylor, or were so afraid of his "friends," that despite witnesses to Neighbors's assassination, no immediate effort was made to bring Cornett to justice. When Cornett finally came to trial, he was, through the ruse of a false report that his wife had been kidnapped by Indians, allowed to slip away. Happily, in May, 1860, Cornett was hunted down and killed by a posse after he attempted to murder Dennis Murphy, the Butterfield station keeper, who was kin to both Patrick Murphy and the cowardly assassin. Rupert N. Richardson, *The Comanche Barrier to South Plains Settlement* (Glendale: Arthur H. Clark Co., 1933), 103-200. Major Neighbors, a Republic of Texas army officer, not U.S., is buried in the Fort Belknap civilian cemetery, a few hundred yards east of the fort. Official records of his murder are not to be trusted, so powerful was the rancor of some Young County residents. Major Neighbors is one of those hero figures of American history almost completely overlooked by chroniclers of the Native American past. The best account of the episode is found in Kenneth F. Neighbours, "Indian Exodus Out of Texas in 1859," *West Texas Historical Association Year Book*, XXXVI (October 1960): 80–97.

38. Ormsby, 47.

39. A. Richardson, 227.

40. Ormsby, 47.

41. At some point after the Butterfield ceased running, a stage station east of the old Franz station was operated by a Swiss immigrant named Cribb, as evidenced by the name Cribb Station Creek, found on maps of western Young County. Descendents of both Franz and Cribb families remain in West Texas.

42. Conkling, Vol. I, 321.

43. In 1864, following the disastrous Elm Creek raid when the settlers in the area resorted to "forting up" because of Indian dangers, the France family was among the twenty five or so families at "Fort Davis" on the Clear Fork River in Stephens County—not to be confused with the U.S. military post farther west. A. C. Greene, "Fort Davis Became Necessity," *Abilene Reporter-News*, 20 August 1959, 1B.

44. Ormsby, 48.

45. Lang, 152.

46. Ormsby, 49.

47. J. W. Williams, "Journey of the Leach Wagon Train Across Texas" *West Texas Historical Quarterly* XXIX (1957): 127.

48. Randolph B. Marcy, *Thirty Years of Army Life on the Border* (Philadelphia: J. B. Lippincott Co., 1963), 182.

49. Ibid.

50. Ibid. W. S. Adair, who for several years wrote a weekly historical column in the *Dallas Morning News*, in 1924 told how Captain William H. Gaston, a pioneer Dallas resident on his way west in search of a runaway slave (whom he never found), survived an "erratic" stage driver to Fort Phantom Hill station in 1860 and found the fort inhabited by two men who took care of the mules but apparently did not serve meals.

51. A. Richardson, 228.

52. Captain John M. Elkins and Frank W. McCarty, *Indian Fighting on the Texas Frontier* (Amarillo: Russell & Cockrell, 1929), 76. Emma Elkins, who as a girl lived at Fort Phantom Hill where her father was a soldier, helped sustain the ghost myth when she wrote about the fort in her husband's book.

53. Ormsby, 50.

54. Ormsby, 51.

55. Abercrombie was said to have inherited a peerage in Great Britain. Whatever the case, the names he put on West Texas did not stick. Abercrombie Peak quickly became known as "Castle Peak," that ubiquitous and unimaginative designation given every tall hump of landscape in Texas that has anything resembling stone as its cap. The range, which passes through five counties, beginning on the east with Callahan County, was baptized by geologists the "Callahan Divide." However, settlers in Taylor and Nolan counties, considering their viewpoints of more moment than those of sparsely populated Callahan, have called the divide the Steamboat Mountains (standing perhaps three hundred feet above the plains), Tonkawa Hills, or simply, "the mountains"—anything but Abercrombie Range.

56. Ormsby's Butterfield reports have been reprinted several times since they first appeared in the New York *Herald* and this is probably the most famous quote of all. His good humor, in spite of all the hardships (remember: this is not a westerner, this is a New Yorker, used to that city's more sumptuous style of life), shows in another personal observation he makes while at Mountain Pass: "There is an old saying that 'every man must eat his peck of dirt.' I think I have had good measure with my peck on this trip, which has been roughing it with a vengeance." Ormsby, 52.

57. Elkins, 55–58.

58. Elkins, 85.

59. Ormsby, 52.

60. Seymour V. Connor, *The Peters Colony of Texas* (Austin: Texas State Historical Association, 1959), 307.

61. Ormsby, 53.

62. Ibid.

63. Lang, 155.

64. Lang, 148.

65. Noah Smithwick, *The Evolution of a State* (Austin: Steck-Vaughn, 1968), 335.

66. C. C. (Tom) Tompkins, *A Compendium of The Overland Mail Company on the South Route 1858–1861 and the Period Surrounding It* (El Paso: G. T. Co., 1985), 297.

67. Ernest William Winkler, ed., *Journal of the Secession Convention of Texas 1861* (Austin: Texas State Library and Historical Commission, 1912), 366.

68. Anson Mills, *My Story* (Washington, D.C.: n.p., 1918), 64.

69. Joseph G. E. Hopkins, *Concise Dictionary of American Biography*, (New York: Charles Scribner's Sons, 1964), 366. Greeley, despite his ardent anti-slavery stand before and during the Civil War, gained a certain amount of Southern favor when, at great cost to his reputation, he joined a small group that signed Jefferson Davis's bond allowing the Confederacy's former president to be released from federal prison in 1867. Greeley urged full reconciliation of North and South for achievement of reforms. The Decatur (Texas) *Advance Guard* newspaper is quoted by Cates in his *Pioneer History of Wise County* (p. 470) as supporting Greeley in his Democratic race in 1872 against U. S. Grant. Greeley's vice presidential running mate was B. Gratz Brown of Missouri. The *Advance Guard* quoted a popular piece of sloganeering:

> Come, let us cheer with lusty throat,
> The man who wears a long white coat,
> And in November let us vote
> For honest Horace Greeley.

Greeley was never taken seriously as a candidate and carried only six states, calling himself "the worst beaten man who ever ran for high office." The abusive campaign, the death of his wife, and loss of editorial control of his *New York Tribune* devastated him and his body and mind broke and he died insane late in 1872.

70. Although travelers didn't often mention boils, perhaps from modesty, the affliction was prevalent. Lack of fresh food was often taken as the cause. "Today we got a dinner of yearling—a rare feast to get fresh meat. . . . Boils may become fewer hereafter. The Drs. Loew & Brown & Peters have 'fine specimens' under their right arms & elsewhere." Llerena Friend, ed., *M. K. Kellogg's*

Texas Journal 1872 (Austin: University of Texas Press, 1967), 87.

71. Clayton L. Thomas, *Taber's Cyclopedic Medical Dictionary*, 16th Ed. (Philadelphia: F. A. Davis Co., 1989), 232.

72. Ormsby, 54.

73. Ormsby, 55.

74. Ibid.

75. Ormsby, 56.

76. Ibid.

77. Lang, 124.

78. Elkins, 86.

79. Ibid. An ambulance, mentioned often in western history, was not a passenger vehicle limited to medical use but was a wagon with springs which gave a more comfortable ride. Because an ambulance cost a good deal more than a regular wagon, having one for private use was unusual.

80. Ormsby, 62–63.

81. Leta Crawford, *A History of Irion County, Texas* (Waco: Texian Press, 1966), 13–28. The community of Arden formed about 1890 when it obtained a post office. It was named for Katie Arden and her husband John, a sheep raiser, who arrived in 1876 after trailing a big flock of sheep from California. Mrs. Arden took over and added to their 20,000 acres after her husband's death. A brick schoolhouse was built in 1916 but closed in 1947. The post office had closed in 1942.

82. More about Camp Johnston station is recorded in Part III.

83. "Apparently the last permanent water as the stages moved up the Middle Concho was in or near the Nathaniel Gocher Survey No. 1943. Surveyors noted a stage stand in this block on July 29, 1859. . . . The date makes it certain that the mail station was the property of the Butterfield interests. This fact puts the writer in the uncomfortable position of being in conflict with the Conklings' study, but there seems to be no way to escape that conflict." J. W. Williams, "The Butterfield Overland Mail Road Across Texas," *Southwestern Historical Quarterly* LXI (July 1957): 11.

84. Ormsby, 63.

85. Ormsby, 64.

86. Ormsby, 63.

87. According to the 1857 map, Lieutenant Bryan established a Camp Concho on one branch of that river in 1849.

88. Marilyn J. Good, ed., *Three Dollars Per Mile* (Austin: Texas Surveyors Association, 1981), 42–43.

89. Kenneth Neighbours, "The Expedition of Major Robert S. Neighbors to El Paso in 1849," *Southwestern Historical Quarterly* LVIII (July 1954): 36.

86

90. J. Marvin Hunter, ed., *Trail Drivers of Texas* (Austin: University of Texas Press, 1985), 977.

91. J. W. Williams, "Journey of Leach Wagon Train Across Texas," *West Texas Historical Quarterly* XXIX (1957): 151n.

92. Ormsby, 75. Jose Policarpo (Polly) Rodriguez, in the dictated story of his life, *The Old Guide*, mentions this same effect. While scouting with Lieutenant W. H. C. Whiting in the trans-Pecos area, Polly Rodriguez tells how one man became excited at seeing "two Indians." Polly told him, "They are not Indians, they are Spanish daggers." He told the man to stop his mules and the "Indians" would stop running with him. On this trip, Henry Skillman, making a useless advance mission, lost Polly's talented mule "that could trail like a dog, putting his nose to the ground to strike a trail and follow it in the night as well as in the day." Good, 222.

93. Ormsby, 66.

94. Lang, 153.

95. Ormsby, 85.

96. Lang, 123.

97. Lang, 153.

98. A. Richardson, 231.

99. Ormsby, 66.

100. Sue Watkins, ed., *One League to Each Wind* (Austin: Texas Surveyors Association, 1964), 154.

101. Ormsby, 66.

102. Ormsby, 68.

103. Lang, 122.

104. John Salmon Ford, *Rip Ford's Texas*, Stephen B. Oates, ed. (Austin: University of Texas Press, 1963), 515.

105. A. Richardson, 233. In the *Junior Historian* Writing Contest for 1953, Bobby McKinney, then a student at McCamey High School, wrote a prize-winning essay on Horsehead Crossing after he flew his airplane over the area and snapped pictures of the crossing. "Since Bobby's article appeared . . . interest in Horsehead Crossing has been renewed and persons in the McCamey vicinity owning airplanes have been making flights, frequently piloted by Bobby McKinney. At present the Crane Chamber of Commerce is working on plans to establish a park at Horsehead Crossing." H. Bailey Carroll, ed., "Texas Collection," *Southwestern Historical Quarterly* LIX (July 1955): 104.

106. Ormsby, 68.

107. Ormsby, 69.

108. Ormsby, 70.

109. Ibid. "But few places can be found more solitary, or that present a more dreary appearance, than all this region of the Pecos. The only life or sign of moving thing is now and then a single deer, a few antelope, a flock of ducks, circling over the lagoons, or a solitary crane winging his way up the course of the stream." Captain S. G. French, T.E., Senate Ex. Doc No. 64, 31st Congress, 1st Session, 1849.

110. Ormsby, 68.

111. The author compared Skillman's drive with other Butterfield drivers and their time "on the box," and visited the mileage in question.

Henry Skillman (1813–1864) was famous for his daring. A native of Kentucky, he stood over six feet in height, and had long yellow hair and beard. He had come early to the southwest, working as a Santa Fe and Chihuahua trader. When the Mexican War broke out, he volunteered as a scout with Doniphan's expedition in 1846, which took over El Paso (now Juarez) from the Mexicans on Christmas Day of that year. Then he became part of the unofficial but useful "Traders Battalion." After the war he had gained a fearsome reputation for fighting the Apaches of northern Mexico. He was awarded the first contract in 1850 for carrying the mail from San Antonio to Santa Fe by way of El Paso on horseback, along with "Big Foot" Wallace. Eventually these two became the most famous stage drivers in the west.

In 1859 Skillman became Overland Mail agent at El Paso. William W. Mills, brother of Anson Mills, said in his history, *Forty Years at El Paso*, that when war came, Skillman was not in complete sympathy with the Confederate cause but joined the rebel army nonetheless. He acted as courier for a Confederate group that had fled the U.S. and formed an emigre colony in the Mexican city of El Paso across the Rio Grande from the Texas El Paso. This group of former residents hoped to regain control of the area from the California Column which, after July, 1862, occupied the far western end of Texas. Serving as liaison between this group and Confederate Texas, Skillman knew the country so well he was able to come and go almost at will, in and out of Texas and Mexico along the Rio Grande. Finally, he was hunted down by a squad under Captain Albert French, specially commissioned to take him alive, but Skillman fought to the death and was killed (some say through treachery) on April 3, 1864, at Spencer's Ranch in what is now Presidio County, near Presidio del Norte. C. L. Sonnichsen, *Pass of the North: Four Centuries on the Rio Grande* (El Paso: Texas Western Press, 1968), 139–40; Conkling, Vol. I, 127, Vol. II, passim.

112. Ormsby, 70–71.

113. Ormsby, 71. "The trail is still plainly visible and, when the river is low, ruts made by the wagon wheels can be seen in the solid rock bottom of the

river at what we know is Emigrant Crossing." Alton Hughes, *Pecos, A History of the Pioneer West* (Seagraves, TX: Pioneer Book Publishers, 1978), 10.

114. "When the first bridge was built over the Pecos on the road to Mentone, some rather deep excavations were required to get adequate foundation for the bridge pillars. During the excavation work an old sweep [oar] was found deep down in the river bed . . . the sweep was in a state of perfect preservation and made of some kind of very tough wood." *Pecos Enterprise*, 1936, 6.

115. Ormsby, 71.

116. Ibid. Ormsby may not have approved of his well drilling experiments, but Captain Pope (later a major-general in the Union army) performed a valuable service with the Topographical Engineers in his many explorations across the southwest, particularly through western Texas; and Ormsby's disapproval of the water hunt appears to have been based more on economics than on the pros and cons of Pope's success. Ormsby wrote: "I believe the appropriations to defray the expenses of these fruitless efforts to obtain water in the Staked Plain were first $100,000, and afterwards $60,000 . . . besides the expenses of two companies of dragoons and a large quartermaster's department."

117. Conkling, Vol. III, plate 36. In general, Ormsby was pleased with the Butterfield personnel. According to R. Richardson, "The district superintendents impressed [him] as being straightforward men, courageous enough for their various tasks. But many of the employees in positions of lesser responsibility seem to have possessed most of the frontier vices with few of its compensating virtues. A group working at Pope's Camp . . . impressed him as being 'the sorriest lot of fellows' he had ever seen. Farwell also thought some of the employees about the stations were 'not equal to their tasks.'" (Rupert N. Richardson, "Some Details of the Southern Overland Mail Company," *Southwestern Historical Quarterly* XXIX (July 1925): 12. Note: Dr. Richardson may have confused Ormsby's quote with a similar statement made about Horsehead Crossing station; the quote can't be found regarding Pope's Camp.

118. Hughes, *Pecos*, 7.

119. Hunter, 977.

120. Ormsby, 72.

121. Lang, 107.

122. Conkling, Vol. I, 388. Marcy's report was published as part of Senate Executive Document No. 64, 31st Congress, 1st Session. It was later (1939) part of Grant Foreman's *Marcy and the Gold Seekers: the Journal of Captain R. B. Marcy, with an Account of the Gold Rush Over the Southern Route.*

123. Ormsby, 73.

124. Conkling, Vol. I, 392.

125. Ormsby, 74.

126. Conklings, Vol. I, 391. The Guadalupe National Park, which includes the Guadalupe Peak area as well as the Pinery, was established in 1961. The park rangers are quite knowledgeable about the Butterfield trail through that region.

127. Ormsby, 75. Ormsby and most writers of his day spelled the word "canyon" as "canon." Ormsby also mentions the first eminence he observed "is sometimes called Cathedral Peak," but that is not the name of either of the two highest peaks of the Guadalupe Mountains. The front peak, El Capitan, with its sheer granite walls, is more dramatic than the higher Guadalupe Peak behind it, thus a great many travelers (including Texans) think El Capitan is Guadalupe Peak.

128. Lang, 122. The Captain Longstreet mentioned was James Longstreet, later a Lieutenant General of the Confederate Army. In the 1850s he was stationed at Fort Mason, Fort Chadbourne and Fort Bliss in Texas. While at Fort Mason, he purchased several acres of land on which the fort stood, retaining the acreage throughout his life. Longstreet's slowness to obey Lee's order to attack at Gettysburg is sometimes cited as a cause for loss of the battle. After the Civil War, Longstreet turned Republican, thereby drawing down the wrath of the South and the studied disregard of Southern historians; e.g., his name was not listed in the original editions of *The Handbook of Texas* (1952). Margaret Bierschwale, "Mason County, Texas, 1845–1870," *Southwestern Historical Quarterly* LII (April 1949): 381, 389.

129. Ormsby, 76. The Guadalupes were legended to contain vast mineral wealth which was scorned by the Indians. Most of the stories follow pretty closely that told by John C. Cremony, who was interpreter to the U.S. Boundary Commission under John R. Bartlett and later a major of the California Volunteer (Union) cavalry—the California Column of Civil War fame in Texas. Cremony told of an Apache warrior named Quick Killer who "for some unaccountable reason . . . conceived a great personal regard for the writer" and told him of finding large, pure chunks of native silver in the Guadalupe Mountains. A few months later, while on a patrol near where Quick Killer said the metal had been found, the Indian agreed to lead the white man there. Cremony wrote: "We then ascended about three hundred feet until we reached a bold and unmistakable mineral ledge, thickly shrouded with underbrush and stunted trees. Quick Killer stopped a moment, examined the place well, and proceeded directly to a spot, which he unearthed for a few inches and displayed several magnificent specimens of virgin silver. I was satisfied, and possessing myself of a goodly lump, we retraced our steps to the command, none of whom were ever made cognizant of these occurrences." John C. Cremony, *Life Among the Apaches* (New York: Time-Life Books, 1981), 289–90. For insight into Apache

fears of gold, silver, etc., see A. C. Greene, *The Last Captive* (Austin: Encino Press, 1972), 65.

130. Ibid.

131. Ibid.

132. Lang, 121.

133. Conkling, Vol. I, 396.

134. Ormsby, 76.

135. J. W. Williams, "The Butterfield Overland Mail Road Across Texas," *Southwestern Historical Quarterly*, LXI (July 1957): 17. The salt lakes in the area were the cause of the El Paso Salt War in 1877, which began from an attempt to convert what was perceived as a public resource to private ownership. The feud quickly burst into a major cultural and ethnic conflict. The "war" itself was fought in El Paso and San Elizario, then the El Paso County seat, not at the salt lakes. Political rivalry was involved; Republican vs. Democrat, Mexican vs. American. Several deaths resulted from the machinations of a powerful Mexican priest who (according to one historian) urged a mob of Mexicans, "Shoot all the gringos and I will absolve you!" They crossed the Rio Grande, forming a rabble that lynched and killed a number of people. The Salt War also involved the only body of Texas Rangers who ever surrendered (they were disarmed, imprisoned, then released in disgrace). Six Mexican citizens were indicted for the several executions at San Elizario and a reward was put on their heads, but though they continued to live just across the river in Mexico, no one ever attempted to collect it. The upheaval of the Salt War led to the reestablishment of Fort Bliss in 1879. Interestingly enough, as C. L. Sonnichsen notes, after all the deaths and disturbances "the question of payment for salt ceased to be a matter of controversy. . . . The Mexicans applied [to the owners] politely for permission to haul salt and paid for what they took." Sonnichsen, 210.

136. Williams, 18.

137. Conkling, Vol. I, 398.

138. Ormsby, 76.

139. Conkling, Vol. I, 398.

140. Ormsby, 76.

141. James B. Gillett, *Six Years With the Texas Rangers* (New Haven: Yale University Press, 1925), 175.

142. John Russell Bartlett, *Personal Narrative of Explorations and Incidents in Texas, New Mexico, California, Sonora and Chihuahua Connected with the United States and Mexico 1850–1853*. Vol. I (Chicago: Rio Grande Press, 1965), 130.

143. Conklings, Vol. I, 400.

144. Bartlett, 130.

145. Conkling, Vol. I, 400–401. Numerous petroglyphs around the base indicates the mountain might have been held sacred by early tribes.

146. Ormsby, 76.

147. Ormsby, 77.

148. Ibid. Gillett disagrees that water became exhausted: "Sometimes the water in the tanks had all been used up by the travelers but there was always plenty of cool rain-water twenty-five feet above the main ground tanks. Often I have watered my entire [ranger] command by scaling the mountain to these hidden tanks and, filling our boots and hats with water, poured it on the flat, roof-like rocks so it would run down into the tanks below." Gillett, 174.

149. Lang, 120–121.

150. Ormsby, 78. Originally established in 1849 as "Post at El Paso," and named Fort Bliss in 1854, it has been located in six different locations in the El Paso area, the last, and present location, in 1893. Fort Bliss is today a major U.S. military installation. Robert W. Frazer, *Forts of the West* (Norman: University of Oklahoma Press, 1965), 143.

151. Sonnichsen, 141.

152. Ormsby, 78.

153. Ormsby, 79.

Part Three

New Routes – Up the Pecos, via
the Guadalupes; Crossing at
Horsehead: to El Paso via
Fort Stockton, Fort Davis
and the Rio Grande

THERE are many places in Texas which can lay claim to being a part of the Butterfield Trail even though Waterman Ormsby did not encounter them on his 1858 journey. The easternmost towns in this category are Decatur, Bridgeport, Wizard Wells, and Pilot Point.

During the first fourteen months of the Butterfield Overland Mail service, Wise County's newly designated seat of Decatur was not on the route. But late in 1859 (about the time of the birth of Decatur's first white baby, Ben F. Allen), Colonel W. H. Hunt and other leading citizens formed a committee to propose to the Butterfield company that the route be changed to include Decatur as well as Bridgeport. As inducement, the Decaturites pledged to open "a traversible road" to the Jack County line and put secure bridges across Denton Creek in northeastern Wise County, as well as the West Fork of the Trinity River at Bridgeport. A state charter for the latter bridge was granted February 11, 1860, and a wooden span was subsequently built.[1] The Butterfield people and the Post Office Department accepted the new routing, and four new stations were opened, although the change added five miles to the route. The first new station, J. B. Brandon's, was on Denton Creek just below where the 1858 trail had swung west toward Earhart's.[2]

The Decatur Butterfield station was at the store of Absalom Bishop on the northwest corner of the town square. Colonel Bishop was the true father of Decatur, envisioning a city perched atop the prominent hill for years before it was built.[3] Cliff D. Cates, in his history of Wise County, drew a romantic picture of the arrival of the Butterfield mail coach.

The stage was due to arrive at Decatur at midnight where it deposited mail and occasional passengers at Bishop's store. . . . The approach of a stage was announced by the sounding of a long note on a bugle. Imagine the sleepy little village of Decatur being aroused from its midnight dreams by the shrill and alarming notes of the bugle coming from the far ravines and hilltops.[4]

From Decatur, the 1860 route reached Bridgeport, crossing the new bridge over the West Fork of the Trinity, then went west across territory now under Lake Bridgeport. A new station was established twelve miles from Bridgeport near Wizard Wells, the village that in the 1920s and 1930s became a well-known spa. The original wooden bridge at Bridgeport collapsed shortly after the Butterfield mail line halted and was not replaced until 1873, when an iron one was installed. The original town near the bridge became "Old" Bridgeport in 1893 after the Rock Island Railroad built through to Fort Worth. A new Bridgeport moved a mile east to the rails, leaving the old one to languish and die.

The route east of Decatur was unchanged until the last month of service, March, 1861. By then Texas had already left the federal union and joined the Confederacy. The U.S. mail was hastily rerouted from Decatur to Denton, bypassing potential trouble spots at Gainesville and Diamond's station. Those last few weeks, the stages went from Denton through Pilot Point and then to Sherman.

The final eastbound Butterfield stage arrived at the Denton square on the morning of March 14. Anson Mills of El Paso, hurrying north to join the Union army, was one of the eight passengers aboard. As related in his book, *My Story*, Mills met an old friend, Judge R. L. Waddill of McKinney in Collin County, where Mills had taught school in 1857–58. Collin County had voted 948 to 405 against secession, and although Texas had been a member of the Confederacy since March 5, Judge Waddill, who was against secession, assured Mills, "The flag is still flying over the McKinney courthouse."[5]

Farther west along the trail, another station may have existed west of the Clear Fork, although Ormsby made no mention of one. One writer notes, "Local legend has it that Thomas Lambshead kept the station at the Clear Fork Crossing or the Butterfield relay station on the west side of the Clear Fork across Lambshead Creek a short distance from the crossing, whose stone foundations can still be seen."[6] Joe B. Matthews, father of Watt Matthews and a founder of the Matthews-Reynolds ranches, also described a relay station west of Clear Fork Crossing to his son. J. R. (Bob) Green, rancher and historian of the region, believes that the structure—whose foundation stones are still visible—while possibly used as a Butterfield relay station, was originally part of Jesse Stem's earlier (1852) farm and Indian Agency layout. Stem had been killed by Indians on February 12, 1854, but his farm remained in cultivation because both Marcy and Neighbors wrote they were impressed by the crops when they passed by in the August after Stem's death. Green feels Thomas Lambshead, an English immigrant, probably worked for Stem. A young man named James F. M. Hamby, who was killed by Indians, reportedly worked for Lambshead near the Upper (Comanche Indian) Reservation.[7]

Sometime early in 1859 another station not on the 1858 Butterfield route was located on the north bank of the Colorado River between the Fort Chadbourne and the Grape Creek stations, about six miles southeast of the present town of Robert Lee. Albert Richardson, who must have hit a particularly rainy season in Texas, writes of arriving there the evening of September 29, 1859, and finding the river impassable: "We slept in the coach waiting for the waters to subside. The vehicle's roof [celerity wagon] was like a sieve, and cold pitiless rain deluged us all night." The next morning, Richardson "awoke cold and rheumatic . . . breakfasted heartily upon pork and mesquite beans; and dried [his] clothes before the fire of the adobe hut-station. The Colorado, usually an insignificant stream a hundred feet wide but now a fierce torrent, compelled us to spend the day here in the favorite range of the Comanche."[8] The Colorado didn't go down until the second day of Richardson's forced lingering, and even when they finally forded it, almost swept away the coach and a six-mule team before the south bank was gained, far down stream.[9]

One exigency of the Butterfield stage ride through far West Texas was the need to herd along a second or third team of mules (sometimes more) to make what were called "flying changes"—quick halts along the long, vacant stretches to harness new teams. Ormsby mentions "a *cavellado* [sic], or drove [of mules] . . . for a change at intervals along the route." When he faced the Llano Estacado (or "dreaded Staked Plain" as he called it), he noted, "We may now be said to have commenced the difficulties of the journey through the great plains or waterless deserts of Texas." He later found that there was not a human habitation, save company stations, in the four hundred miles from Fort Chadbourne to Franklin.[10]

The Camp Johnston station was a meal and change station. Richardson stopped there for dinner on October 1, 1859, after having spent the two-day delay on the bank of the Colorado River. He reports, "Our spirited little landlady, reared in eastern Texas, gave us a description of an attack on the station by one hundred twenty Comanches who were held off by the stocktender, her husband and herself three weeks before." The lady declared "we won't be driven out by worthless red-skins." Richardson says iron-pointed arrows, with feathers, were still sticking in the cottonwood log fence that surrounded the station.[11]

This site remained important. After the Civil War a post office called Johnston Station was on Ben Ficklin's mail line, which followed the Butterfield Trail through this area. During the Civil War the Butterfield mail road was used by a number of Texans wanting to reach Union territory or simply escaping the dangerous climate of the Confederacy. Noah Smithwick, heading for California, described using the recently abandoned Butterfield stations:

> . . . we struck the United States overland mail route to California, and in the dismantled and deserted stations were constantly reminded of the disturbed relations between the two sections of the country. . . . At the head of the Concho a protracted rain came on and, availing ourselves of the deserted

station buildings, we awaited fair weather. Leaving the head of the Concho [and] the Mustang ponds being the last living water until we reached the Pecos . . . we lay by before beginning the long, dry march. There was no station at the ponds, but as the next station out—Johnson's [Johnston's]—had to haul their water from there, there had been a stone house built for protection in case of attack.[12]

Between Head of Concho station and Horsehead Crossing, there was another Butterfield station, built probably in 1859, or at least after Ormsby and Farwell had made their trips. The Conklings claimed to have discovered this station, having found no mention of it on the company timetable. The Conklings dubbed it "Llano Estacado." It was later discovered that had indeed been the official name of it. The Reverend Mr. Tallack mentions it, arriving there June 30, 1860, after a torturous forty-five mile ride from the Pecos River: ". . . never was the sound of the post horn so welcome as today at noon after sixteen hours' fasting. . . . On dismounting we found a dish of dried apples stewed, fried steaks, and hot coffee, and never ate a breakfast with keener relish." Williams reports that newspaper items of the time proved the existence of "the man-made and man-supplied oasis."[13]

Shortly after Ormsby rode the Butterfield stage, the company broke up the long, arduous ride up Captain Pope's new road (on the far-western portion of the 1858 trail through Texas), by establishing a meal station about half way between Emigrants Crossing and Pope's Camp, naming it Skillman's for the great driver. Farwell, in his San Francisco newspaper reports, said that Skillman's station was twenty-five miles from (south) Pope's Camp.[14] The Conklings, writing in the late 1920s, found the station was about seven miles north of Porterville in Loving County.[15] The Butterfield company also set up a small relay camp thirty-six miles northwest of Horsehead Crossing, about five miles west of present-day Grand Falls, for the exchange of teams. It was not, however, a passenger station.[16]

On August 1, 1859, Postmaster General Montgomery Blair ordered a major segment of the Butterfield Overland Mail route changed. After that date the upper route, from Horsehead Crossing up the east side of Pecos River and through the Guadalupe mountains to Franklin City, was abandoned. The new route crossed the Pecos at Horsehead Crossing, going southwest to Comanche Springs—called "*Agua Ancha*" (wide water) by the Indians—at newly established (March 23, 1859) Camp Stockton, then joined the San Antonio and San Diego Mail line, which was also the military road, to El Paso.

One reason the route had been shifted was so Butterfield could service three forts in the region that were getting no direct mail from the east: Camp Stockton, which on May 3, 1860, became Fort Stockton; Fort Davis in the Apache, or Davis, Mountains; and Fort Quitman on the Rio Grande. Water was more easily obtained on the new route and there were more people along the Rio Grande. Ten stations were abandoned on the Guadalupe Mountains route and sixteen stations added on the "lower route." There wasn't much difference in mileage, the lower route being only sixteen miles longer.

Using the new route meant the Pecos River had to be crossed, regardless of its high, steep banks and floods, so the Butterfield company added a ferry near Horsehead Crossing by which passengers and mail from either direction could be ferried to a mail stage waiting on the other side.

In June, 1849, Major Robert Neighbors had reported on Horsehead Crossing to General William S. Harney, new commander of the 8th Military Department: "The banks are low, bottom firm and hard, and the water more shallow . . . yet the depth is too great for fording, and a good ferry boat will be required."[17] Albert Richardson, making the trip in October, 1859, recalled "crossing the swollen river in a skiff," while the Conklings refer to the boat as "a scow ferry."[18] Of whatever size or kind, the ferry boats were not capable of carrying horses and wagons aboard.[19]

Noah Smithwick, hurrying with his family to California to escape the ardent Texas Secessionists, reached the Horsehead Crossing in April, 1861, a month after Butterfield service had ended, and complained, "Here the work of vandalism had already begun in the destruction of the ferry boat."[20] Horsehead Crossing was later (1866-67) used by Oliver Loving and Charles Goodnight in establishing the Goodnight-Loving Trail, which went up the west bank of the river to higher points in New Mexico and Colorado.

The Butterfield, leaving the Pecos, went in an almost direct southwestern line to Fort Stockton's Comanche Springs. Richardson remarks, "We soon struck the old trail of the Comanches to the City of Mexico," which was true in regard to the Comanches but inaccurate as to its ultimate destination.[21] There are no traces of intervening stations or relays although stops were probably made at Diamond Draw or Comanche Creek if recent rains had created ponds. The Butterfield line entered Fort Stockton south of the springs and the fort, going to the station, which was on what is today Gallagher Street and South Main in Old Fort Stockton.[22] Richardson, riding the Butterfield stage a short time after Camp Stockton was established, referred to it as "a military post of three or four edifices with pearly misty mountains in the background." He notes also that this is where "we reached the well-trodden mail road from San Antonio to El Paso."[23]

Anson Mills, who had a short time earlier surveyed and laid out El Paso (for which he received $150 and four lots), in 1859 also laid out and surveyed the town of Fort Stockton. Well before the various U.S. Army explorations of the 1840s and 1850s, the Comanche Springs were well known, although by a variety of names, as the destination of travelers and traders from as far away as Chihuahua and New Mexico. The waters there came gushing out of a large opening and formed a series of tree-lined streams, creating an oasis in the otherwise barren region. Eventually the waters flowed into the surrounding countryside, sinking into various marshy places and disappearing. The famous springs, which for centuries flowed millions of gallons of water a day—the Conklings reported the flow in 1935 at sixty millions gallons daily "of fine clear water"[24]—gradually lost flow after prodigal irrigation pumping began in 1949, and ceased to flow at all in March, 1961.

Fort Stockton was never popular with the troops, either before or after the Civil War. It was abandoned for the several years of that conflict. Burr Duval, who kept a diary on an 1880 trip from San Antonio to the Big Bend, reached Fort Stockton early in January and reported, "The soil is strongly impregnated with alkali and the parade ground of the post is white and shining as though it were strewn with salt. . . . The redeeming feature about the post, and the only one I can see, is a magnificent spring which supplies it with water."[25]

From Fort Stockton the westward mail road followed the road to El Paso already in use by the San Antonio–San Diego mail run, as well as military movements to Fort Davis, so most facilities on this route had already been set up.[26] The first stop on this road after Fort Stockton was the Leon Water Hole station, famed for the food served by the stationkeeper and his wife. (An 1857 map calls the site *Agua Delgada*, or "narrow water," in contrast to the size and volume of Comanche Spring, or *"agua ancha."*) A historical marker on Interstate 10 commemorates the legendary Mr. and Mrs. Isaac Rude:

On their way to California from Tennessee in the 1850s, Isaac J. and Sarah Isabella Rude settled in West Texas. In the Davis Mountains, Rude built and operated a station for the Butterfield Overland Stage; here passengers had meals. . . . Soon Butterfield had Rude moved to Fort Stockton and built another stand. In 1859, when a stop was added at Leon Water Hole . . . Rude built and ran the stand there. The food served was the best on the route, said journalist Richardson. Sarah Rude (1834-1916) carried a pistol under her apron [and] when Indians attacked the Davis Mountains stand, the men loaded guns and handed them to Mrs. Rude, a calm, sure marksman. Just over 5 ft. tall, she butchered and skinned beeves to feed her family when her husband was away. Later [Isaac Rude] became a prosperous businessman in McKinney. He died in 1902.

The Reverend Mr. Tallack gave an unusual sidelight to the stage stand and also praised the food at Leon Hole when he came through in 1861:

> Took supper at Leon Hole Station, so named from a deep moorland tarn, whither troops of antelopes come over the plains to drink. It is said never to have been fathomed, though sounded with a line of five hundred feet. An emigrant once threw in here, over night, the shrunk wheels of his waggon [sic], and, on coming to draw them out in the morning, was astonished to find that they had entirely disappeared in the depths of what . . . he had assumed to be an ordinary pool or temporary accumulation of water in a prairie hollow.
>
> At this station we had for supper some excellent bread, the best on the route; and there was a refinement about the spot very different from the rugged aspect of the generality of Overland stations and their inmates. This was owing to the presence of a cheerful matronly woman (the wife of one of the station-keepers), and two gentle girls, her young daughters, bright "prairie flowers" not often seen in these rough Far-Western wilds.[27]

Some ten or so miles west-southwest of Leon Water Hole station was Hackberry Pond, which, despite the name, is not on Hackberry Draw, a few miles farther west. Hackberry was a watering place only, said the Conklings. They earnestly suggested the modern traveler of their day use the old mail road, to wit:

> Leaving Highway 290, at any convenient gate leading south, and driving from five to eight miles, the old track will be

crossed. The driver of a car [may] . . . by easing down the banks of an occasional arroyo with the aid of a shovel, be able to drive . . . over the hard and almost level desert country.[28]

The Conklings, in their rough and rugged off-road tracing of the Butterfield Trail, make modern four-wheel drive explorers seem a trifle timorous. In the Preface to their monumental set, they noted they traveled nearly 7,000 miles in their "seven-passenger, 1930 model Buick that, although subjected to the severest tests in many hazardous situations—frequently digging our way in or out of an arroyo—never once failed us."[29]

The next station was named Barrilla Spring, in Jeff Davis County, although the spring itself was two miles north, at the southernmost tip of Reeves County (in that confusing area where Reeves, Pecos and Jeff Davis counties meet). The word *barrilla* is a Spanish word for a kind of herb that grows nowhere in the vicinity of either the Barrilla Mountains or Barrilla Spring. Some authorities on the region feel, with the Conklings, that the word is a corruption of *Varela*, from Francisco Varela, an early settler whose name is found given to the spring on early maps.

After Barrilla Spring station, the road passed through rocky Limpia Canyon, with Limpia station the next Butterfield stop. The way Limpia Creek cuts through its mountainous course means that every road or trail, even today, must hug its banks and (literally or figuratively) wade its waters many, many times before reaching Fort Davis. Burr Duval noted this when he reported, "About 10 miles from Barrilla Springs . . . we entered Limpia canon, following its tortuous windings, crossing Limpia creek an incredible number of times to Fort Davis."[30]

Although one reason for shifting the Butterfield run to the Davis Mountain route was to avoid Indian troubles on the Guadalupe route, in the long history of wagon and stage use of the Fort Stockton-Davis Mountain route, Indian attacks were more frequent and persisted longer. The original San Antonio-Santa Fe run of 1850 and later the San Antonio-San Diego line to El Paso were constantly beset by Indian troubles, and freight fees showed it.

Edward F. Beale, explorer and surveyor of the West (also the lieutenant in charge of the army's first camel experiment in 1857, through Texas to California), stated on July 7, 1857,

> We were passed on the road this morning by the monthly El Paso mail on its way up [to Santa Fe], by which I received, forwarded by some friends at San Antonio, a box about two feet square, for which the moderate charge of twenty dollars was made! The dangers of this road, however, justified any price for such matters. Scarcely a mile of it but has its story of Indian murder and plunder; in fact from El Paso to San Antonio is but one long battleground.[31]

Stories of attacks and death well before and long after the Butterfield Mail run are more frequent along Limpia Canyon and on the way from Fort Davis to Barrel Springs, Van Horn Wells, and through Quitman Canyon, than they ever were on the upper route. The Butterfield was fortunate; the company lost few animals and never had one of its stages attacked in the two years it ran via Fort Davis—even as travelers, emigrants and soldiers were losing their lives on that pathway. Some Butterfield drivers in Arizona reached informal "treaties" with the Apaches there through small bribes of corn, food, etc. There is no record of this occurring on the Texas portion of the trail, except at a station.

Limpia Station[32] was ten miles by road from Barrilla Spring station, and much of Highway 17 is over the same path as the old mail road. The Conklings report that Limpia station was probably only a "swing" or change station—in other words, no stops were scheduled and no meals were served. Only the teams were changed, and not always that, because mention is made that the twenty-eight mile run from Barrilla Spring to Fort Davis was often done without a change.[33]

Four miles west on Limpia Creek is Wild Rose Pass, famous as a landmark long before the coming of the mail wagons. Spanish conquistador Antonio de Espejo, first white man through the mountains, used it in August, 1583. A later interesting visit involved Lieutenant Beale and his camel caravan that stopped and camped at the pass on July 16, 1857.[34] Unfortunately for history, the modern road doesn't use the true pass, but takes a lower divide just west of it—although it is unfair to imply there is less beauty on the later pathway; it is quite lovely. The pass follows a three-mile canyon between Star Mountain at 6,350 feet and Major Peak at 5,822 feet.

Albert Richardson, making his way through Limpia Canyon, and the Conklings, years later, repeat a story that, though found in other histories, bears the suspicious overstatement of myth. Richardson reported that several months before he made the trip in October, 1859, a San Antonio-San Diego mail coach was ambushed by a party of Apaches who killed the driver and carried off the mail sacks.[35] The Apache party, arriving back at its hiding place, is supposed to have ripped open the mail sacks and become so fascinated by such picture magazines as *Harper's Weekly* and Frank Leslie's *Illustrated Weekly*, that they were caught off guard by a detachment of Fort Davis troops who (quote the Conklings) "completely annihilated them." The Conklings added "This sudden retaliation evidently quenched the desire for any further literary leaning in other savage breasts, for it was thereafter regarded by them as bad medicine to even look at an illustration, and to touch one of the magazines was courting death."[36] Here one finds a rare misinterpretation by the Conklings. What Richardson actually wrote was, " . . . killing fourteen and *routing* the rest." He then added that the Apaches believed the papers had revealed their whereabouts, " . . . and still supposing that pictures can talk, they avoid them with superstitious dread."[37]

Fort Davis station, twelve miles southwest of Wild Rose Pass, was not located at the fort but was on Limpia Creek a short distance northeast of the fort. This site was a locality of sorts originally known as La Limpia or, by the Comanches, Painted Camp.[38] Established in 1854, the fort was first called "Post on Limpia." It was then named for Jefferson Davis when he was Secretary of War, well before he became president of the Confederacy. The camel experiment by the army sent the beasts through Fort Davis in 1857 and 1858. The original fort was turned over to the Confederates in April, 1861, then was reoccupied by Union troops from El Paso after the Confederates departed in 1862. Indians and scavengers almost destroyed the post during its short vacancy. When U.S. troops were sent to Fort Davis after the Civil War, a new complex had to be built. The buildings standing today are a "new" Fort Davis, erected in the years following the reoccupation of the fort site in July, 1867.[39]

The town around Fort Davis seems to have grown up with the 1854 fort, as was usually the case with frontier forts, but it was not recognized as a town until several years after the fort was established. This area was at the crossroads of the old Chihuahua Trail (used by traders coming up from that northern Mexican city), and the regional mail routes. It was a lovely spot, and had water, but it was a dangerous post. It has been said that in the fourteen years following its rebuilding in 1867, Fort Davis troops engaged in more Indian battles than those of any other military installation in the country. The Conklings said of it, "The only other military post on the whole route that is located amid such natural beauty, is old Fort Tejon in California."[40] Burr Duval felt, "The country surrounding the fort is by far the most enjoyable to look at I have seen in western Texas."[41]

Ten miles west by southwest from Fort Davis, the mail road led past a formation known as Point of Rocks. While not a stop, it was an old watering place from a seep spring below a huge granite ledge. In 1935, Captain Jim Gillett, who had owned land in the area since 1890, unveiled a monument at Point of Rocks to "Ed Waldy [Walde], John M. Dean, August Fresnell and all other stage drivers who traveled this route. Fearless heroes of frontier days. By their courage the west was made."[42] Although a modern highway through this section originally followed the mail road rather closely, slowly the old road southwest and northwest of Fort Davis has been lost to erosion and engineering changes. At many points, what must have been the Butterfield roadway now offers a patternless series of gullies and washes, impossible to trace without a surveyor's notes and equipment. Because of the sudden force of rain-filled streams coming off the mountains, water crossings in this region have been especially vulnerable to this process.

Some sixteen miles from Fort Davis is Skillman's Grove, between Barrel Springs and Dead Man's Hole. It was a camping place for stages, emigrant wagons, and soldiers, and from time to time was a stage stand. In 1890 the annual Bloys Camp Meeting began there, and it continues to the present. A 1914 traveler described the place as "a beautiful 'park' in the mountains."[43] This large, astonishing sweep of oak trees was named for Captain Henry Skillman, although he did not own the land. He first used it for a camp site in 1850 on the San Antonio-El Paso mail line. Captain Skillman was also commander of Fort Davis for a few months when it was in Confederate hands.

Not far west of Skillman's Grove the mail road—and the modern state highway—pass over what Richardson calls "the highest ridge between St. Louis and El Paso." Pointing out that the mules were, to begin with, "so wild they could only be caught by lassoing them," Richardson adds, "When we started [down from the ridge] they proved altogether unmanageable." His adventure, from this point, is worth a full retelling.

In the headlong race, while the coach was poised on two wheels, I sprang out. The vehicle barely avoided capsizing; and after a circuit of a mile, the driver brought his riotous steeds around again and stopped for me to re-enter. "My friend," observed the colonel [who had gotten on at Fort Davis], "you are fortunate to escape a broken neck. Whatever happens, always stick to the coach." "And," added the [California] general, "never jump out over a wheel!"

Scarcely had these golden axioms been uttered, when the spirits of our mules again effervesced. The coach was transformed into a pitching schooner, which the bounding billows of prairie tossed and rolled and threatened to wreck. I kept in the vehicle; but both my military companions jumped head-long over a hind-wheel to the sure and firm-set earth. After that climax, equilibrium was restored; but the colonel picked up with a sprained ancle [sic], and the general, with a severely bruised foot, both seemed in doubt whether to laugh or fight, when their own wise counsel was repeated to them.[44]

Another six miles brought the mail stage to Barrel Spring station. The name is believed to have come from soldiers having sunk bar-rels in the ravine below the spring to catch the water. The spring was described as coming from "beneath a large boulder of granite" by Captain S. G. French when leading an 1849 wagon train from San Antonio to Paso del Norte (Mexico). The mail station at Barrel Spring was reportedly rebuilt three times after destructive Indian raids, and in 1870 was rebuilt for Ben Ficklin's mail line.[45] Captain Gillett in 1890 bought the Barrel Spring Ranch with the old stage station on it.[46]

Thirteen miles northwest of the Barrel Spring station was the Dead Man's Hole station, located on the southwestern side below El Muerto [The Dead Man] Peak. The Conklings point out that the fireplace in the Butterfield station (not to be confused with the Ben Ficklin station of a later date) was unique. "It was built almost in the center of the room, of smaller selected rock slabs and formed a huge stone stove, nearly five feet square at the base."[47] The name of the spring is said by Barrie Scobee to have come from the fact that a man was found shot and killed in the spring when the first San An-tonio-El Paso mail coach ran the route in 1854.[48] Which was named first, the peak or the spring? Whichever actually honored whatever slain man, the Conklings noted that "in spite of the sinister sound-ing name, it would be difficult to find a lovelier or more romantic lo-cation than the site of this old mail station."[49]

Leaving Dead Man's Hole, the mail road eventually worked its way a few miles northeast of the present-day small town of Valen-tine. At that point it parallels the present tracks of the Southern

Pacific Railroad and the modern highway (U.S. 1-10), close to the forgotten siding of Chispa. Valentine was the connecting point with the Southern Pacific for the twenty-six mile Rio Grande Northern Railroad which ran from the mines at San Carlos, near the Rio Grande, to Chispa. The Rio Grande Northern was chartered in 1893 but was abandoned in 1899. It held an even more interesting distinction: it used one of the only four railroad tunnels built in Texas. However, the tunnel was used as an automobile roadway for years after the rails were removed.

The old stage road crossed the Southern Pacific and the modern highway near the town of Lobo—once a ranching supply point and later headquarters for regional mica shipments. Van Horn's Wells, at one time a series of ponds, furnished water for Indians, explorers, mail drivers and, later, steam locomotives. A historical marker on U.S. Highway 90 locates Van Horn's Wells as one-half mile west of the roadway and states that the wells were named for either Major Jefferson Van Horne—who passed the site in 1849 en route to establishing the "Post at El Paso," the predecessor of Fort Bliss—or for Lieutenant James J. Van Horn, stationed at the wells to fight Indians in 1859. Beginning in 1880, the town of Van Horn grew up 12 miles north. The name similarity has caused questions of what is named for whom that are still unsettled.

Heading from Van Horn's Wells toward Eagle Springs station,[50] the old road recrossed the route of the Southern Pacific, about a mile and a half southeast of Hot Wells—not to be confused with Van Horn's Wells. The Eagle Springs station was a few miles due west of Hot Wells on the northern slope of Eagle Mountain. The Conklings pointed out that "as the station was located in a canyon with access to it through numerous passes, it probably suffered more from Indian depredations than any other station in this portion of the route. . . . [I]t was destroyed three times at different periods in its history."[51]

From here the Butterfield route ran half a dozen miles south of Sierra Blanca before turning southwest over Quitman Pass, through Quitman Canyon, to First Camp on the Rio Grande. This stretch of roadway today pretty well follows the old mail road, as the narrow pass doesn't allow much deviation. This piece of the trail was also used in the U.S. Army's 1916-1917 campaigns against Pancho Villa's guerrilla forces. The Conklings reported, when they traveled this road, that "some of the concrete pads laid down at that time on the numerous crossings over the dry washes are still in use."[52]

It is interesting to note the historic symbolism, if you will, of the fact that the remote and deserty hamlet of Sierra Blanca, on the general route of the stagecoach and mule trains, marks the coming together of several modern modes of swift transportation, swifter than John Butterfield or Ben Ficklin at their most farsighted could have envisioned. The former Texas & Pacific Railway (now Union Pacific) comes from the east and parallels U.S. Interstate Highway 10, and is joined by the Southern Pacific from the southeast paralleled by U.S 90. Above them all, the transcontinental jets begin descending to land at El Paso—the goal of the mail stages, the railroads, and the highways.

The First Camp on the Rio Grande, located on a terrace above the river at an ancient spot, was always called by that name, but there was never a town located there. (Realignment of the river has severely altered the spot today.) On October 4, 1859, Albert Richardson reported: "At daylight we reached the Rio Grande and looked across it upon Mexican territory. Three dirty blanketed barefoot men smoking cigarettes, shivered over the fire on the river bank, where two Mexican women cooked our breakfast of frijoles."[53] Without wishing to make early travelers sound too brave or stoic, notice, in reading the accounts of their torturous journeys, how seldom there is a complaint about the heat or the cold unless it somehow prevents the continuation of the journey.[54]

The Rio Grande highway, from First Camp to old Fort Quitman traces pretty well the mail road, but the river is a different proposition. The lazy and acute loops and turns of the Rio Grande have been straightened to below the site of First Camp, swapping small portions between the two nations whose boundary it forms. The Conklings, not overlooking a detail, point out that the river rectification project of the mid-1930s "greatly altered the site(s) and destroyed sections of the old road as well."[55] Fort Quitman, established in 1858, was not a Butterfield station but merely an exchange point for dropping off or taking aboard passengers and mail. Richardson, with a touch of vinegar in his words, wrote:

> At Fort Quitman, whose whitewashed adobe buildings look like marble, we left the colonel [who with the general had chided Richardson for jumping from the careening stage], so lame that his Irish servant lifted him from the coach like a baby. The general while asleep had lost his hat overboard, for the second time within forty-eight hours. Unable to purchase a new one he wrapt his head in a fiery red comforter, like a sanguinary and turbanned Turk.[56]

Richardson seemed pleased with the Rio Grande country along the river.

> We continued up the sandy valley of the Rio Grande, from five to forty miles wide, and bounded on the west by a notched line of mountains. We passed Mexican villages, where bright-eyed, dusky-faced, half-naked children were playing about the streets, and through open doors women were visible . . . gossiping and smoking cigarettes.[57]

Rio Grande station on the Butterfield, only a change station, was twenty-eight miles northwest of Fort Quitman. Also known as Birchville, it was a camping place on the San Antonio-San Diego line in 1857, and was named for James E. Birch, founder of that line. The Conklings felt that, based on some of the relics found there, the owners of the line might have had ambitions toward putting a city at the spot, but until Butterfield people built a station there, no building had stood at Birchville. In 1870 the building was rehabilitated by Ficklin and named Pierpont Ranch station. (Pierpont was an El Paso landowner from before the Civil War.)

The Butterfield route led past, or across, the area where the town of Fabens was to be laid out in 1911. Fabens should receive historical recognition as the southwestern terminal of the Rio Grande Valley Traction Company, an El Paso interurban electric railway which was placed in service August 30, 1913. Unfortunately, the extension from Isleta (or Ysleta, whose name *isleta* means "little island"), through Clint to Fabens lost money from the start and was abandoned in 1918, but service to Isleta continued to 1932. Corporately, the RGVT was later absorbed into the El Paso City lines which crossed the Rio Grande to Ciudad Juarez, the last electric railway to cross a U.S. border. Although the El Paso-Juarez rails were in place in 1993, service was interrupted in the mid-1960s with the building of a new international bridge, and was not resumed. Although missed by the Butterfield Trail by some two miles, historical recognition might also be made of Clint, founded in 1909 and named for Mary Clinton Collins. Clint gained international fame in the 1940s and 1950s as the post office drop for ordering such items as "bless cloths" and plastic "glow-in-the-dark" statues of Jesus (suitable for mounting on the dashboard of the car) offered by radio evangelists.

The 1857 Topographical Engineers map, when examined closely, shows the island formed by the old windings of the Rio Grande, which included the cities of Ysleta, Socorro, and San Elizario. For nearly two centuries these cities were on the Mexican side of the river, but they were moved to the Texas side on January 12, 1849, when the Rio Grande in flood diverted its main channel a few hundred yards westward. The old bed often carried so much water that the stages and wagons used fords located below modern Clint near Socorro. The Rio Grande Rectification Project of 1933–38 so totally changed the river system south of the city of El Paso that it is almost impossible today to find the old bed among the watery maze of laterals, canals, interceptors, and drains.

San Elizario is one of the most historic spots in Texas, but since it was not founded by Stephen F. Austin, it hasn't been recognized as such by many Texas historians. It was the last station on the 1859

Butterfield route before Franklin, and the station building was located near the old Spanish presidio for which the town was named. It was a meal and change station. In 1870 the Ficklin station was at the same location, in the charge of Luis Cardis, who, though of Italian origin, was an opportunistic political leader for the Mexican national elements in the area and whose shooting death (but one of many surrounding the so-called El Paso Salt War) led to the mob deaths of J. G. Atkinson, the San Elizario postmaster, and Judge Charles Howard, the man who had killed Cardis. San Elizario, for several years the largest town in the area, was the first county seat of El Paso County. It was established in 1772 as a presidial town, but the presidio (military post) was moved across the river into Mexico in 1814.

For two centuries the many towns and villages along this part of the Rio Grande were a separate world, paying little attention to which side of the river they were on. And that world was quite old, in the North American time frame. Juan de Oñate, who led the initial colonization of New Mexico in 1598, crossed the Rio Bravo in the area of San Elizario, and because of the river passage, the whole region became known as El Paso del Norte (The Pass of the North) or simply, El Paso. Early maps show villages such as Colonia Militar, Guadalupe, and San Ignacio along the Rio Grande, and reference is made to them by writers of that time, but only San Elizario on the east bank was of a size to be called a town. The treaty that ended the Mexican-U.S. War was the first event to sunder this hitherto boundary-less situation, putting part of the "El Pasoans" in the United States away from their Mexican brothers. (Breaking up these ethnic communities had a great deal to do with the internal fights such as the Salt War, and with the bitter resentments that prevailed in the region for more than forty-five years after the towns became part of the U.S.)

The Butterfield Overland Mail line was not the first such service, by any means, to include San Elizario in its schedule. San Elizario had been a station on the first horseback mail trip between San Antonio and Santa Fe from 1850 to 1853. After that it was a station for the Wasson-Giddings first mail coach routes, and when the San Antonio-San Diego line began in July, 1857, San Elizario was again a major stopping place. On the 26th of that month, the previously mentioned Lieutenant Beale, commanding the army's first camel experiments, led his twenty-five pack camels through San Elizario, Socorro and Ysleta, reaching Franklin the same day, then plodding on toward California. Beale reported the appearance of the camels created much excitement, with the residents crowding the streets and even following the camel train into camp for a closer look.[58]

The next little village on the old stage and mail road was Socorro. In modern bus terms, it was a flag stop, the stage only pausing to pick up passengers if so signaled. Richardson, riding through on the Butterfield coach, noted, "Water is conveyed from the river through ditches to every portion of the farms. In this sandy soil and rainless climate, no crop can be raised without irrigation." Then he added, "Passing the pleasant, shaded Mexican hamlet of Socorro, with quaint old churches and low houses of adobe, and Ysletta, [sic] a Pueblo Indian settlement with its tall white cathedral, we reached El Paso."[59]

Ysleta del Sur, the "Little Island of the South," founded in 1680, claims to be the oldest continuously occupied town in Texas, although Nacogdoches disputes the claim. The Tigua Indians established Ysleta after coming out of New Mexico following Popé's 1680 uprisings against the Spanish. The county seat was moved from San Elizario to Ysleta in 1874 and it remained the El Paso County seat until 1883, when the seat was moved permanently to the city of El Paso, rapidly becoming a major population center for the entire ancient Rio Grande region. Historian Anne E. Hughes has written, "Though the beginning of Texas is commonly associated with the small group of missions established by Massenet in 1690 on the Neches River in Eastern Texas, as a matter of fact, the true beginnings of what is now Texas are to be found in the settlements grouped along the Rio del Norte in the El Paso district."[60]

Anson Mills was contractor and builder of the Butterfield station in El Paso, situated in the heart of the city, which was completed less than a month before the arrival of the first Overland Mail coach. Mills, never hesitant to claim his place in history, insisted it was due to his personal efforts that the name of the town was changed from Franklin to El Paso in 1859. He said Benjamin Franklin Coons (or Coontz),[61] was "an undesirable citizen."[62] Whatever Coons was, or wasn't, he passed from the El Paso picture. His name, however, persists in "Franklin Mountains," "Franklin Street," and the "Franklin Canal" there.

The two Butterfield routes, upper and lower, came together at Stephenson's Concordia ranch (today Concordia Cemetery is a reminder) and from there went to the Franklin station. C. L. Sonnichsen writes, "A permanent reminder of stagecoach days in El Paso is preserved in the titles of the downtown streets, some of which were named for the destinations of one or another of the stage lines. The westbound coaches left town by way of San Francisco Street . . . [and] by the same process St. Louis (now Mills) was labeled."[63] The Butterfield station was at South El Paso Street and Overland Avenue—the latter named in 1859 for the Butterfield line—occupying two acres of ground between El Paso and Oregon streets. The walls were twenty feet high and nearly three feet thick. The main entrance, on El Paso Street, was a vestibule leading to the patio. There were thirty rooms built around the 43 x 72-foot patio. The 52 x 106-foot corral contained rooms for a cook, blacksmith, and wheelwright, as well as a harness repair shop and storage. There was a well and a tank watering trough inside the corral.

The station was so large and substantially built that in 1860 a second story was added. This Frontier Hotel, according to the Mesilla (New Mexico) *Times* at the time the El Paso hotel opened, advertised large, airy rooms, careful servants, good meals, and a fine bar. The Butterfield Company also kept a large stock of goods at the station and (according to the Conklings) "carried on a mercantile business of no mean proportions along with the mail and passenger enterprise."[64] After the Butterfield stage ended its run through Texas, this station was a residence, sheltering important families through the years such as those of Judge Gaylord Clarke, Albert J. Fountain (two "good guys" during a period when the bad guys were trying to take over El Paso). It was home also to the well liked Judge J. P. Hague, and the well hated Judge Simon Newcomb, a Radical Republican appointee of Governor E. J. Davis, later removed from the bench by the State Legislature.

Richardson, describing the town in August, 1859, said its "four-hundred inhabitants [were] chiefly Mexican." He continued,

Its business men are Americans, but Spanish was the prevailing language. . . . [H]abitual gambling [is] universal, from the boy's game of pitching quartillas (three cent coins) to the great saloons where huge piles of silver dollars were staked at monte. In this little village, a hundred thousand dollars often changed hands in a single night. There are only two or three American ladies; and most of the whites keep Mexican mistresses. Slavery is only nominal in western Texas, as negroes could easily cross the Rio Grande into Mexico, where the natives sheltered them. . . . The American residents believed in the inalienable right of the white man to bully the inferior race.[65]

El Paso had already become famous for its brandy and wine when the Butterfield stage arrived for the first time. John Russell Bartlett gives a lengthy description of viniculture at the Pass:

There are both white and purple varieties [of grapes]. Large vineyards . . . are seen within the town and the district adjacent to El Paso. Careful cultivators cover the vines during the winter with straw. With the first opening of spring the vineyards are irrigated, or rather inundated; for the water is suffered to flow over them, and there to remain until the ground is thoroughly saturated. This is generally all the water they get.

As may be supposed from the abundance of this fruit, it is exceedingly cheap, and forms a large portion of the [inhabitant's] food.[66]

He also described the winemaking process: "The grapes are thrown into large vats, and trodden by the naked feet of men; after which they are put into bags or sacks of raw ox-hide and pressed." As for the quality, Bartlett, a New England political appointee, ethnologist, and Rhode Island librarian, turned up his nose: "The wine of El Paso enjoys a higher reputation in certain parts of the United States than it deserves. I have drank little that was above mediocrity; and it served me as it does most others who are not used to it, causing a severe headache. Brandy . . . is also made from the grape. It is of a light color, and is known in New Mexico as 'Pass Whiskey.'"[67]

The American influx into the El Paso del Norte region had begun shortly after Alexander Doniphan and his Missouri army, moving toward Chihuahua, captured the town on Christmas day in 1846. By the end of the Mexican-U.S. war, a considerable number of Americans had become acquainted with the Rio Grande's upper valley and a detachment of U.S. troops was at El Paso del Norte. The first military installation on the U.S. side was called, simply, "Military Post at El Paso"—the El Paso being on the western, or Mexican side, of the river—or, in C. L. Sonnichsen's *Pass of the North*, "Post Opposite El Paso." By 1854, after much shuffling of troops and temporary locations, the army post was named Fort Bliss, and five moves and five miles later, in October, 1893, the present site of Fort Bliss was opened.[68]

The Butterfield stage, after leaving the station, went out San Francisco Street and worked its way through the Pass, between modern Sunland Park and the river, past the old town of Fronteras. Much of this part of the trail is now under U.S Highway 80 and the tracks of the Santa Fe Railroad. The mail road then passed La Tuna on the way to the Cottonwoods station at the northern edge of Texas, almost in Anthony, developed by the Santa Fe Railroad.

Richardson tells of an adobe station about twenty miles from El Paso where dinner was served. This was probably the El Paso-Santa Fe mail line's station at Los Tres Hermanos (The Three Brothers) ranch, which was owned by the three Mills brothers, Anson, W. W., and Emmett. (Emmett, who was in charge of the station, was later killed by the Apaches.) This station was just within the southern boundary of the present town of Vinton. The Butterfield line passed through western Anthony and crossed the Texas-New Mexico line, which sits on the 32nd parallel, heading for Fort Fillmore and Mesilla, New Mexico.

Notes

1. Cliff D. Cates, *Pioneer History of Wise County* (Decatur: Wise County Historical Society, 1971), 299–301.

2. Michael Collins, *Cooke County, Texas: Where the South and the West Meet* (n.p.: Cooke County Heritage Society, 1981), 6–7. The Conklings believed Brandon's station was near "an old trading post known as Fitzhue [sic] station." This was usually referred to as Elm Station, established by Colonel William Fitzhugh in 1847, a few miles southeast of Gainesville. Fitzhugh led a company of U.S. Mounted Volunteers patrolling a line across north Texas from Warren's trading post on the Red River, south to Bird's Fort and Johnson's Station (now Arlington, Texas). Elm Station, or Fort Fitzhugh, was a single row of log blockhouses with a stable, all surrounded by a log fence. Cooke County was organized there and the first county officials appointed there in 1848. Fitzhugh divided his company among Elm Station and Hickory Station, which was a short distance southwest of modern Denton on Hickory Creek. The mounted Volunteers (rangers) were disbanded in 1849.

3. Cates, 109. Bishop was an interesting, though paradoxical, figure in Texas history. Cates, the Wise County historian, speaks of "his fiery rebelism in Texas" and ascribes it to Bishop's early association with arrogant Robert Toombs, Georgia politician and Confederate governmental malcontent. Bishop was a captain of militia during the 1837 Seminole War in Florida where he and his men intercepted and held John Howard Payne, playwright and actor who wrote the song "Home, Sweet Home." Bishop, claiming he was ordered to

detain all "unknown or suspicious characters," wouldn't free Payne. The actor had attempted to obtain justice for the displaced Cherokees in Georgia, thus was probably looked on as a suspicious character by the militia. But by whatever interpretation, Colonel Bishop was notably bull-headed, and even though recognizing Payne, pretended to hold him strictly by the book. Afterward, in his memoirs, Payne referred to Bishop as "Smooth and silky Absalom." Cates says Bishop was very active "in that phase of politics which surrounded the enforced removal of the Indians of Georgia to reservations—becoming so radical as to necessitate his removal from Georgia."

4. Cates, 109.

5. Anson Mills, *My Story* (Washington, D.C.: n.p., 1918), 64. Anson Mills had attended West Point for nearly two years when he was dismissed in 1857 because of deficiencies in mathematics. Chagrined, he fled to Texas where in 1857, Judge Waddill secured him to teach in McKinney for a year in a frame building which Waddill had erected in his own yard. Mills went from McKinney to El Paso where, as a surveyor, in 1859 he laid out the Texas townsite and suggested the name El Paso to ease confusion over the three separately named settlements on the Texas side of the Rio Grande. Mills voted against secession and joined the Union army, attaining the rank of captain. In 1866 he patented an ammunition belt that was used by armies the world over and made him wealthy. After the Civil War he remained in the army, eventually accumulating fifty-four years of federal service, including twenty as a member of the International Boundary Commission. Although he and his family lived in Washington, D.C., where he died in 1924, Anson Mills never lost interest in El Paso. And despite his mathematical shortcomings at West Point, he was a brigadier general when he retired from active duty in 1897.

6. Frances Mayhugh Holden, *Lambshead Before Interwoven* (College Station: Texas A&M University Press, 1982), 25.

7. Randolph B. Marcy, *Thirty Years of Army Life on the Border* (Philadelphia: J. B. Lippincott Co., 1963), 182.

8. Albert Deane Richardson, *Beyond the Mississippi: From the Great River to the Great Ocean* . . . (New York: Bliss, 1867), 228. Unless some stationkeeper had discovered a method unknown to the author (a native of the region) for making the bean of the mesquite tree a palatable dish, we question that menu.

9. Ibid.

10. Ormsby, 62–63.

11. A. Richardson, 231.

12. Noah Smithwick, *The Evolution of a State* (Austin: Steck-Vaughn Co., 1968), 167.

13. Walter B. Lang, *The First Overland Mail: Butterfield Trail* (Washington,

D.C.: n.p., 1940), 152–53.

14. Lang, 123.

15. Porterville was abandoned in 1930 after a Pecos River flood left only a 1910-built church which was moved to Mentone.

16. Grand Falls was named for a former six-foot falls in the Pecos River.

17. Neighbors to Harney, June 4, 1849. Letters Received, Army Headquarters. Olds Records Sec. (Washington, D.C.)

18. A. Richardson, 233; Roscoe and Margaret B. Conkling, *The Butterfield Overland Mail 1857–1869*, Vol. II (Glendale: Arthur H. Clark, Co., 1947), 14.

19. After the Civil War (1872) stages could cross the Pecos on a bridge of pontoon boats. This point was known as Camp Melbourne Crossing or more often, Pontoon Crossing of the Pecos. August Santleben writes,

... in 1872, when returning from Chihuahua, I crossed the Pecos River at the Horse-head ford on a pontoon bridge belonging to the United States army. The military authorities had constructed it for temporary use to facilitate the movement of troops and government wagon-trains. The structure was not capable of sustaining heavily loaded prairie schooners like mine, consequently I was compelled to divide my freight ... and had to carry each lot over separately. The laborious undertaking consumed almost the entire day. August Santleben, *A Texas Pioneer, Early Staging and Overland Freighting Days on the Frontiers of Texas and Mexico* (Waco: W. M. Morrison, 1967), 145.

20. Smithwick, 338.

21. A. Richardson, 233.

22. In 1875 when Pecos County was organized, the county seat was St. Gall, named for Peter (Don Pedro) Gallagher, an Irish-Texan entrepreneur and a large landowner of the community. The "zero" stone marking the center of St. Gall is still in place, located on the courthouse square, several yards east of the old Butterfield station site. Fort Stockton was chosen county-seat name over St. Gall in an 1881 election. Gallagher, born in County Wicklow, came to Texas in 1837 and was a member of President Lamar's ill-advised Santa Fe Expedition of 1841. He was captured and held prisoner at Mexico City's Castle Perote before being released. His diary gives an account of this misadventure.

23. A. Richardson, 234.

24. Conkling, Vol II, 15.

25. Sam Woolford, ed., "The Burr Duval Diary," *Southwestern Historical Quarterly* LXV (April 1962): 497. Burr Duval was a nephew of John C. Duval "first Texas man of letters" according to J. Frank Dobie.

26. The first usable road to the El Paso country had been north out of San Antonio, developed by the San Antonio-El Paso-Santa Fe mail run, later by the

San Antonio-San Diego line. A road north and northwest to El Paso and Chihuahua from the Texas interior had been desired for years, and after the Mexican-U.S. war ended in 1848 and this *terra incognita* began to open up, it became imperative.

The route along the Rio Grande offered water, but for vehicular travel the mountain ranges of the Big Bend made passage almost impossible. Six months after the close of the Mexican War, a group of San Antonio citizens attempted to make a commercial connection with northern Mexico, sending Colonel John Coffee (Jack) Hays and thirty-five Texas Rangers under the command of Captain Samuel Highsmith to find a practical wagon road to Chihuahua by way of the Big Bend and El Paso. Presidio del Norte, the farthest point, was reached after a fifty day "death march." The survivors dragged in after one hundred seven days of futile effort. James K. Greer, *Colonel Jack Hays, Texas Frontier Leader and California Builder* (College Station: Texas A&M University Press, 1987), 217–37. Some route had to be found safe from Comanche and Apache danger, but, most important, it must have sufficient water to save the travelers from extinction. Thus, the Trans-Pecos region, and the terrible Llano Estacado, with their waterless and vegetation-less reputations, were avoided. But the discovery of gold in California sent the forty-niners scuttling westward by every route available, deadly or not, and the public demanded ways be found and marked for the argonauts. In 1849 the army began a series of expeditions and explorations throughout the southwest, mapping and marking across West Texas and the Trans-Pecos region, so that by 1857, when the Butterfield engineers began laying out the stage road, they were assured of a workable, if not infallible, series of maps and official notations.

The army used the Topographical Engineers, an elite branch whose members—Robert E. Lee was one—carefully added "T. E." behind their name and rank. Lieutenant Colonel Joseph E. Johnston headed a series of "surveys and reconnaissances" which went on for five years and included expeditions by Lieutenants F. T. Bryan, M. I. Smith, W. F. Smith, Nathaniel Michler, and the greatest explorer, Captain Marcy, probing west and northwestern Texas. During the 1850–54 period, Major W. H. Emory mapped the U.S.-Mexico boundary and led mapping expeditions among the waterholes of the Big Bend area. In more northern parts of Texas, Lieutenants James William Abert (the artist), James Hervey Simpson, and Amiel Weeks Whipple, all of whom became high ranking officers of the Union army in the Civil War, explored along the 35th parallel. This became important to Butterfield history in 1857 when Captain Whipple proved to be an ardent supporter of this route as bids were being received for the overland mail contract. He reported that in the highest passes along the 35th parallel "the deepest snow found was but eight inches deep, and the mercury was never down to zero." Waterman Ormsby wrote, "The eulogium of this route by Capt. Whipple was unequivocal" and helped cause the great Northern outcry when the 32nd parallel (southern) route was chosen. Others, including fellow explorer Simpson, represented Capt. Whipple (to quote Ormsby) "as having thrown too much coleur de rose around his reports."

27. Lang, 151.

28. Conkling, Vol. II, 22.

29. Conkling, Vol. I, 17.

30. Duval, 498.

31. Leroy Hafen, *The Overland Mail* (Glendale: Arthur Clark Co., 1926), 73.

32. A mile or so west of the Butterfield site, Ben Ficklin constructed a rock station between 1869 and 1872. Across the creek on the west bank from the Ficklin station was an early Limpia post office which is sometimes confused with the Butterfield station.

33. Conkling, Vol. II, 23.

34. J. Lloyd Mecham, "Antonio de Espejo and His Journey to New Mexico," *Southwestern Historical Quarterly* XXX (October 1926): 135.

35. The San Antonio-San Diego line was called "The Jackass Mail" because pack mules were used originally to carry passengers and mail from Yuma to San Diego.

36. Conkling, Vol. II, 25.

37. A. Richardson, 233–34.

38. "This creek [Limpia] is followed for a distance of about twenty-five miles to the Painted Comanche camp; and here the road to Presidio del Norte passes to the southward and westward while the road to El Paso del Norte strikes northwestward toward the pass in the mountains on the Rio Grande." Lieutenants William F. Smith and William H. C. Whiting, Topographical Engineers (1849); Sen. Ex. Doc. No. 64, 31st Congress, 1st Session.

39. John C. Cremony, *Life Among the Apaches* (New York: Time-Life Books, 1981), 251–52. "General Carleton dispatched Capt. E. D. Shirland and his company, C of the First California Cavalry Volunteers, to retake Fort Davis, in Texas [in 1862]. Upon Shirland's arrival he found the fort deserted by the Confederates; but also discovered that they had left three men behind who had been seized with small-pox. These poor fellows were abandoned to their fate; but the Confederate troops had scarcely left the place before the Apaches arrived, and with their usual precaution they made careful inspection before trusting themselves into the building. In the course of their investigations they discovered the three sick men, and recognizing the disease with which they were afflicted, filled their bodies full of arrows shot from between the iron bars of the windows; and without attempting to enter the fortress, went on their way

toward their own fastnesses. A few days afterward, Shirland, at the head of twenty-five men, encountered over two hundred of those same Apaches at the place known as 'Dead Man's Hole' and killed twenty-two of them without sustaining any other loss than that of a single carbine."

40. Conkling, Vol. II, 28.

41. Woolford, 498.

42. Conkling, Vol. II, 28.

43. B. C. Tharp and Chester V. Kielman, ed., "Mary S. Young's Journal of Botanical Explorations in Trans-Pecos Texas, August-September, 1914," *Southwestern Historical Quarterly* LXV (January 1962): 379.

44. A. Richardson, 235.

45. Conkling, Vol. II, 31.

46. Ben Ficklin, a key figure of western staging history, in 1859 helped organize and became general superintendent of the Central and Overland California and Pike's Peak Express Co. He became known as the man who projected the Pony Express. After the Civil War, although he had been a Confederate officer, he received a government contract for weekly mail service from Fort Smith to San Antonio with a branch to El Paso by way of the Concho country. He established the Concho mail station as headquarters for the operation of his stage lines, growing into the town of Benficklin, which in 1874 became the first county seat of vast Tom Green County. Benficklin was washed away in the awesome Concho River flood of 1882 which killed fifty people. But by then Ben Ficklin, the man, was dead, having choked to death on a fishbone in 1871 while eating dinner in Washington, D. C.

47. Conkling, Vol. II, 32.

48. Barry Scobee, *Old Fort Davis* (San Antonio: Naylor Co., 1947), 34.

49. Conkling, Vol. II, 33.

50. Springs is sometimes spelled in the singular but there was apparently more than one seep spring.

51. Conkling, Vol. II, 34.

52. Conkling, Vol. II, 39. In 1992 no such concrete crossings were visible.

53. A. Richardson, 236.

54. M. K. Kellogg, whose 1872 Texas journal has been quoted, was an exception. Although a well known and well-thought-of artist, he was a whiny, spoiled, self-centered valetudinarian who complained about the weather, the food and his companions—his attitude brought on, perhaps, by the fact that his wife of eleven years, the beautiful actress-author Celia Logan Clarke Kellogg (twenty-three years his junior) had divorced the fifty-four year old Kellogg and married another. Our modern expectation of having central heating and air conditioning, even in our rolling vehicles, has made us far too aware of

ourselves. We won't tolerate physical discomfort, going to extreme lengths to avoid it rather than finding methods or psychological means of accepting it. Could 20th (or 21st) century man have made it as a Southwestern pioneer?

55. Conkling, Vol. II, 41.

56. A. Richardson, 236.

57. The old mail road and the modern highway come together a few miles southeast of the little town of Fort Hancock. Hancock was the last frontier fort to be built in Texas. Camp Rice had been set up in 1881, but a new Camp Rice was built a few miles to the northwest in 1884–5, and in May, 1886, the name changed to Fort Hancock. It was abandoned late in 1895. The Conklings report the fort site "on a marshy flat near the river . . . subject to periodic flooding, could not have been worse." The buildings were mainly of red brick, some of which stood until about the mid-1930s when the remaining brick walls were razed and the land put under cultivation.

58. The camels were a success as beasts of burden across the Southwestern deserts. Colonel Robert E. Lee, commander of the army's Texas Department in 1860, reported he was completely sold on them—of course, Robert E. Lee didn't use those words—and in his report to the Secretary of War he used words and phrases such as, "endurance, docility, and sagacity" and said "but for whose (camels') reliable services the reconnaissance [test expedition] would have failed." But getting American soldiers and officers to use the camels did not follow. It was, one officer said, "a horse and mule army," determined to remain that way. At the beginning of the Civil War, the Confederates took over the camels at Camp Verde, Texas, and in the Arizona Territory, Bethel Coopwood, a Confederate officer and spy captured fourteen of the beasts, but no one knew what (or how) to do with any of them. (Coopwood, later a Texas lawyer and historical writer, had fourteen children.) Only one camel seems to have "served" throughout the war. General Sterling Price, Confederate officer of Missouri, used one to haul his camp equipage and supplies on his Arkansas campaigns. In 1866, Coopwood bought the remaining Camp Verde herd at auction for $31 per camel and as late as 1878 still had some forty camels on a ranch at Elgin, Bastrop County, Texas. (Taken from Colonel Martin Crimmins, ed., "Colonel J. K. F. Mansfield's Inspection Report of Texas," *Southwestern Historical Quarterly* XLII (October 1938): 141–42; Frank B. Lammons, "Operation Camel," *Southwestern Historical Quarterly* LXI (July 1957): 20–50; Walter Prescott Webb and H. Bailey Carroll, ed. "Texas Collection," *Southwestern Historical Quarterly* XLVIII (July 1944): 107–108; Walter Prescott Webb, et al, ed. "Camels," *Handbook of Texas*, Vol. 1, 274.)

59. Richardson, 237. Bartlett, the Boundary Commissioner, was quartered at Socorro with the Commission in 1851. He said that so many "worthless and

vagabond men" had been discharged at Socorro—from various emigrant trains—that it had become dangerous to live there. Then, "after several murders had been committed, and horror and dismay filled the breasts of the orderly part of the community," help was asked of the U.S. Army post at San Elizario, which assistance was denied. When Edward C. Clarke, the Assistant Quartermaster of the Boundary Commission, was murdered at a *fandango*, the alcalde being "a weak and sickly imbecile," members of the Commission were compelled to take matters in their hands. Helped by volunteers from the Mexican community, three American hardcases, dismissed earlier from the Boundary Commission by Bartlett, were tried, sentenced, and quickly hanged from a cottonwood tree, guarded by a detachment of American soldiers sent from El Paso by Colonel Van Horne. A few days later a fourth desperado, the leader of the terrorist gang, met the same fate on the same cottonwood. John Russell Bartlett, *Personal Narratives of Explorations and Incidents in Texas, New Mexico, California, Sonora and Chihuahua Connected with the United States and Mexico 1850–1853*, Vol. 1 (Chicago: Rio Grande Press, 1965), 158–59.

60. Anne E. Hughes, *The Beginnings of Spanish Settlement in the El Paso District* (Berkeley: University of California Press, 1914), 303–307.

61. Coons was a young St. Louis trader and freighter operating out of Santa Fe. His Coons Rancho contained the former ranch and houses of Juan Maria Ponce de Leon, the first white man (1827) to cross the river from the west side to get a large grant on the other side, both sides then belonging to Mexico. Coons Rancho was later leased to the government to become the predecessor of Fort Bliss. When the name Franklin was submitted to the Post Office Department there was found to be another Franklin, Texas, so the Post Office Department made it Franklin City. (Old Franklin, as it is now called, was county seat of the original Robertson County, which included such sites as Waco and Fort Worth.)

62. Anson Mills, *My Story* (Washington, D.C.: n.p., 1918), 51–52.

63. C. L. Sonnichsen, *Pass of the North: Four Centuries on the Rio Grande* (El Paso: Texas Western Press, 1968), 141.

64. Conkling, Vol. II, 59–61.

65. A. Richardson, 238.

66. Bartlett, Vol. 1, 185–6.

67. Ibid. Captain S. G. French, reaching the El Paso area in 1849, in his official report noted: "The grape is extensively cultivated on the irrigable lands, and in size and flavor is perhaps unequalled. The wine it yields, however, owing perhaps to the mode of manufacture or making, is rather indifferent." Senate Ex. Doc. No. 64, 31st Congress, 1st Session.

68. In 1865–66, while Maximilian and his French forces were occupying

Mexico City and eventually even Chihuahua in the far north corner of the nation, President Benito Juarez was driven to Paso del Norte where he set up a cabinet-in-exile, supported greatly by the United States, but vowing never to leave Mexican soil, making the Mexican city of El Paso, for that time, capital of Mexico. In 1888, with the Texas city of El Paso growing in size and international importance, causing increasing confusion, the Mexican city of El Paso del Norte, in honor of the national hero, was renamed Juarez.

PART FOUR

Modern Travelers on the Butterfield Trail.
The Past Is Not Past:
The Trail's Still Down There

I F you fly over Mountain Pass in Taylor County, Texas, you can see in the chalky earth below two faint white tracks which follow the north edge of the hills, climbing toward the low summit of the pass. And if your imagination and your sense of history are as good as your eyesight, you should hear the clatter of hooves and wheels, the pop of a whip, or the faint cries of a brass bugle heralding the approach of the stagecoach, for this is one of the few visible traces of the actual road of John Butterfield's Southern Overland Mail through Texas: the Butterfield Trail. Most of the remainder of the trail has been plowed under, paved over, overgrown by mesquite and scrub oak, or lost midst the maze of mechanical tracks created when an oil well is drilled and sustained.

There is a challenge to the modern traveler trying to follow in any fashion—foot, horse, or auto—the old Butterfield Trail. But arduous as the effort becomes, my wife and I found the job not just rewarding but exhilarating when we traced the trail in the 1990s.

In much of Texas crossed by the Butterfield stage, you could have found more people along the road in 1858 and 1859 than might be found today. It was a lonely passage, and it remains a lonely passage when you depart the main-traveled roads—and if you go where the Butterfield went, you usually depart any significant highways.

Because of local legends, many Texans believe the Butterfield stage ran through their town when, in fact, it came nowhere near. Usually the stage line in question was one that merely carried mail to or from the actual Butterfield line. So powerful has been the popular image of the Butterfield stage that even today western stage lines tend to be referred to as "Butterfield" and any stage as "the Butterfield stage." Butterfield's Overland Mail Company, first of the true overland systems, also inspired the subsequent use of "Overland" in a number of stage line names that had no connection with Butterfield Overland Mail and were not "overland" (reaching to the West Coast) at all.[1]

When the Butterfield Overland Trail was being constructed through the state of Texas, there was no thought of real estate development along the way such as would be practiced later by the railroads. Sherman, Gainesville, Jacksboro, and Franklin City (El Paso) were the only towns the original route traversed. A year later the Butterfield stage passed through Decatur and Bridgeport. On its very last trips, it stopped in Denton and Pilot Point.

In West Texas the trail missed even the sites that would later be chosen for building up towns and cities. Starting at Fort Belknap in Young County, the old trail misses Woodson by one mile, passes Albany by ten, and skirts where the town of Fort Griffin would rise in 1867. The stage line cuts a mile north and northwest of where Abilene now sits, misses even the suburb of Tye by a few hundred yards, goes well below Merkel, and fails to touch Bronte on the way south. San Angelo wouldn't be established until 1868, across the river from Fort Concho. The old Butterfield stage road misses both locations by two miles to the northwest, and passes a few miles above such later towns as Big Lake, Rankin, and McCamey.

A routing change in 1859 did put the line through Fort Stockton, but it was more military post than town at the time. The same was true of Fort Davis on the 1859 route. Some measure of the remoteness of the Butterfield route can be imagined by knowing that on the entire transcontinental line, excluding the terminal cities, there were only four towns with newspapers: Fort Smith, Arkansas; Sherman, Texas; and Los Angeles and San Jose, California.

The stage, moving across Texas in 1858, was not bound by most of the same things that control highways and roads today. It was able to go as straight from Point A to Point B, in most of its running, as the terrain allowed. Once past some frontier edge such as Fort Belknap, there were no private property lines to observe and drive around, no fences or walls to impede the direct passage. Only in a few places did the stage use a precisely designated route; even the military roads were merely described. The pathways might have had names or been shown on maps, but as for offering a given course, these were indicated rather than specified. That is why it is so hard, almost impossible, to travel, mile by mile, the Butterfield Trail across Texas.

Although the Texas portion of the entire transcontinental trail is the longest of any state along its route, that fact really did very little for Texas, despite what opposing senators from the North might have thought it would do. The essential loneliness of the trail itself, even today, is evidence enough that whatever hopes for greatly increased settlement might have been aroused, they were not realized. The trail, therefore, contributes to the mystery of the frontier—why people did things, why people went places; why this push, this need to go west, this urge to westering that has been the basis for many books, many stories, many novels—and the Butterfield Trail is simply a 2,785-mile extension of that idea; the country through which it passed was secondary to where it headed, because it headed for the Pacific Ocean, at that time the ultimate destination of an ambitious America.

* * * * * *

We drove rapidly over . . . prairies and blossomed plains, till about sunset we entered the dark and tangled jungle which for many miles skirts the Red River.[2]

The Reverend William Tallack is speaking from aboard a Butterfield Overland Mail coach approaching the Texas landing of Colbert's Ferry in the summer of 1860. If he were to revisit that "dark and tangled jungle" today he might not find himself altogether confused. Despite decades of being traversed by the major highway to and from Texas and Oklahoma, the area alongside the old mail road has gone back to being "a mixture of forest, garden, swamp and jungle . . ." as the modern traveler will note, picking his way along the ghost of the highway.

Starting at the point the Reverend Mr. Tallack described, my wife

Judy and I stood looking over the rolling Red River, caught in the powerful tide of imagination the river brought on.

Time has a way of making history repeat itself, and a century and a third after the Butterfield Overland Mail stage entered Texas at this point, the country surrounding the old Colbert's Ferry landing has returned, if not to its primal state, to a place which sees fewer visitors in a 1990s year than passed across it in one 1860s week.

True, the stone piers of the last toll bridge—a structure which almost started the Red River War between Texas and Oklahoma in 1931—stand in the midst of the river marking the waters where Colbert's Ferry passed, but the approaches have gone back to what they were before Ben Colbert put his slaves to work in 1858 spading a road up the Texas side.

Now, if you have an ounce of the romantic in your bones, it is easy to stand on that south bank and see the ferry being poled across the river, the Butterfield Overland Mail coach and team aboard. Then, imagining the scow reaching Texas, watch the coach passengers, even the women, getting out of the coach to climb the steep bank afoot.

In our age of fierce independence and personal rights, we wonder why stagecoach passengers so easily consented to getting out and walking so often. We wouldn't put up with it today. But they had to. The stage couldn't go with them in it at times. It was a part of life—and part of the implied contract. A surviving set of instructions for nineteenth-century travelers has this polite but firm stipulation: "When the driver asks you to get off and walk, do so without grumbling. He will not request it unless absolutely necessary."[3] Their lives did not lead them to expect the accommodations that we demand without a thought. They were not bounded by speed, convenience, and time. If the coach were late arriving, or the passengers had to get out and push—the men, at least—nobody promptly filed a law suit upon reaching his destination.

Tracing the Butterfield Trail today calls for a lot of romantic imagination, especially along stretches of the road that pass through the more densely settled parts of Texas. That short, wild stretch from the Red River southward is preserved only because the river crossing to Texas went through a series of transportation evolutions.

The Red was not a good river to ford in this stretch, so first there was the well-used ferry. Then came a wagon bridge which the devilish old Red promptly washed away, succeeded by a series of better built bridges of varying success. Ultimately the Red was tamed, the crossing elevated above the flood plain, by the Missouri, Kansas and Texas Railroad, which assured its passage with a high, steel bridge in 1872. After that the mails, as well as the greater percentage of Texas-bound passengers, began moving by rail. The coming of the railroads also caused the creation of Denison and the erasure of the Butterfield's path across that area. Once you leave that ragged bit of roadway that runs south from the Colbert's ferry landing, you go almost altogether by landmarks—a street name here, a historical marker there. The final evolutionary step (since an airplane pays no attention to such things as rivers, no matter how wide or dangerous) came with the automobile, which slowly—but with certainty—eclipsed even the railroad in its demand for a safe and suitable way across.

Judy and I began tracing the Butterfield Trail with the guidance of Judge R. C. Vaughan, a native of Denison with a lifelong involvement in Grayson County history, who knew the territory intimately. But it is impossible to follow the actual trail across modern Denison, although certain topographical features which must have determined the early route remain, especially in the northwestern part of town. The mail road crossed Duck Creek near Munson Park,[4] a crossing where the Conklings, in the 1930s, found "a well preserved section of the old road." South to Waterloo Park lake, once the municipal water supply of Denison, the Butterfield stage watered at Sand Springs, a notable landmark hard to get to today. Its inscription rock is marked with travelers names from 1840 to our own century. Undoubtedly some of the initials and names were carved in the sandstone by Butterfield passengers when the coach made a brief water stop here—there was no station. Today the springs, which once were described as "boiling," do little more than seep.

Another landmark presumed to have been on the route even though not officially recorded as such is Cook's Spring, flowing into Iron Ore Creek near Park Avenue, about where the Butterfield crossed that watercourse. Located in a deep hole, the spring is a private facility, but has for decades been open to the public for recreational uses. After running a few miles southwest and crossing over the Midway area, the mail entered Sherman at the modern intersection of Broughton and College streets, probably along the same roadway that is now used by the Southern Pacific Railroad, only a few feet east of the intersection. It is an unpretentious area west of famed and venerable Austin College, organized in 1849, the first collegiate institution in Texas to offer a graduate degree.

From that intersection (although neither street was there in 1858), the coach crossed over to Pecan, going south along Travis to the courthouse square. The Butterfield station stood on the southeast corner of the square and its stables stood on the east side of the 200 block of Travis. The stage reportedly stopped at Bird Anderson's hotel on the north side of the square, then wheeled around to Jim Darnell's hotel on the west side of Travis near the station. The post office, with W. Bradley as postmaster, was a small log hut on the south side of the square. Waterman Ormsby remarked that he "had barely time to run a few steps to the post office to drop [New York] a letter" before the stage resumed its journey on the first trip west, so the postal hut must have been quite near.[5] Standing on the east side of Travis at the courthouse square, if you look down, a hitching ring or two will remind you that time hasn't removed all traces of an equine past in Sherman.

From the courthouse square the Butterfield stage left Sherman, going west by way of Crockett, Elm, and Washington streets, the route now commemorated by an unusual marker at Washington and Rusk streets. The seven-foot monument consists of a mill stone, said to have come from the first ox mill in Sherman, mounted on a base which celebrates the passage of the Butterfield stage over the spot. From that marker, the trail went in a southwesterly direction, crossing Post Oak Branch and Sand Creek within the modern city limits, then generally following the present Highway 56, an old roadway in use since the 1850s. Highway 56 follows the Marcy trail, for decades the way west. Although this road is along the Butterfield Trail, it is impossible to know precisely where the stages actually ran. But somewhere, undoubtedly, your automobile treads criss-cross the iron wheel marks hidden somewhere beneath the asphalt.

Despite the fast-food places, the quick-stop grocery stores and the filling stations—not to mention the wrecking yards, car lots and tire shops—that line either side of a modern highway going into and out of most Texas towns, there are a few relics of another motoring age still around. Reaching Whitesboro on the way west, there is a narrow highway underpass beneath the old Texas & Pacific Railway line just as you come into the main part of town. The underpass has "1930s" all over it, and the insignia of the T&P is cast in the concrete of the overhead as you enter. If you have the memory for such things, you recall how such underpasses—narrow because the cars were smaller and speeds were much slower—were found on every major highway. And if you "left the pavement" (as back-roads driving was termed), then using an "underpass" likely as not involved driving between the pilings of the railroad bridge.

On the western edge of Whitesboro—the town wasn't formed until 1860—was Diamond's station, all traces now gone. A state historical marker refers to the site as "Diamond Horse Ranch" and makes the barest mention of it being a Butterfield station, which is just as well, perhaps, when we recall the villainy of the stationkeeper and his brothers.

Leaving Whitesboro, the Butterfield Trail passes along present Highway 82, where the country is unusually pretty on the way to Gainesville. At that town you still drive on California Street, where the Butterfield station was located, but commercial buildings, some from the nineteenth century, have long since replaced the station.

137

This place marks the edge of the Western Cross Timbers, a designation important to settlers early in the nineteenth century. There were two long, narrow bands of thick timbers running north and south from the Red River, one just east of the Trinity River, the other several miles farther west of that watercourse. The Eastern (or Lower) Cross Timbers, in more fertile, well watered soil, contained larger oak and blackjack which furnished logs for building, fuel and fencing. Its dense growth formed an obstacle to travelers, who had to find "holes" in the tangled barrier. The Western (or Upper) Cross Timbers initially marked the edge of the lands roamed by the much feared plains Indians such as Comanches and Kiowas. Due to its drier, thinner soil, the timber itself is mainly smallish oak growth (called "scrub oak") and post oak. The Western Cross Timbers helps create a more interesting, more soothing, landscape than what the traveler encounters farther west.

Outside Gainesville going southwest, you have the opportunity to follow rather closely the old trail—that is, if you can map your way through a number of Farm-to-Market (or worse) roads: FM 51, then 1630, then a series of nameless but enticing rural byways that pass through quiet pastoral country which, we can be sure, saw more in wagon days than today. Following the Butterfield, you drive down a gravel road and pass through the once-was village of Hood, a ghostly place with an old church and an old school, both abandoned. Driving around the sharp turn that leads past the church, you half expect the forgotten houses and stores suddenly to come awake and be filled with the people who built the homes, worshipped in the church and attended the school.

This is all very pretty country, very secluded. Looking across rolling waves of grass that sweep over the low hills, you get the feel of riding through unexplored, unoccupied country. The site of Doctor Davidson's station, between Williams and Wheat creeks, can be reasonably guessed at from the road, as we turn off our gravel path onto Highway 373 just before it turns into 922. It is very wooded, very lost, because there aren't many people around here—and never have been apparently. A short drive along the latter road takes you to Rosston, now reduced to a handful of houses and a colorful, and unexpected, general store with not only the usual soft drink machines but an ice-vending machine on the front porch.

Again, the Butterfield Trail took out across pastures and fields now fenced and cultivated. Sixty and more years ago when the Conklings were tracing the trail, most of the farmers still lived on the land they tilled, many having inherited their acres from fathers, mothers, or grandparents. Tales and legends, as well as myths, were still fresh on the land, and almost everyone knew his next-door neighbor. Sitting around the stone fireplaces or listening to supper table talk, their memories went back to the pioneer days, so locating old station sites, often with foundations and hearths in place, was much simpler. Time after time (especially in this area) the Conklings report identifying forgotten rock piles and corrals, or discovering Butterfield employee names in half-gone cemeteries, led there by someone who still recalled hearing tales of the old stages from youth. Sixty years ago the roads were most often lanes, mostly dirt, creeping around fenced corners, twin tracks leading to isolated houses—it was decades before electricity and the telephone came into general use here—and someone could, and was always willing to, send the inquirer to a neighbor if the information was not at hand. You can't do that now. That was before whole communities abandoned their lifelong rural lands to disappear into some larger city.

But as is often the case if you possess a few historical clues, you can still negotiate a series of unnumbered country roads which parallel and often touch the Butterfield's path. Whether you are actually on the trail or just nearby, you get a feel for the nature of its passing. Although there are fences and wide, smooth fields long-cultivated, where generations of plowing have erased even memory traces of the trail, nevertheless you can hear an ancient quietness—if you will lower your windows and turn off the air conditioning—broken then by the iron tires of the stage and now by the crunching of gravel under your modern wheels.

At Forestburg the community has made a nice bow to history with a restored log cabin, although a nearby historical marker reveals nothing about the log cabin and virtually nothing about Forestburg. You will observe, as you pass along the ghost of the Butterfield, that quite a number of historical markers leave much to be desired in the way of information, accuracy and originality. A few miles south along FM 455 is another marker, at the Butterfield Trail crossing as it ran southwest toward Decatur. It is accurate, but a carbon copy of several other markers along the trail.

Just inside the northern edge of Wise County, north of Denton Creek, was the site of Connelly's station. This area is today a part of the Lyndon B. Johnson National Grasslands. When they passed near it in the 1930s, the Conklings said the route "might be in its picturesque aspect, a transplanted section of the New England Berkshires." Along this pleasant rolling and open country can be found the site of Uz community, established in the 1870s (according to a marker), reaching its peak of importance and population at the turn of the twentieth century when it had homes, stores, a cotton gin, school, post office, and a telephone exchange. The marker notes a boll weevil infestation that destroyed the cotton crop, which was the basis for the town's existence. Alas for Uz, Texas, unlike the Biblical land of Uz, there was no "man whose name was Job" to preserve its fame.

Somewhere in the midst of the Lyndon B. Johnson National Grassland is the place where the Butterfield Mail road changed in 1860, going directly from Davidson's station to the town of Decatur, abandoning that stretch which continued west. FM 730 twists and turns along what was undoubtedly several miles of the original trail—and it is lovely traveling. Don't let the grassland designation alarm you with visions of flat, brown prairie. This is the sort of country you drive through and wish you could stay, buy a piece of land and finally live the life you've always thought you wanted—although you may also note that of those hundreds who once lived here, only a handful remain. But it is still a "land of dreams" landscape.

If you would approximate the later mail route out of Rosston, then you must twist your way around and back to the village of Greenwood—the road once connecting the two points is gone—and proceed straight southwest to the place where the citizens of Wise County built a bridge over Denton Creek to lure the Butterfield mail to come through Decatur. Using this back road, or continuing on from Rosston, you arrive at the back door, i.e., the preferable historical entrance, to Decatur. The original trail, leaving the site of Davidson's station, crossed U.S. Highway 81 just north of Alvord and reached Earhart's station, which was located a little over two miles west of where FM 2127 intersects U.S. 81.

Decatur sits high atop a plateau which puts it, on all sides, a few hundred feet above the surrounding territory. Visiting Decatur, get off the main highways and tour the old town. The charming courthouse square, where the Butterfield station was located, is full of fine old store fronts, and the courthouse alone is worth a swerve from the major highways. If you have continued on FM 730 from the LBJ Grassland, stay on it right through town; it circles the square. The imposingly prominent main building of the former Decatur Baptist College, built in 1892, is now a museum. The school, which claimed to be the oldest junior college in Texas, moved to Mountain Creek Lake near Dallas early in 1965 and has become Dallas Baptist University.

But the showpiece of Decatur sits east of the downtown in splendid isolation. The elaborate "Waggoner Castle" was built in the 1870s by Dan Waggoner, who came into the country and eventually owned or controlled hundreds of thousands of acres to the west and into the Texas Panhandle. Already a wealthy family, the Waggoners added oil to their empire with the famous Electra strike near that North Texas town which was named for a Waggoner daughter.[6]

West of Decatur, following now the "new" Butterfield route which began in 1860, you pass a finger of the Cross Timbers with some sizable oak trees. You can wonder as you drive these verdant but empty spaces, what must have been the reaction at some isolated station, say on a late night, upon hearing the coach horn as the Butterfield stage approached. The hustling about that began, the arrival of the coach, the jingling of chains, the stamping of animals, the crunching of the extra-wide wheels on the rutted path, the hostlers leading off the worn teams and harnessing and hitching up the fresh ones. Inside the station, the questions being asked of driver and passengers—news not being a daily thing of morning newspapers or evening television—the relief the passengers must have felt, seeing the dim lamps of civilization before them, alighting to a meal, skimpy as we might think it now. Almost any stop was sure to be a delight (as passenger Waterman Ormsby makes clear) for the travelers; an occasion to "wash up," or for the ladies, perhaps, a chance to "pick daisies" in a more private fashion. The activity, the noises, the voices, the simple importance of this spot—now lost to memory and almost, *almost* to history.

They say that in some little towns where the railroad has not run for forty years, you may still hear, on certain apt nights, the ghostly wail of the 10 o'clock local, laboring up Nine-Mile Hill. Would I care to drive alone down one of those remote Cooke, Wise, or Montague county lanes, late night, past some forgotten station—at the hour when the stage was due?

From Decatur to Bridgeport the modern highway must follow the old mail road fairly closely. Bridgeport, which came into existence because of the Butterfield Overland Mail, shows more outward appreciation of that heritage than any other place along the Texas route. Approaching the town, you see a large, colorful, reasonably accurate sign depicting a Butterfield stagecoach with lead and wheel teams pulling, which was erected by the Chamber of Commerce to welcome you to Bridgeport. Downtown, one long stone wall has been decorated with a mural of a Butterfield stage, this one pulled by six horses or mules: wheel team, swing team and lead team. Going south through town, you come to a marker telling about the toll bridge, built over the West Fork of the Trinity in 1860, and the site of the old town of Bridgeport, which occupied a meadow some 50 feet to the east of the river crossing. As the historical plaque states, the wooden toll bridge fell in shortly after the Butterfield ceased operating in 1861. The town moved over about a mile to the railroad when it built to this point in 1893, despite the fact a sturdy iron bridge had replaced the fallen wooden one in 1873.

Standing on the modern replacement bridge and looking down into the murky waters of the West Trinity, you are convinced you can see evidence of the pilings of the Butterfield wooden bridge—but, of course, that could be more of the romantic imaging that can afflict a pilgrim and, like a mirage, convince him there are lakes and cities out there where nothing dwells. But the scant stream circulating through the channel brings another question to mind: why was a bridge necessary? Despite its unimpressive flow today, in those other days the West Fork of the Trinity became a torrent several times a year. Lake Bridgeport, on its watershed, has greatly controlled the flooding and helped supply Fort Worth with water since 1931.

Although it is not a notable arena for history, Bridgeport is the sort of town in which you should take time to inspect the details. For instance, set into a hillside behind an automobile sales yard ("the old Chevy place") is a set of big wooden doors covering the entrance to its last coal mine—Bridgeport, through the 1920s, being a major Texas coal mining center. For years "Bridgeport coal" was a separate listing in the market reports of Texas newspapers. In the small downtown, on the main street, you can find an ancient cast iron step to a door that was long ago bricked over (the entrance to a store gone even longer), which proclaims brightly "Gainesville Iron Works." A few yards away another cast iron plate bespeaks, less clearly, the name of "J. R. Stevens." Both were put down for permanence, guaranteed to last a lifetime. And they have lasted, still visible at the foot of a wall of modern brick—even if the lifetime hasn't.

I like to inspect the back ends of old towns; look at the stone and brick walls with old, fading signs painted on them that recommend certain plows, wood stoves, spring buggies, Battle Ax chewing

143

tobacco, or Coca-Cola in bottles and at the soda fountain for five cents. I like to see where quaintly narrow and arched windows, now eyeless, once looked out, where doors high up along the wall opened onto outside stairs that perhaps were of fancily twisted wrought iron—marked by brick blankness now—or maybe a faint notice that Winton automobiles or Wichita trucks are for sale here.

The Butterfield stage run out of Bridgeport crossed the Trinity bridge and went directly west. The route is now thwarted by Lake Bridgeport, although you can drive around the south end of the lake, through the retirement and resort community of Runaway Bay, then north to the road which passes through the famed but faded village of Wizard Wells. Once a health spa and mineral water health resort, Wizard Wells slowly lost importance as the mineral water health treatments lost popular favor and the Rock Island Railroad, a mile south, dropped passenger service. Local owners made a brave effort to keep freight service between Bridgeport and Jacksboro as Texas Export Railroad in the early 1970s, but they failed and the rails were pulled up.

The 1860 stage route ran slightly north of Wizard Wells. (It was originally named Vineyard for George Washington Vineyard. When the Rock Island Railroad built through in 1898, another town, some two miles south, became Vineyard.) The stage line, from a few miles above it, paralleled modern U.S. 380 into the Jacksboro station, south of the town square.

The 1858 Butterfield route, which had passed far north of both Decatur and Bridgeport, followed a southwest course from the Earhart station location on the banks of Big Sandy Creek, and it, too, passes through many roadless acres laced by the maze of West Fork (Trinity) bottoms. But highway 1810, while paved, sticks close enough to the old roadway to furnish the atmosphere of the run, going by Cundiff and Maryetta, four miles west. It's a pleasant drive, but if you are bound to drive over a stretch of the old trail, there is a gravel road off to the left less than a mile west of Cundiff which, in its eleven miles or so, uses more than two miles of the mail road.

The passage is more than worth the extra mileage involved in traveling it. The West Fork of the Trinity station was located on the north bank, just east of where the present road crosses the West Fork.

This is where Albert Richardson tells of spending the night in a barn waiting for the river to go down, then crossing on a slippery log to the south bank where another stagecoach was waiting. Later, flood-marooned passengers were sent across in a dug-out. The mail road fording place can be seen a few hundred feet downstream from the spidery iron bridge that crosses the river. The Trinity riffles across the fording place in a beautiful series of ripples with the sunlight sketching each wavelet, seen through the branches, into a separate figure. This crossing area is not only one of the prettiest along the Butterfield, it is also one of the few specific sites that remains very much the way Richardson and the Conklings saw it. In fact, the iron bridge from which the Conklings observed the ford back in the 1930s still remained in the 1990s, replacement of the plank flooring with concrete being the only change.

The Jacksboro station site is marked by a lovely granite column erected by the State of Texas in 1936, celebrating the centennial of the Republic of Texas. As mentioned, too many of these Butterfield markers are only mildly useful because they repeat the same general information with no relation to the site other than to say, "Here ran the Southern Overland Mail . . ." before wading off into several lines of hyperbole. But at least the granite monuments have a permanence lacking in later historical markers made of cast aluminum which, in time, not only fade to unreadability but are frequently blasted by bullets, in the annoying Texas tradition of impulsively firing rifles and pistols at anything that makes a target at the moment.

The Butterfield Mail left Jacksboro across what later (1867) became Fort Richardson, now a partially restored state park. A slender iron bridge north of the fort is sometimes said to have been used by the mail stages, but this was actually a bridge over Lost Creek on the old Rock Island Railroad branch to Graham, long since abandoned, and the bridge moved to Sewell Park.

In following the Butterfield Trail west out of Jacksboro, you go over a true country road; it is gravel, and the turnoff is hard to find although it is right in town. Finding and driving the road is well worth making the extra effort because, in several of its miles, it traces the tracks of the old trail. This is one of the most interesting parts of the westering pathway, another one of those stretches where there were very probably more people 140 years ago than now. Not even the ubiquitous beer can is seen.

A lot of times the passengers had to get out and push on roads like this, especially in bad weather or when going up these rather sharp inclines. About a quarter of the way to Fort Belknap (which this road led to) is the Winn-Hill cemetery. A marker there states that this was on the Butterfield route, also that the cemetery is all that is left of the Winn-Hill community; named, incidentally, for a William H. Wynne. (The orthographics of the situation are not explained.) Occasionally you will see a utility pole, but looking off to and up at the surrounding horizon, you may well view what you would have viewed in 1858, or 1758—or, for that matter, 1058. Shortly after passing the cemetery, you ride over a particularly picturesque section. The unfenced lane proceeds through a tunnel of densely crowding bushes and trees, crossing a little watercourse on an old fashioned, and very narrow, little iron and wooden bridge: a postcard view. Only after reaching State Highway 16 and seeing the modest county road sign at that intersection do you realize you are on famed Monument Road, passing just a few yards from the site of the Warren Wagon Train Massacre of 1871—the massacre that led to the unusual trial of the Kiowa chieftains in Jacksboro.

Ida Huckabay, in her book *Ninety-four Years in Jack County*, describes the original monument from which the road takes its name:

In the winter of 1872 Troop F of the 4th Cavalry, under Capt. Wirt Davis, erected a monument on the site of the massacre. The monument, eight feet high of native oak, was pyramidal in shape with a cross atop, and painted olive color. The plinth carried the inscription in black. The monument was made by the Quartermaster at Fort Richardson.[7]

M. K. Kellogg told of visiting the monument in September of 1872, and repeated its inscription: "Sacred to the memory of seven brave men killed by Indians at this place on May 18, 1871 while in the discharge of their duty defending this train against 150 Comanche Indians." On the other side were the names of the men with "Wagon Master N. S. Long" above the teamsters. Kellogg, an artist, was with a commercial expedition seeking to confirm mineral deposits in north and west Texas. He sketched the monument, adding a tree for scale.

His journal entry for September 9, 1872, records:

10:25 A.M. came to Monument to 7 men massacred—50 yds left of road [going east] . . . Temporarily encamped just beyond monument near pool of water from 11 to 1 P.M. & lunch. Sketch some sunflowers & thistles on a low hill near monument [where] the Comanche Chieftain Satanta said on trial he was there blowing his bugle and looking on at the massacre but had no part in it—only wanted to see if his young men could fight! . . . 2:45 P.M. at Cross Timbers: We have now passed the most dangerous prairie in all Texas—if rumors be true—and not an Indian![8]

This rather strange wooden memorial disappeared decades ago—although there is one historic photograph of a group of men seated on the monument—and the State of Texas erected a granite one in 1936. It is on private property, but at least the bronze embellishment on the stone has not been vandalized, as is so often the case with anything bronze or copper. The wording reads: "BURIED HERE are the remains of seven teamsters . . . employed by Henry Warren, government contractor, who were slain by Indians under Satanta, Satank, and Big Tree, Kiowa and Comanche chiefs, on May 18, 1871 while hauling forage between Jacksboro and Fort Griffin."

147

This has been a road of tragedy, and far more people, red as well as white, died than just those remembered by monuments. When you turn west onto Turtle Hole Road (it is marked), you are nearing the spot where Brit Johnson and fellow teamsters, all Negro, were slain. Kellogg, breaking camp at 6:10 A.M., wrote, "open, treeless prairie, noted for Indian massacres, the most dangerous place in the region. At 7:10 stop to view graves of the men who were killed two years since—Negroes—one Brit Johnson a famous Indian fighter."[9]

Most of the time the Turtle Hole itself is little more than a wide puddle, invisible from the road, but there is often an enormous sky with high, dark clouds that seem to isolate the entire region. When the open land assumes this almost sinister quality, it becomes easy to feel yourself, in momentary dismay, alone and liable to unknown dangers. Despite the fact that for nearly three years the Butterfield stage went across these bloody valleys and pastures in safety, that ominous aura thickened so that by the 1870s the section had gained an almost supernatural reputation for danger—although looking out across the peaceful meadows today, you can't believe that there could have been as much violence and as much death as there was.

The Warren wagon train dead, the numberless Indian warriors, Brit Johnson and companions, unknown settlers, male and female— their spirits, for those who know history, hover over these innocent appearing meadows, these often dry creeks and waterholes. I believe that sometimes we don't really appreciate history until we go where it happened.

Farther along the westward route, south of U.S. 380 some four miles from Fort Belknap, is another tragic spot, called today "Stem's Gap." Although the low hills on the southern horizon scarcely attract our gaze as elevations, we must remember that getting horse-drawn vehicles cross country caused much more concern about elevation, and the lack of it, than it does today, when driving something being propelled by several hundred horses, not just two, four, or six. So Stem's Gap was an important landmark on the road between two hills on the way up to the Jesse Stem farm on the Clear

Fork of the Brazos. The place name was given in 1854 after Stem and a companion, coming through the gap, were murdered by a pair of renegade Kickapoos. Here, like so many other places throughout this region, there is often a dark and bloody past lurking behind the innocent names.

We arrived at Fort Belknap on a warm, cloudy day, a good time to see the old post because it takes some of the modernity off the reconstructed buildings—although there are several remaining old timers. The Butterfield stage line went right through what is now the central part of the Fort Belknap Park, marked on the west side by a monument which explains the significance of the military road. Fort Belknap, as is true of so many partially reconstructed posts, is slightly disappointing. You can get the rawness of the frontier much easier when on some deserted outpost such as Fort Phantom Hill, standing on the barren parade grounds, the wind sweeping across, so that your imagination not only can reconstruct the buildings but also regain the atmosphere of the time and the place.

But Fort Belknap was the mother fort of those broad and unknown lands beyond the Brazos, and many of the famed—and infamous—figures of the Civil War served here. Explorers, bold settlers, California gold seekers, and renegades passed through on their way west to a greater destiny or to death.

The old Fort Belknap cemetery is about three-quarters of a mile east of the modern park, at the end of a dirt road, the graves lying amidst a grove of live oaks. The central gravestone and a historical monument marking it belong to Major Robert S. Neighbors. Explorer and Texas state Indian agent, he tried to work with, among other tribes, the Comanches, achieving a workable understanding with them. But white man jealousy and greed led to his assassination in 1859 on the streets of Fort Belknap. (See footnote 37 in Part II.)

Leaving the fort, the old mail road went directly west. A seam of bituminous coal is still exposed where the road plunged into the Brazos, but it must be found on foot. The Butterfield trail here emerged into the arid loneliness of West Texas, so different from the green loneliness of, say, Wise or Montague County. You can't follow it by automobile now, but the nature of the country—and the tragic history of it—can be sensed almost immediately.

You are scarcely a mile out of Newcastle (the coal mining town that replaced Belknap village in 1908) when you cross the Brazos beside a picturesque but abandoned multi-span steel bridge—one of those 1930s constructions that looked like a real bridge and made you feel safe, high above the waters—a bridge of the sort that marked an important crossing of an important watercourse. You knew you were approaching a significant barrier. Crossing between the high steel arches, the chords and arcs, you reached the other side acknowledging you were at a different boundary, a consequential shore. The majesty of steel, even in abandonment, forms a stately contrast, alas, to the nearby low-railed, concrete passageway across the Brazos that replaces it—one so like all the anonymous structures in almost universal use on Texas highways today. These modern bridges that seem to scorn the idea of being a bridge, denying that anything difficult to cross lies below its standardized piers and support pieces. Unromantic, unhistoric, the water below is unseen and indistinguishable without the standard highway sign bearing the river, the creek, or the draw's name.

Not many miles west of the river is the site of another bloody event, the Elm Creek raid of 1864. The mail road crosses that creek just at the point of Proffitt Cemetery, where a state marker is orotund and somewhat inaccurate. The largest raiding party in Texas history, composed of swift Comanche and Kiowa raiders (a settler with a spy glass counted over 700 Indians), came out of the Texas Panhandle and attacked fourteen homes, mostly located in the Elm Creek valley, killing a dozen persons and kidnapping several women and children. This raid, which took the life of his son and resulted in the capture of his wife and two daughters, led to the saga of exslave Brit Johnson's search for and eventual success in rescuing not only his family but other white hostages. Later, as noted, Brit himself was killed and his body badly mutilated, possibly from revenge when he was recognized by his attackers.

These raids and ambushes already mentioned were not by any means the beginning or the end of bloodshed and tragedy. Inside the Proffitt Cemetery there is a large brick enclosure marked "Common Grave" that contains the bodies of three nineteen-year-old boys (including a Proffitt) killed in another raid on Elm Creek in 1867.[10]

Although the Butterfield road today cuts through pasture and roadless ranch lands, there is an easily located landmark which doesn't require leaving the comfort of your vehicle: Cribb Station Creek, found on all Young County maps. The Conklings seemed to have confused Cribb Station with the James Madison "Matt" Franz station, several miles over in Throckmorton County. One Young County historian noted: "Cribb Station was the first stop west of Belknap on the Butterfield Overland Mail Route where Ben Cribb ran the stable and a store in the pre-war days."[11]

South on FM 578 you come to the site of Murray, formerly known as Fish Creek and once quite an important Young County spot. Today it offers a very pretty white frame church built in 1907 for a Methodist congregation that had outgrown several log cabin and schoolhouse meeting places originally located two miles west. The building is quite photogenic and worth locating, whether tracing the Butterfield Trail or not.

Franz (or France or Frans) Station is today a pile of stone along the bank of Middle Kings Creek, near the right-of-way of the long abandoned Cisco & Northeastern Railroad (which ran northwest). The pilings for a former railroad trestle remain nearby. The station site can be viewed from Highway 1710 a short distance north of Woodson. From Franz Station the road, all abandoned, went southwest to Clear Fork Station, on the east bank of the Clear Fork of the Brazos River.

I have been describing the difficulty of actually following the Butterfield route, but much of that comes from easing along in a modern air conditioned, low-to-the road automobile. With a four-wheel

151

drive vehicle and a strong spine (and permission from the landowners), it is still possible to drive along parts of those backwoods Butterfield trails. But one of the best ways to make the trip mile for mile is by air; a helicopter would be ideal. To see what could be found of the Trail, after more than a century, a few years back I joined rancher Bob Green of Albany who piloted his Tri-Pacer (which we dubbed "Celerity Wagon II") from Fort Belknap westward.

From that point above, the mail road can be plainly seen entering the Brazos west of Fort Belknap by way of a cut slope, although a sand and gravel works in operation on the west bank eliminated some traces of the fording place. West of there the trail crossed several acres of land now heavily timbered with scrub oak which disguise the actual roadway. We were reasonably sure that by using the Brazos crossing and the next station as headings we could now and then see a depression, even across cultivated ground, made by the passage of the coaches and wagons. Traces are apparent north of Woodson, and from the air you tend to see any number of piles of rock which could have been the site of Franz station. The old C&NE roadbed helped make our decision as to which was which.

The landscape changes abruptly at the edge of Throckmorton County and you see the open ranch country coming with the sharp distinction of a rug giving way to plain floor. Some of the ranch roads undoubtedly follow the old stagecoach tracks, although it is impossible to differentiate. Fortunately, a visit by car to Clear Fork Station is possible, with permission, and the old well used by the station is still in place. Only a repair of the curbing (dated 1907) is not part of the original well. When the Butterfield engineers first came through in 1857 they found a strong spring nearby and that possibly had something to do with locating the station here. But the spring went dry, as West Texas springs all too often have done, so the well was dug early in 1859. A modern rock house sits on the foundations of the station. Although it has been many decades since the F. R. Stribling ranch operated here, this is still referred to as "the old Stribling place." It is now part of Lambshead Ranch. Watt Matthews, the legendary manager/owner of Lambshead, in the 1980s marked the trail across the ranch with a stone monument at a steep hill that is called Butterfield Gap. Watt, while in his nineties, proudly drove his pickup up the rocky trail to display the many historical sites to ranch visitors. It was in this area that Ormsby noticed two bluffs "whose position reminded me forcibly of East and West Rock as seen on entering New Haven harbor," features still prominent in the lonely landscape.

Southwest of the Stribling ranch house by less than a half mile is the crossing of the Clear Fork of the Brazos where Waterman Ormsby took his bath and had to clamber wet aboard the stage, sans clothing, when allowed so little time. The cut down bank is easily seen, although not negotiable by vehicle. It is thought that at one time there was a corral and a sort of relay shed on the south side of the Clear Fork crossing, used both as a remount pasture and as an eastbound stage stop when the river was too high to be forded. Continuing west, the trail rode over the still lonely vastness of the Lambshead. From the air this whole region is a network of trails, but again, by using Clear Fork Station as your visual base and taking a southwest heading, parts of the present ranch road fit the past perfectly.

The Butterfield crossed a part of what is now the J. H. Nail Ranch, then ten or twelve miles northwest of Albany crossed Bluff Creek at a site marked by the remains of an ancient rock corral—the kind built before barbed wire was introduced. As the trail crosses U.S. Highway 180, about eleven miles directly west of Albany, there is a simple marker at the site. The old Texas Central, later the Missouri-Kansas-Texas Railroad, ran along here out of Albany. Just across the road from the Butterfield monument is a set of pens called Budmatthews, named for Watt's father, the late Judge J. A. (Bud) Matthews of Albany. After 1900, when the railroad built west out of Albany (where it had stopped in 1882), Budmatthews saw thousands of cattle loaded onto the cars to be shipped all over the west. Today, the railroad is long gone, but the pens are preserved, although little shipping is done from here. Regardless, I hear the whistle of the little Katy steam locomotive when the wind is just right and the automobiles and pickups leave a quiet space on the nearby highway.

After the trail crosses the highway, it enters the ranch known as the Old Conrad place. About a mile inside the ranch the road is easily traced from the air and, thanks to a later owner, you can follow it on the ground. It was here that Bob Green and I and the late historian/playwright Robert Nail actually drove the Butterfield Trail, got our wheels in the ruts and let them guide us. In fact, the car took a sudden lurching thud and we realized we had hit all that was left of Smith's Station on Chimney Creek: a pile of rocks from the chimney. But I wouldn't recommend driving the Butterfield Trail in some low slung sedan of the present; besides, the rock chimney has now been re-erected to commemorate the station site.

The road leading away from Smith's Station is easily followed, albeit on foot, because it is quite distinct, cutting across Chimney Creek where Butterfield's engineers used blasting powder to cut the way through a limestone ledge. The Conklings found the remains of the station's corral, which was gone when we visited the site. A few months after that visit, I was getting gasoline at a station a few miles down Deadman Creek when I mentioned to the proprietor, Grady Smith, about finding the big stone corral was gone. Grady, who had been manager of the ranch, said well, sure, he knew where it went. The state highway department had come along looking for material for their rock crusher while rebuilding the Albany-Abilene highway and he told them to go ahead and use that bunch of old rocks down there at the creek. *Sic transit gloria historia!* I must admit there does seem to be a touch of poetic justice, perhaps, in using the materials of one form of transportation, the stagecoach, to make another superior form of transportation, the modern highway.

The Frank Conrad Ranch house, which is located a mile southeast up Chimney Creek, was thought by many to have been the Butterfield station because of the stalls it supposedly had in the basement to protect the stock from the Indians. The beautiful old stone house sits on the brow of a sharp hill and has a two-story rear and a single-story front. However, research proved that the Conrad house wasn't built until a decade or more after the Butterfield ceased running.

Chimney Creek was also named after the Butterfield stage stopped running, probably because of the limestone chimney of the fallen station. The stage road ran across the present Buck Nail Ranch into Jones County, crossing the pasture where the lost city of Rising Sun flourished briefly a century ago. As this is mostly cultivated land, all traces of the Butterfield trail, even from the air, have been lost. However, a winding but passable county road going south off 180 leads by the gate of the Rising Sun cemetery, which is (as it should be) the city's last remaining evidence. Seeking perhaps a surviving community, you go west again to Nugent (surviving mainly via a Baptist church). On Highway 600 you cross the Clear Fork of the Brazos on a modern bridge that replaced one of those wonderful old nineteenth century iron-and-plank contrivances.

There is a lonely beauty to this country, without being isolated or even remote. Too bad the old Butterfield Trail couldn't have been preserved as a historical pathway, for it rides over a most legendary landscape—not only with the majesty of mountains or the enticing depths of the forest, but with a high sky and a rolling openness that inspires you to stretch out your mind and, who knows, expose your soul. Maybe this is why so many of the old ranching families, some wealthy and traveled enough to be able to live wherever they choose, cling to the family acreage; it owns them, not vice versa. And if you linger too long, or are a tad romantic to start with, you may find yourself perilously close to being owned, too.

It is too bad that lack of roads means you can't approach Fort Phantom Hill from the east or northeast, as the Butterfield stage did, because coming from those directions you are able to see why the ghostly name was attached to this unspectral elevation. The Butterfield station, which used the old guardhouse, is in fair condition. The fireplace and hearth where meals were prepared for Butterfield passengers could today be used for the same thing. The little rock magazine which the agent used for storage has been nicely repaired, although the copper lining the building once had to protect the munitions from flash-fire is long since gone. The commissary, unfinished at the time the post was abandoned and used by Butterfield agents as a stable, may remain in about the same shape as it was when the stage came through.

And yet, visiting the remains of Fort Phantom Hill today in broad daylight—the chimneys, fireplaces and foundations, the few standing walls and silent parade grounds—brings on a moment of historical apparitions, visions and sounds associated with neither the bright sun nor the moving wind. Is it the name Phantom Hill that starts the visioning process, or does it depend on knowing the history of the spot, seemingly cursed from its creation? Because it had so short a military life, did the unrecorded tragedies remain stuck to those lonely stone chimneys, unerased by later, bolder events?

My apologies for lingering over what was a relatively unimportant U.S. Army outpost. But if I must point to one spot, one place, and say this is where I found history or where history found me, then it must be Fort Phantom Hill. Being a native of Abilene and born less than fifteen miles from the old fort, I knew, from my earliest recollection, it was where something "historic" had happened near my relatively unhistoric hometown. Visiting Fort Phantom Hill, as I often did, clambering over the stone magazine, searching among the chimneys, letting my young mind embrace whatever imaginative adventures it was creating, I felt the past take on immediate importance for the first time. That grip has never loosened. It only tightens as I approach this little hill that disappears—phantom-like—while the boy reappears, phantom-like, when I come to it.

Tracing the trail westward, you go down a slight bluff on a neglected little road that you find just a few yards south of the fort. Go an additional hundred feet and find the old fort's cemetery which, despite a popular legend, does not contain the grave of Robert E. Lee's child. Incidentally, the grave of the cowboy who requested, "Bury me not on the lone prairie," won't be found locally, either, despite persistent West Texas legend. The legend of the Lee child has a slightly better basis. Colonel Robert E. Lee camped among the remains of Fort Phantom Hill at least twice in 1857–58 while in command of Camp Cooper.

That gravel road follows closely the Butterfield Trail, skirting the bluff above the Clear Fork valley, although the stage line never crossed this frequently powerful river. Near where the old trail crossed U.S. 83 is a modern, but ironic, tribute to the mail company, the "Butterfield Trail airport" for private planes. The old road went across this deceptively flat country in fairly straight fashion, but surely, in those days, they must have had real problems getting through the sudden freshets when there was rain. Today in wet weather, the researching traveler may well be faced with a washed out culvert or a dangerously slippery section of county road (as did this traveler). But eventually you emerge and go south to the edge of the town of Tye. Originally Tebo, it was whimsically called, in my youth, "Tebo Tye, Taylor County, Texas." At Tye you join I-20 west and come to the marker for the Butterfield crossing which the Taylor County surveyor located and the Daughters of the American Revolution's Abilene chapter erected in 1929. Pause a while here and you will again be given an ironic composite shot: a B-1 bomber or some other faster-than-sound military jet will descend right over the monument to the Butterfield stage, Tye being home of Dyess Air Force Base, a major SAC base since 1955.

After crossing I-20, you reach a territory where you and the Butterfield Trail can, as often as not, become one. Threading a couple of county roads, heading always southwest, you are soon within sight of Castle Peak, or Abercrombie Peak as it was called in Butterfield days. A pair of state historical markers tell of the peak's historical importance and of the 1871 running fight between Texas Rangers and Comanches that took place all New Year's day from the marker to the Mountain Pass station site.

Castle Peak (although I prefer honoring Colonel Abercrombie, who founded Fort Phantom Hill), begins to separate itself from the blue-tinted background of the Callahan Divide as you drive around its perimeter. It emerges suddenly into an impressive formation, even if it doesn't rank as much of a mountain. Ormsby's comment that at a distance it "much resembled the turrets and abutments of a lofty fortress" remains true. Castle Peak may not be much of a natural wonder, but you are able to view it almost as Ormsby (or Colonel Abercrombie) viewed it, for there are no power lines or buildings to mar the sight, and the peak itself grows loftier and more intriguing as you pursue the old mail road at its feet. How fascinating it must have been, in that earlier time, for a New York reporter like Ormsby, moving by stagecoach his first time west, to be encountering such a solitary spectacle, even if within a few days he would be enveloped in real mountains and deep canyons.

Making a turn south, you regain the stage route and start the slight incline up Mountain Pass. Don't look for a sharp rise, but instead accept the historical definition of both words: in the days of stagecoaches and wagons, these were mountains, this was a pass. Mountain Pass is one of my favorite spots on the Butterfield Trail for at least two reasons—no, I think of a third. First, the road follows exactly the Butterfield route. It has to; there's no room on either side for weaving in and out of the path. Second, this is a very lovely little dell, if you will, wild without being savage. It has not changed a great deal since white men first used it—the undisturbed hillside rocks and the juniper trees lining the pass, the turkey vultures sweeping the skies around, the sound of canyon birds, mysteriously near but never discernible. Were you a Butterfield passenger, hanging out the window to absorb the scene, you would have smelled, seen, and heard, what you may smell, see, and hear today. And that third thing I mentioned: clear, running water. A little stream crosses the road unbridged in the pass, coming from some spring source higher up the way. It is unusual to find clear running water in this part of Texas, and the Mountain Pass station was located so as to be along the creek this spring-fed rivulet eventually becomes.

Here again, although only a few hundred feet above the surrounding countryside, you feel uplifted, inspired, cleansed of something soap and water has nothing to do with. And history has spent a lot of time here. Butterfield's Overland Mail was not the only stage line or wagon train that used this pass. Army troops, moving from Fort Phantom Hill, Camp Cooper, Fort Belknap, to and from Fort Chadbourne, all came this way. In fact, a small army detachment was ambushed here, in 1867, costing the troopers two lives. (Appropriately, Mountain Pass is still on a mail route, driven over by a rural carrier.)

The road up the pass rises to a plateau instead of descending into a valley the way a pass should; the region behind is almost as high as the hills. The Butterfield Trail continued directly south of Mountain Pass, but the land it passed over is today fenced off and it has been years since it was usable. When viewed from the air, however, once the summit of Mountain Pass is crossed, the wheel marks of many wagons and coaches can be discerned.

A later way through the hills was found a few miles to the east, using a low natural opening called Coon Hollow. That is the way the modern road (U.S. 277) takes from Abilene to San Angelo. Coon Hollow, while coming later than Mountain Pass, has its own interesting history. One of the last stage runs in Texas used this passage until 1909. At that time a newly opened railroad, despite being several miles longer, made the trip quicker—and a good deal more comfortable. Until recent years brought the widening of Highway 277, you could see where the Coon Hollow stage road hugged the side of the hill above a long ravine.

All this hilly section offers reasonably pretty country—skirting, but not touching, such communities as Shep, Happy Valley, Hylton and Bump-Gate. But it is still a very lonesome stretch of the Butterfield Trail, especially if approached at dusk when the absence of farm and ranch house lights increases the wide open quality of the landscape. However, modern times are apparent: when a house is seen, so are television dishes and antennae sprouting from every roof or yard.

The modern Butterfield traveler must take Highway 89 over to

277, a pretty drive of some eight miles. At U.S. 277 there is a suppositious historical marker headlined "In The Vicinity of Coronado's Camp," which conjectures Coronado might possibly, maybe could have, perhaps, passed here. Maybe I'm being unfair, but Coronado is memorialized in a suspiciously large number of Texas sites which are many miles removed from the reasonably true path of that wandering conquistador. Coronado's possible visit is commemorated while, on the other hand, many seventeenth and eighteenth century explorers who really did *pass here* and *camp here* are neglected.

Proceeding south on 277, itself an unusually scenic highway, you parallel the Butterfield Trail, which lies west by two or three miles. In fact, when U.S. 277 was modernized and paved in the 1930s, it was dubbed "The Butterfield Trail." At the community of Shep you may once again ride over the ruts of the old mail road. You leave 277, turning west on one of the several country lanes that end up touching this section of the old trail, going through Shep the short distance to the road that was the Butterfield Trail. The old mail road runs south beside a deserted Baptist church, which reminds those of us old enough to have memorized the poem in school, of James Whitcomb Riley's schoolhouse by the road, "a ragged beggar sunning."

Somehow, once you are on this county road, you know you are again on the Butterfield Trail. You feel history. It is gravel, not rough and rutted, as are some other sections that you discover farther west, but it has the same looking-back, unused quality. Therefore, it is not surprising, within a few hundred yards from the old church, to find a marker which states that the Valley Creek station was along this road. Valley Creek itself is another site of unexpected beauty, its clear waters rippling in from the west.

Such live liquid is exceptional in dry West Texas, although there are a number of so-called seep springs in this immediate area. The most soothing is Fern Spring, whose water dripping from an overhanging limestone ledge creates a deep, fern-surrounded pool in which you are able to read the date on a coin at the bottom, so clear is the water. Unfortunately, even at this distance from the towns, the ranchers have to keep the locations secret and the gates locked around their springs or the basins would quickly fill with beer cans, fast-food plastic, and disposable baby diapers.

The county road continues southwest, twisting between the low hills, the path pretty well following where the Butterfield went. How can we suppose this? Well, there isn't any place else a road can go, short of using the modern earthmovers, front-end loaders, and bull-dozers to demolish the landscape the way Interstates are built. No, this road, save for certain sharper corners around fenced property, is still slightly throbbing with the iron-tired wheels of other days. At the former town of Hylton—one building still remaining—turn south again onto what looks to be an impassable track, but isn't. You get back on 277 about where the Butterfield would have hit it, and although there are several inches of gravel and asphalt between you and the Butterfield, it's down there all the way to Fort Chadbourne, which lies on private property just south of the highway. The small cemetery on the highway, which contains the graves of many im-portant regional figures, is open and interesting. Very few military graves remain in the old fort and camp cemeteries. In about 1907 the army reinterred most of its frontier dead in military cemeteries in San Antonio and other official burial places. Perhaps it makes good sense, but it leaves a page of history blank in our minds.

Fort Chadbourne is falling down. The owners can't be faulted too much because it is a massive job to stabilize and reclaim the bar-racks and outbuildings that are still standing. But Chadbourne is worth it. Not only was a lot of American history involved here; this was a well built fort to begin with. Stone masons were brought up from central Texas rather than leaving the construction to the sol-diers, as was the case in many pre-Civil War frontier installations. The Conklings, in 1933, thought it was the best preserved early fron-tier fort standing along the old Butterfield route. Most of the adobe structures they found are now gone. You can't help but sympathize with the Conklings who indignantly observed, "In no other country

161

would monuments of such historic value as the chain of old frontier posts and the first mail stations, suffer such callous neglect and wanton destruction."[12]

The Butterfield Trail continued southwest from Fort Chadbourne, passing by the site of the later civilian town of the name and that town's cemetery, but then moving across pastures, fields, and places where the present road does not go. (A Butterfield marker where the road recrossed 277 is effusive and full of errors.) After passing through Bronte (named for Charlotte, of the writing sisters), then going west toward Robert Lee (not "Robert E. Lee" as some atlases have it), you find another marker for the Butterfield crossing on Highway 158. It has the same errors, but just beyond the marker, turning off south, is a rough little gravel road that leads down to near where the Colorado River station was situated. (Warning: the road turns to dirt its last mile.) The Colorado River is well controlled at this point because of the big E. V. Spence Reservoir west of Robert Lee, so you won't have to remain on the river banks all night during a downpour the way Richardson did in 1859.

Passing through the unusually active town of Robert Lee, the traveler goes south to another very rugged road leading east to the river at a point just across from where the station was located. A sand and gravel works here has changed the landscape to such a point that the river seems naked and embarrassed at its vulnerability. However, if you continue on that same road you quickly turn back southwest and are once again on the old stage road for about two miles before reaching the modern highway south.

From this point the Butterfield Trail moves in an almost direct southwestern heading, but it is lonely, vacant and nearly impenetrable. Even by air it becomes indiscernible due to the numerous creeks and draws along the watershed—the water headed northeast goes into the Colorado, while just a few yards away the water flowing south becomes one of the Concho rivers. The Conklings tell of two landmarks in this section of the mail road, Butterfield Peak and Butterfield Gap. Except for foot or four-wheel mobility (and owner permissions), they are both inaccessible.

If the intrepid historical traveler wishes to come near Grape Creek station, he may do so, but only after traveling all the way south to San Angelo and back up northwest on two county roads. At this point (you may have to get directions), the East Fork of Grape Creek can be ascended. The creek itself is modestly pretty, but the station site, as is the case with so many Butterfield installations today, is on private property. There are several branches of Grape Creek, so be careful which you follow. There have been those of us who have gotten lost.

To follow the Butterfield Trail, it is almost impossible not to go to San Angelo, even if the Butterfield stage didn't touch there—in fact, neither the town nor its Fort Concho were there in the Butterfield's time. What is surprising about the Butterfield Trail west of San Angelo is not how little you can find, but how much; at least, how easily it may be traced. You can't always ride on it but you can come close to finding where it was and ride alongside it.

From San Angelo the historical traveler must take U.S. 87 northwest to Carlsbad, the former Texas State tubercular hospital. The mail road crossed at Carlsbad and a marker is installed, but be cautious because it is easy to overlook the marker and find yourself in Sanatorium, the institution that adjoins. The reason I am being so precise here is because the road from Carlsbad that the stage followed west is difficult to find, but very much worth the finding. It is delightful. Getting on this back road, you tread on the old pathway for several miles before it swings off to the west on its own and you emerge on Highway 853, to start across Irion County.

Not far west from where you join this highway you ford Big Rocky Creek a short distance north of the location of the first, short lived Butterfield station. The stage forded Big Rocky just before the creek feeds into the Middle Concho River. You can find evidences of many crossings. Right downstream from the modern highway there is a wide flat area which would have been perfect for fording.

Surely this is one of the superbly lovely places on the entire Texas run, and we can imagine how welcome the sight was to the travelers. The water, clear and cold, flows strongly, and there is evidence that when the creek is up it can be wicked—an entire slab of paving was tossed up on the bank like a huge quilt when we crossed it. We saw hundreds of monarch butterflies following the creek, and then we saw four deer up the road, pausing cautiously and then crossing very carefully, but unfrightened by the near presence of humans. The whole thing is quite tranquil. We didn't want to leave. Of course, at the crossing you can find evidence of modern American road culture, but looking up or down stream helps overcome that.

Not far west along the creek are the remains of the town of Arden—the old post office first turned into a community center (with, oddly, a sidewalk and turnstile), now fallen into a cactus and mesquite choked derelict.

Continuing on the paved road, you reach the point where it turns sharply south, but the Butterfield traveler continues west on a gravel road. For a matter of some twenty-two or twenty-three miles, this road either follows directly or crosses the stage road, forced to do so by the fact that even now the Middle Concho prevents much deviation. It is a very exciting road. Shortly after leaving pavement, the gravel road crosses the edge of Camp Johnston, the 1852 predecessor of Fort Chadbourne, which was put to use by the Butterfield company as a meal and change station. A small town grew up around the location. You can't see it from the road, but the site is not far south of the barbed wire fence that faces you at a right-angle turn. This was also the old Goodnight-Loving Trail, opened in 1867, and virtually every mile of this road, or any of the cattle trails joining it, has seen death and bloodshed and heartache—only partially brought on by the Comanches, Kiowas or Apaches.

As you drive west, you recognize you are entering a different, even a separate, country. Just a few miles eastward was another Texas. Because you are in touch with nothing but yourself and what you are driving, imagination should come easily. Your air conditioned, four-wheel drive vehicle becomes, instead, a rocking, racking, iron-wheeled celerity wagon, lurching over the bumps and ruts and rocks that shock absorbers and heavy springs take in their stride. But it's not just the physical changes of the landscape. There is a changed feel to things—not the high sun, not the winds, the brown grass or the long-viewed, wide open terrain, but the unseen agency some land has that starts your emotions moving in and out involuntarily. Again, you have to wonder what must have gone through the minds of those passengers, what effect that unseen agency must have had on them—or were their literal fears too powerful for any other emotion to impinge on? The problem in the days of the Butterfield was that they couldn't admire the beauty for thinking of water and fearing Indians. The road is rough, but the surroundings—the environment, the hills (we're in valleys, too)—create a beautiful piece of arid and exhilarating land. But you don't hear much about the beauty of it in the accounts of cautious travelers.

The Butterfield Trail is to me a piece of unresearched past: my own past. I find myself in virtually every mile of it, and I can find an excuse wholly removed from any professional role in traversing it. That sounds rather heavily mystical, perhaps, but history is a mystical study. What is it but the sum of the experiences of every person who has ever lived? At the risk of sounding like Walt Whitman, I become Waterman Ormsby, at least in those days he traveled over this very piece of earth I am traveling over right now. I become a soldier at Camp Johnston, used to living in huts and on dirt with conditions the soldiers of even a decade later would scorn to put up with. I can even become a Comanche or a Kiowa, recognizing this is a strange epidemic that has no name but is endangering not just my present importance but my past—my land, my god, the number of me.

It is difficult to transcribe. I feel a direct identity with land. Mine is not the identity of some, who can find the secrets of the earth, know the life of the animals, seek out the rootings and blossomings of the plants. I have never felt nostalgic for the buffalo. But I like the vastness of land; land powerful enough to affect lives. That's what history has meant to me in most cases, not just studying the past as a field of research, although that is important, but studying the past as an extension of my own persona. That sounds like an egotistical approach to things, and I suppose an even more egotistical approach to history, because if history teaches us anything, it is the

165

unimportance of egotism. But history must include people, whether me or Waterman Ormsby, or J. B. Nichols, the stage driver who assured Ormsby that while he did not know the road, or how far it was to the next station—he wasn't lost. History should become an attempt to locate yourself. But the life a historian too seldom studies is his own.

Approaching Highway 163, if you decide not to try the ranch road that leads northwest near where Kiowa Creek and the Middle Concho met around Camp Charlotte, you must turn south because the region directly ahead where the old mail road led is now uncrossed except perhaps by a ranch pickup trail. Camp Charlotte, which was established seven years after the Butterfield Overland Mail ceased to operate, was a stockade type fort with overhanging defense posts at the corners, rare in the Southwest.[13] It was established as a subpost out of Fort Concho but remained a settlement for many years when the various mail runs and cattle trails used its services.

Along the paved highways of this region, every few miles you will see a dead deer by the side of the road, hit by a speeding car or truck. In no more than ten miles on Highway 163 we counted eight. And there will often be a vulture body nearby, evidence of the usually cunning vulture who just couldn't quite give up his meal in time to save himself. Is there a parable in this?

The Head of Concho Station was located out in this trackless (today) region, situated where Centralia Draw is joined by South and North Mustang Draw and East Snow Draw. There is a trace of caliche road that leads to the vicinity, but it is private, and even if the gate is unlocked when you enter, there is always the possibility that you might get locked in—with the ranch headquarters twenty miles away. At any rate, Head of Concho was the last sure place for water as the Butterfield headed for the Pecos River. Most of the early explorers and trailmakers mention the location before there was a habitation of any sort there.[14]

Highway 163 goes south to Barnhart, where you then head west alongside the Santa Fe's Orient Railroad (Kansas City, Mexico & Orient was its original name). When this line opened in 1909 disaster was predicted for it, and very nearly occurred. For decades the Orient limped along, forecasts of its demise coming annually. Oil play in the 1920s energized it for a while, but its connection at Presidio with the newly completed Chihuahua al Pacifico railroad of Mexico in 1964—making Santa Fe's Orient a transcontinental route to the Pacific Ocean—was the line's ultimate salvation, although some stretches today have been abandoned.

At Big Lake we turned north again on Highway 137, heading for Stiles where the Butterfield line ran along Centralia Draw. Stiles, the town, did not come along until several years after the celerity wagon had passed. It's a longish detour up to Stiles, made necessary because there are no east-west roads—you go up, then must come right back down—but the extra mileage is worth it. You see a whitish building in the distance, beckoning to you several miles before you reach the "town," and when you have arrived you discover this building, the old courthouse, is about as lonely a building as you'll find. There is a paintless, weedy county barn and a ranch home about half a mile west, but there is nothing else to Stiles.

Judy and I spent a fascinated hour looking around the carefully dressed limestone courthouse, abandoned in 1923 when newly oil rich Big Lake took over the county seat. A tragedy took place inside this courthouse in 1914 when Sheriff Japson killed his former friend and partner, cattleman Jim Belcher, and then took his own life.[15] But the old courthouse is of a classic simplicity and beauty. It offers the same face on all four sides, with a chimney at each corner, and stands resolutely in solitary splendor on what was once the courthouse square. The vestiges of a small park occupy one corner of the square. A friend, who had been a pretty, young (unmarried) schoolteacher in Big Lake during the 1940s, said there was a big dance at the Stiles courthouse every Saturday night and oil people and lonesome cowboys (not to mention school teachers) drove thirty, forty, even fifty miles to attend. The courthouse is still in solid condition, seventy years after its abandonment, but once the windows go—and some are missing—and the roof starts opening itself to the sky, deterioration will become devastation.

The Butterfield Trail followed the depression of Centralia Draw, which runs but a few yards to the south of the courthouse. From there it continued southwest through more unreachable range lands. Although it has been a ghost town for several decades, there are dozens of stories about Stiles and the country around it, a desolate, terrifyingly lonely place for the few women who followed their rancher husbands out here late in the nineteenth century and early in the twentieth. One storyteller describes a cowboy living in a remote line shack in that region west of Stiles, who upon entering the shack one winter night couldn't get his lamp lit because something kept blowing out his match. Imagine his terror when, on finally making a light, he found, staring at him from inches away, a mad woman hanging from the rafters. She had been puffing out his match each time he tried to strike it. The cowboy, so the story says, fled the shack, jumped on his horse, and rode furiously to "civilization." The woman? The storyteller said she had lost her mind from being left alone so much in the wide and sparsely settled country.[16]

Lonely country or not, the mail road crossed what became some of the most famous oil fields in Texas, from whose depths have been pumped a billion gallons of petroleum. In 1923 an oil well named the Santa Rita #1 came in and marked the beginning of the extraordinary wealth of the University of Texas at Austin. Within a few months other wells in the vicinity were brought in and shortly the University was receiving millions of dollars worth of royalties from university lands set aside years before (1876) by the State of Texas. There is a large measure of irony here. The university lands, designated before there was a University of Texas, had been pushed westward again and again until they embraced the sorriest acreage, the roughest, most arid kind of terrain. Thus, the University of Texas, from holding thousands of acres of twenty-five cent an acre land—

if it could be sold at all—overnight became the nation's richest state university.

As the Colorado mining boom left ghost towns all over the Rockies, so the oil booms of Texas contributed lost communities statewide. There are three historic examples of once thriving towns west of Big Lake on U.S. 67: Best, Santa Rita, and Texon. There is no direct Butterfield connection, but they are worth making the slight detour it takes to progress among them. Best, like the other two, was a product of the petroleum bonanza days. Named for oil man Tom Best, it was an oil camp during the boom days from 1924 until late in the 1930s. At one time there were 3,500 residents, making it, as one chronicler states, "a lively community characterized as the town with the best name and the worst reputation." Santa Rita, just a hop, skip and a jump along the ties west on the railroad, is site of the first University of Texas well. The derrick and old style works are still in place (the original drill rig is on the university campus at Austin), but Santa Rita, too, is more ghost than flesh.[17]

Texon, named for the oil company that brought in the Big Lake field, was a company town which, legend says, began in 1923 with two wooden shacks, an oil derrick, and a hamburger stand. Texon had a hospital, schools (it and Best furnished some of the toughest football players in Texas), theater, and recreational facilities including a community center, a golf course, a famous semi-pro baseball team, and a modern library. It held onto its population of just under 2,000 until after World War II; then, as the oil faded, so did Texon, finally disappearing in 1962.

This "detour" is interesting and historic, but it can create a hollow feeling in even the unhistorical breast at the recognition that here, on these mesquite-crowded lots, among these dark, rusty warehouses, in the buildings that sat on those bare concrete foundations—whole lives were lived with no thought that things would ever change. So who among us is safe?

The historian may, leaving Texon, go northwest on Highway 1555 for about eight or nine miles, passing, a couple of miles to the west in a private pasture, the Llano Estacado Station. The Conklings said the station, though in ruins, had suffered less from destruction than many others along the route. The ruins are now covered with cactus and mesquite brush. Today the highway makes a sharp western turn and the traveler finds himself paralleling the Butterfield again. However, Highway 1555 doesn't continue west, so you are forced to return to U.S. 87, this time at the town of Rankin. The Butterfield Trail crosses the highway about ten miles north of there. Three miles west, near the old mail road, is the site of Dr. George Washington Elliott's ranch house, built in 1880, the first house in what became Upton County. When it was built, its water had to be hauled fifty miles from Head of Concho. In 1905 it became headquarters for San Antonio rancher Mayer Halff's famous "Quien Sabe" and Circle Dot ranches. The town of Upland, only two or three miles north, became the first county seat of Upton County when it was organized in 1910. In an effort to increase population, Halff once sold lots at Upland for the cost of notary fees. Rankin was made county seat in 1921 after Upland had been bypassed by the railroad, and Upland slowly became a ghost town.

From Rankin, to follow the old trail, you go northwest on Highway 329. About midway toward Highway 2463 stands the intersection of Highway 329 and China Draw. To the east, China Draw created "Wild China Ponds"—as often cursed for having no water as blessed for having it. "China Ponds" is such an intriguing name, this oriental designation here in the middle of a semi-desert; how disappointing to discover the draw and ponds were named for the chinaberry trees that grew there.

At Highway 2463, the Butterfield traveler is able to continue west on a gravel road which almost precisely follows the old mail route. This is harsh, high and dry country, this clear upland region which puts you on your own for spiritual exhilaration, like some zealot in the desert. Along about here, when the Mustang and Wild China

Ponds had proved illusory, the explorers, trailmakers, emigrants and stagecoach passengers began to feel the lack of water, the lack of landmarks, the lack of anything other than mesquite brush, buzzards, and stinging things underfoot. How many of them must have wondered, seeing only heat and dust ahead and around them, "where am I and what the hell am I doing here?" But fortunately for my wife and me, on our four stout radials, with our ice chest full of moisture, the road gets better after awhile, and today's traveler can safely reachieve the historical rhythms of the celerity wagon without having to endure its crawling pace. But despite modern luxuries, these are pickup truck roads, not really for passenger vehicles.

As our little county road starts to turn northward, we are treated to the unmistakable appearance of Castle Gap dead ahead, looking as if some monster from the age of dinosaurs had bitten a huge chunk out of the range of hills extending across the horizon before us. We know that the Butterfield came rolling across where we are. The hills themselves are unremarkable; it is what has happened in this bite that counts. There are too many references to Castle Gap in the early records of exploration and literature to recount them one by one. There are treasure tales and murder tales and Indian attacks centered around this innocent gap, and tales of things stolen—from cattle to food to wives. Rip Ford tells of sharing a mule with a Comanche warrior at Castle Gap in 1849 when the expedition with Rip Ford and Robert S. Neighbors was near starvation. He reported "mule meat was found almost as palatable as beef."[18]

The Butterfield line passed through the gap but had no station there, although some writers assert otherwise. A ranch house occupies the eastern entrance to the pass and the old mail road seems to have been eroded away into a wide, dry wash. The road through the pass is long gone. Patrick Dearen wrote: "Ever since a wagon route first had been cleared through the gap in 1839, water from infrequent rains had drained down the arroyo on the road's north side and a shallow depression on the other. But sometime after 1910 a fresno crew working for treasure hunter Billy Pool shoveled thousands of cubic feet of dirt across the ditch and altered the flow of the runoff onto the road bed. The water began to gouge out great chunks of the trail and eventually closed the gap as a practical route."[19] The west end of the gap is pocked with holes, including a mammoth one, where treasure hunters have moved tons and tons of earth trying to catch the elusive wealth of Maximilian—the mythical jack-loads of silver, of gold bricks, or (once again) Coronado's wraith.

Here is another spot where even from the air the trail is lost, lost to the *real* treasure of Castle Gap, antedating Coronado, or even Maximilian—oil. Oil activity over the past sixty years has eliminated any identifiable traces of an original roadway in the maze of service roads and trails going from well to pump to tanks. The Conklings point out that even in the early 1930s when they walked Castle Gap some of the oil wells had been drilled in the mail road itself.[20]

The most famous landmark on the entire Butterfield Trail across Texas is supposedly visible from the gap: Horsehead Crossing on the Pecos River. But getting to the crossing from the east side of the river takes permission from landowners and use of private roads.

After circling north around Castle Gap, you reach U.S. 385 and turn south toward McCamey. There's a little fence-post telephone system about six or eight miles out coming into McCamey, probably not in operation, but most unusual for this day and age. There was a time, and not too long ago, when nearly every Texas ranch or isolated farm was reached by a strand of message wire strung atop posts of a barbed wire fence. Many of the lines just went to nearby neighbors and weren't connected with larger telephone systems.

The Butterfield station, on the east side of Horsehead Crossing, was around an S-curve of the river, northwest of the crossing itself. The Butterfield stage didn't use Horsehead Crossing until mid-1859. The original (1858) road went along the east bank of the Pecos River and today is not only impassable but can't be found. Agriculture and oil obliterated the road, erosion and flooding by the river have turned and twisted its bed so that we can't be sure where the east bank road might have been. Therefore, to continue tracing the route toward the Guadalupes, the traveler must get to the other side of the river. So at McCamey we must join U.S. 87 west, crossing the Pecos at Girvin (most notable for being the site of a huge electrical power plant), and turning immediately northwest onto Highway 11. About eleven or twelve miles along, a marked road leads off to the right. It is paved, although not always well, and it leads directly to the west bank of the Pecos River where a 1936 granite monument informs you that what you see below where you are standing is Horsehead Crossing.

Horsehead Crossing is romantically adequate if slightly disappointing as a dramatic landmark. It is remote and inhospitable, with nothing around it; it is lonely, populated only with ghosts. But if the wind is right, surely you can hear the urgent voices, war cries, bellowing cattle and frightened horses—otherwise, why have you come this distance to gaze on this spot? You are both astonished that it is as ordinary as it is—no spectacular wide, rushing water, no lovely ripples over rocky shoals—and that such a place could have seen so much history and tragedy and disaster.

My wife and I stood, looking at the shallow trickle of water that is now the Pecos, trying to picture the crossing when making the swim from shore to shore, whether with horses, cattle, or wagons, was always a thing of tension, full of danger from the elements, from drowning, from starvation, from thirst, and from the Comanches, who crossed here on their fearsome war trail to Mexico. Despite its absence of drama, the crossing today is rather pretty, involving a turn with a nice little vista upriver, which is better than the flatness of the river along so much of its West Texas length. The ultimate satisfaction gained from standing and looking over Horsehead Crossing is that it enables you to imagine it in a more romantic age, and to convince yourself, "I am there."

After leaving Horsehead Crossing, we continued to drive northwest on Highway 11. We made an interesting Pecos River discovery on the west shore that had nothing to do with the Butterfield but seems significant of the whole section. Driving along the highway, we turned back toward the river along a gravel lane which the map indicated led to Abell oil field and a bridge we might use across the Pecos. But when we reached the end of the road at the river we found only the skeleton of an old, narrow iron bridge. And while the river here could theoretically be forded by auto or truck, a system of barriers has been thrown in the path to make it impossible. This lonely abandoned bridge, now bereft of everything but truss, sills and abutments, somehow symbolizes the history of this river. Once as important as any in the west, the Pecos is now dammed and controlled into a mineralized drainage ditch with salt cedars being the predominant vegetation; more pest than beauty.[21]

The Goodnight-Loving Trail of 1867, and the hundreds of thousands of head of cattle that followed it, used Horsehead Crossing and went along the west side of the Pecos on the way to Mexico, California, and New Mexico.[22] A sign that this area has seen more prosperous days comes along the maze of roads along the river's west bank, where abandoned irrigation farming is marked with broken down gates and weedy ditches. Here and there an ancient barn slopes its way earthward, and even the few road signs are hand-painted, not the product of efficient state or county upkeep. There is a kind of tragedy about certain aspects of western irrigation. The water-filled ditches and *acequias*, in the old days, became lined by beautiful trees, usually cottonwoods. But when irrigation is abandoned these huge old trees quickly die, leaving gaunt and ghostly skeletons which slowly fall, making the desert bleak and sadly harsh again.

Driving the west bank is an uninspiring trip, except for stopping in the town of Pecos to eat and view the museum down by the railroad tracks. Pecos claims to have been the birthplace of the rodeo in 1883. Going northwest on U.S. 285, travelers might wish to veer briefly across the Pecos to see Mentone, the county seat of legendary Loving County, least populated (around 61) and last organized (1931) of the 254 Texas counties. This is storied country; vast and vacant, but full of legends, myths and tales of death and deliverance. Ghosts wait along the forgotten trails that once supported lives.

Night was falling as Judy and I reached Orla, presuming from its prominence on our map that it would supply some sort of resting place. But be not deceived by the modern county maps, in case dark might catch you there. Orla has no sleeping facilities. It is simply the only town mapmakers have to show in that thousand square mile area, so they overdo it. We discovered that Orla once had a motel, but it went the way of its drive-in movie. Dark fell on us after we left Orla.

We knew that the old Pope's Camp at Pope's Crossing was now submerged beneath the waters of Red Bluff Lake. Hughes has stated that the remains of the camp could still be seen when the lake level is low. The crossing is under the lake waters "near Arms camp." Hughes says:

> The river crossing was a natural one and had been used by the Indians many, many years before Pope and his party came to the area. There was a large Indian camp on the west side of the river at the crossing and, even as late as 1930, many artifacts of all kinds could be picked up at this old camp site. The trail from [Pope's] camp to the river crossing was very well defined and could probably still be traced [1974] if it were not under water.[23]

We had found the Pope's Crossing monument on the highway— backing the car around so we could read it by headlight—and we ventured down the dark road in the direction the monument indicated, our vehicle sadly thumping over an abandoned railroad dump. We found the place where the monument said the Butterfield trail reached the west bank, and discovered ourselves in a deserted village. It was spooky, on a dark, cold night, driving among the houses, seeing no radiant television screen through any window, or evidence of any humans but us. And the already dim path became dirt and, without warning, led into the lake. If your headlights aren't on bright, or you are not watching closely, your vehicle could become bogged, or worse. I could imagine wide-eyed, dripping mules charging out of the dark water, dragging a wet stagecoach, rocketing by us into the night. We were uneasy until we got ourselves back to the main highway. Perhaps we both had read the opening pages of too many science fiction stories.

From Pope's Crossing the Butterfield route went cross-country. It forded the Delaware River a few miles due west of the crossing—named for the Delaware tribe, not the state—then continued to Delaware Springs station at the headwaters of the river, nearly forty miles west of the Pecos. This is where three different springs combine to form the river. Early explorers speak of how sweet the water of one spring among the three was, and how disgusting the other waters were. Marcy suggests (in 1849) that "at no distant period" a health resort will undoubtedly be built around the springs, affording what he calls "a place of fashionable resort for the 'upper ten thousand' of New Mexico." Or was that formidable frontiersman masking a joke? Be that as it may, today you can't get to the springs. They are on private property and approached, if at all, by a dubious ranch trail.

Roads of any kind are scarce-to-rare out here, and Highway 652, which connects U.S. 62/180 with U.S. 285, is a lonely trace to travel. But the land is high, and was cool and lovely when we passed over it. On Highway 652, as you are driving through absolutely empty country so far as people and other vehicles are involved, you suddenly cross a well-kept railroad track. A paved private road leads along it to a large molten sulfur layout at Rustler Springs. Other than this unexpected rail crossing, we neither saw nor met another person or vehicle along the entire 43-mile distance of the highway. The Butterfield Trail does cross it, just northwest of the Delaware River bridge, but the juncture is unmarked. We almost hated to gain U.S. 62/180, we liked 652 so much.

Going southwest, the U.S. highway continues in beauty, with the Guadalupes facing you. You almost wish the road weren't so up-to-date and wide. What an experience it must have been for the early automobile and truck travelers, edging their way, the automobiles using second—maybe even first—gear, the trucks in one of those old compound gears several shifts below "grandma." We were extra fortunate because a storm was darkening the air and now and then a tiny snowflake would hit the windshield. We passed three deep canyons which headed up into the mountains, including McKittrick Canyon, whose ecosystem is so fragile that only a few persons at a time are allowed by the National Parks people to visit it. Then we pass over Nickel Creek, where a lot of history was made by the California-bound emigrants pausing there, though there is nothing there now.

There was a little camp-like settlement called Pine Springs near the entrance to Guadalupe Mountains National Park, but Judy and I found it abandoned. I thought back on a time several years ago when it seemed the end had come for me at Pine Springs. I discovered that while a friend and I were standing only a yard or so away, the old woman who operated the grocery store-cafe-service station was pumping diesel fuel into the hot muffler of an 18-wheeler rather than its fuel tank. After a scrambling retreat, we shouted for her to stop and she reluctantly withdrew the nozzle. The truck didn't blow up, but I don't believe she was convinced she endangered herself and us. I think maybe she thought we were trying to cheat her out of the sale of a few extra gallons of fuel.

When we arrived at the Butterfield station called The Pinery, the flakes were coming stronger and the bite in the air was quite pronounced. Somehow the weather seemed to enhance the ruins of the old station, causing us to wonder just what the stationkeepers and their crew must have thought of all the beauty around them, even while wondering how they were going to keep warm.

We often mention that stagecoaches were not air conditioned, but we must also remember they were not heated, either—and the Butterfield Overland Mail ran summer and winter. We tend to think of "hot, dry Texas," overlooking cold, snowy, freezing, icy Texas. Most of the Texas stations were heated by wood, especially through West

Texas and beyond the Pecos. Three or four near Fort Belknap and Bridgeport may have used local coal. The station meals were cooked on wood (or buffalo chips) in an open fireplace. Winter tested the mettle of passenger, driver, agent, and especially the agent's wife. There is plenty of winter where the Butterfield ran, especially on the Llano Estacado and in mile-high mountains like the Guadalupes. Too bad all the passenger accounts seem to have been written in summer or fall. Kenneth Neighbours does write that, "On the fifteenth of April, on the bare and almost sterile plain between the head of the Concho and Castle Mountain, the party was assailed by a cold, wet norther. The cold was intense, and it snowed and sleeted for hours. There was nothing visible for miles but bushes."[24]

Another thing we overlook about the Butterfield stagecoaches is that they ran day and night without anything we would even consider to be night lighting, just the soft yellow glow of oil burning outside lamps, or candles inside the coach. Yet, somehow the Butterfield Southern Overland route had one of the best accident records of any stage run. Stages overturned in a few instances, but only one fatality was recorded. In the Choctaw Nation (now Oklahoma), a runaway team smashed a coach against a tree, killing a passenger from Missouri and badly injuring the driver and four other passengers.

Standing at the Pinery, feeling the rough remnants of the station walls, it is easy to find yourself back in that time, even though the headquarters building of the Guadalupe National Park is nearby. We watched the thick dark storm clouds come rolling over Guadalupe Peak, sweeping down upon us, only to dissipate into delicate flakes that floated to earth more like goose down than snow. Although our clouds were of a different hue, we were able to share a high moment with Ormsby, remembering what he wrote about "the gorgeous appearance of the clouds . . . assum[ing] . . . all sorts of fantastic shapes."[25]

Higher mountain passes can be traversed on American highways, and higher mountains can be viewed in storm, but nowhere but the

Pinery can you do all this at a former Butterfield station. It is the only station ruin located on a national highway—U.S. 62/180 is less than 400 yards away. Guadalupe Pass, at 5,534 feet in altitude, was the highest spot on the original route, and Guadalupe Peak is, after all, the tallest in Texas.

In 1958, to celebrate the centennial of the beginning of the Butterfield Overland Mail, a six-foot stainless steel pylon, honoring early day air mail pilots who crashed and died flying over the Guadalupes, was carried mule-back to the top of Guadalupe Peak and permanently installed there by Noel Kincaid, manager of Hunter Ranch. American Airlines, which had commissioned the monument, had flown in several writers, I among them, from newspapers along the Butterfield route in Texas and Oklahoma for a celebration held in the broad valley at the foot of the peak. A number of us, some no doubt inspired by the workmanship of two professional bartenders, arranged various chairs and tables so that we could prance across the upright steel needle before it was installed above, thus enabling us to brag that we had cleared the top of Guadalupe Peak in one jump. Mr. and Mrs. J. C. Hunter, of Abilene, owners of the ranch and the Pinery at the time, were present for the ceremony but, being of a "dry" persuasion, partook not of the high-jinks.

The beauty of the surroundings and the grand scenes that the road seems to frame is accomplished without today's motorist giving much thought to acceleration, so easy is the modern grade. However, heavy wind currents push hard against the side of a fast moving automobile that might not have bothered a laboring stagecoach or slow-moving covered wagon. The modern highway and the old road have to share a narrow defile. From time to time, on either side of the modern highway, you are able to see remnants of the old stage and wagon road through the pass, especially where the highway, twisting southeast, goes across and above the roadway of the mid-nineteenth century, for which the Conklings found the remains of dry wall masonry retaining walls defining the early passage. The Butterfield stage had to travel 2800 or so miles in 600 hours to fulfill the twenty-five day transcontinental schedule.Thus, they had to maintain an average speed of nearly five m.p.h.[26] They would have to have gone twice as fast on some other portions of the trail to make up for how slow they could travel up the incline at Guadalupe Pass. It is possible that a good deal more of the old road survives than we notice driving an automobile through the Pass at 60 or 65 m.p.h. Why, at a sacrifice of history and beauty, do we of today demand everything be made easy?

Leaving the pass, the change in scenery is dramatic. One minute you are under the 8,000-foot magnificence of El Capitan Peak, the next you are facing the saline desert of Salt Flat. Fortunately, the Texas Highway Department has established roadside parks which afford not only a wonderful view of what is above but of what is ahead. We stopped at each, increasingly wondering why people live in cities when this sort of beauty has been here for eons.

The Butterfield road is close alongside the mountains, passing through the salt lakes across what is now Dell City. Unable to re-trace the old road, we must take Highway 1576. Salt Basin, and the immense chain of salt and gypsum "lakes," become unbelievable. We saw them by day, but by moonlight the salines are said to be fantastic, "a lunar landscape," the Conklings considered them. The basin is lonely and remote, but it is hard to imagine a stagecoach here—it is too much like a movie set, almost contrived, unnatural. Some film producer hauled in this glistening expanse, we think. This couldn't have been the real frontier. But it was. The Salt Basin and lakes, like the Guadalupes, are worth the time and trouble to visit, Butterfield trailing or not.

We continued on Highway 1576 for nearly seventeen miles to a gravel street north of downtown Dell City, leading directly west, then switching northwest toward the New Mexico line and the Cornudas Mountains. Selecting the way from Dell City through this remote part of Otero County, New Mexico, can be tricky. There are no direction signs. From time to time you can come to believe that you are lost, and from time to time you can be lost. My wife, who acted as navigator on our Butterfield Overland expedition, saved us from an uncertain fate—definitely one of numerous wasted miles—when she made the driver back up for nearly a mile, predicting correctly that said driver should have taken one specific gravel trail instead of another. But Cornudas Mountain,[27] the original "Horned Peak" of the Spaniards (it appears to have two horns), where the Butterfield station was located, can't be missed. If you have taken the correct trail you go close enough to know it is the place. Thorne's Well, inside the mountain, has gone dry and is on fenced property, but you have been riding fairly close to the old road all the time you are approaching the mountain.

Within a few miles northwest out of Dell City you reach solitude; lovely, high, clean and bracing solitude. This is the impressiveness of far western country: nothing much changes. The country is too vast, the mountains too rugged, the sky too high, the vistas too long. It won't be tamed by puny man, even with his bulldozers, his concrete, his never-to-be-gotten-away-from electronic world. For a while you see signs of a buried telephone line along one side of the road, but pretty soon the ranches end and so do the cable locations, and except for now and then a barbed wire fence, you have the countryside to yourself. We did come upon a herd of eight or ten antelope grazing roadside. They hardly moved away, much less fled, until our car was within fifty feet of them. Such beautiful animals and so graceful in flight, once they decided we might be dangerous. Both Ormsby and Tallack praised the beauty of the antelope on their Butterfield trips.

The Butterfield stage made good time through here, sometimes doing 12 m.p.h. The automobile can make good time, too, but the road can be tricky on the turns, the gravel sliding dangerously under a speeding vehicle—although I can't imagine wanting to speed. We saw one other traveler: a propane truck taking fuel to some off-the-road ranch.

Would this be a wonderful country to live in? It would for someone who had thoughts and ideas that needed to ferment, that needed to be worked on, worried with, refined, improved by pruning and polishing, then put on paper, or through whatever medium the composer worked. To a lot of other people it would be a lonely hell, I suppose, beautiful or not. We live in a congregating world that is becoming more congregational. As William Cowper said, "Oh solitude, where are the charms / That sages have seen in thy face?"

The road from Cornudas station to Ojos de los Alamos (Cottonwood Springs) is approximately the old stage road. There has been no reason to change the route, since there is nothing to keep away from or get past, no creeks or ravines to avoid. All around are singular mountains, sometimes giving the impression that there are three together, then slowly separating as you approach or change angles. Your westward climb (which is gradual enough to be unnoticed) takes you by Wind Mountain, which, locals say, "sings" to the listener when the wind comes from the right direction—"a strange, low wailing cry like a great wind harp that issues from the crags of its serrated crest," say the more poetic than usual Conklings—although they, as we, seemed to have missed the sound.

The 1858 traveler saw much we see today, and we see very little more than the long ago travelers did. Although this swing up into New Mexico is mostly noted for the Butterfield stations along its route, it was also used by army explorers, emigrants, and freighters, too. It is many miles out of the way on a direct route from the Guadalupes to El Paso, but in those days water was the compass. And God help you if you lost your compass.

For the historian seeking to regain the mood and effect of a former time, the first rule, after ascertaining the validity of the spot, is, "Don't look up." The jet airplane has made historical purity a sporadic thing. There is no place where time has been allowed to stand still if it is on the flight path of a modern airplane; cities of the desert, the untrodden wilderness, the mountain-top hermit, the isolated fort or mail station, all lie under the contrails of the oblivious jet.

When the Conklings made this run in 1931, they reported the sixty-mile section between Cornuda station and Fort Bliss, in El

Paso, as the sole remaining portion of the whole route between Tipton and San Francisco that was still virtually undisturbed and unaltered and that could be comfortably driven. Today, that sixty miles has been reduced to a total of about thirty, but the alteration in mileage does not represent an alteration in the views and the landscape. The Conklings found, "winter or summer, there is no drive more pleasant and inviting and filled with more fascinating interest than to follow over this old way . . . few fences, no disfiguring road signs and pole lines, and no indication of habitation."[28] Except for the addition of a few utility lines, and the gate to one large ranch complex (apparently a corporate-owned retreat), the same can be said of the road today until it starts southeast toward Texas again, crossing the state border within sight of Cerro Alto and leading almost directly south between a set of solitary mesas and mountains until U.S. 62/180 is reached. The old road turned west shortly after passing Cerro Alto and took two routes to reach the Hueco Tanks; one called the north pass, one the south. Both have long since been fenced.

To reach the Hueco Tanks station you continue on the highway west, twisting through more ups and downs of the Hueco Mountains, and then turn north on the park road that makes a direct eight-mile run north to Hueco Tanks State Park. Today this area is famous around the world as a rock climbing and bouldering site. The mountains surrounding the Tanks are, in actuality, huge separate rocks, with a natural amphitheater within the four major parts: North Mountain, East Mountain, East Spur, and West Mountain. A would-be developer once put a dam across one end of the open area and created a lake, but the water leaked out through fissures in the rock. The development turned out to be something of a scam, so fortunately, this DisneyLand approach near the Hueco Tanks fizzled. A longer, leak-tight dam was built at a different site in 1970 when the state opened the park.

As rock climbers are a unique group, their guidebook on climbing the rocks around the Tanks is worth buying at the store that is on the road just outside the park gates. Although it has nothing to do with the Butterfield station—in fact, doesn't mention it—the book is worth owning for some of the amusing names the individual climbs have acquired. A series of climbs on East Mountain starts with "World's Hottest Gossip," goes to "Hide Pounds Fast," and eventually includes such astonishing titles as, "Mom Sells Kidney to Buy Furniture," "Bigfoot Is a Woman," "Kidnapped By Monkeys," and "The Astonishing Flying Guru." Do not ask a non-rock climber the significance of these, but given their adventurous spirit, some of the early-day travelers might have fit right in with the modern group.[29]

The inscriptions, as well as the pictographs, are to be found in several areas of the rocks, not just at the north end where the Butterfield stage stand was. The inscriptions near the water hole itself are protected as much as possible by the park rangers, but decades of neglect have allowed a lot of the Indian pictographs and pioneer *paso por aqui* names to be obliterated by present day pop sayings and obscenities. There is an interesting inscription by one J. Nardboe, who was at Hueco Tanks in July of 1856. Johan Nardboe was the son of one of the first Norwegian families to come to Texas. Several Narboe (as the name came to be spelled) families had Peters Colony grants which underlie large parts of Oak Cliff in Dallas.

A growing menace to Hueco Tanks rock art comes from gang graffiti. Felt markers, spray paint and charcoal mar several sites thought to be between 1,000 and 2,000 years old. Most of this damage is irreparable. In 1880, Burr Duval, writing of another Trans-Pecos location, admonished:

On the face of the cliff are numerous Indian picture-writings in red ochre. . . . It struck me as rather singular and suggestive that in all these "picture writings". . . there nowhere appears anything obscene. Give the cultured Saxon a piece of red chalk and tell him to draw something and the chances are ten to one it will be a nasty figure or an obscene idea expressed somehow. So much for our boasted civilization.[30]

184

The Butterfield station site was at the north end of North Mountain and is marked a few yards west of the old ranch house of former owner Silvero Escontrias—that ranch house now part of the park. The park is entirely surrounded by a cyclone-type fence. Picnic facilities are free here, but campgrounds have a modest nightly cost. The park also has an entrance fee, but it is also modest and worth the effort. It is difficult today, in the confines of the park, to imagine the Butterfield station, the stage arriving, the hostlers out with lanterns to take care of the teams while the passengers were fed. The magnificent and overwhelming view of the mountains themselves tends to wipe out the thoughts of former historical sites, although there are a good many other than those associated with the Butterfield Overland Mail line.

Leading southwest away from the station site is an old portion of the Butterfield road, named "Butterfield Trail," but regardless of the noble intent of the developers (it is outside the park), it is as rough a stretch as a wheeled vehicle can sustain. But at whatever cost, it should be traced for the five miles it can be traversed. It gets better as you go, and the present road which turns directly south, while not in the Butterfield stage's path, catches the spirit of that enterprise, clanking over a series of mesas and plateaus before regaining our old friends, U.S. Highways 62/180. From this point the highway leads alongside modern Fort Bliss (you come to a corner of the reservation as you depart the small section of old Butterfield Trail), and passes El Paso International Airport—suitably juxtaposed to the old road to be considered a nice historical contrast. If you seek as much authenticity as possible, stay on U.S. 180 south of Concordia Cemetery—remnant of Concordia Ranch, one of the original "towns" of El Paso—until you get to Highway 478. Turn left (when headed west) onto San Antonio, paralleling a canal, until you get to Raynor, where you take a right (north) over the canal. Go two blocks to Magoffin (I didn't say it was simple), where you turn left on Peña, which almost immediately becomes Magoffin again. On Magoffin you will pass the site of Magoffinville, another of the early "towns," and then after rejoining San Antonio (it doesn't go through from its canal-side stretch), turn left almost anywhere to Overland Street. Continue to El Paso Street, and you have arrived at the place where the Butterfield station for so many years marked the heart of old El Paso. C. L. Sonnichsen notes, "The glory of the Overland line's mid-point, the El Paso terminal, is long gone, replaced by brick commercial buildings a couple of blocks from downtown El Paso."[31]

* * * * * * *

Although the 1858 Butterfield Trail had taken my wife and me through the Guadalupe Mountains, across a part of New Mexico, and delivered us to El Paso, we were not through with tracing the Butterfield Overland Mail's path across Texas. To do this we had to return to Horsehead Crossing, this time on the west bank, and follow the 1859 rerouting which sent the Butterfield mail coaches southwestwardly, swinging by Fort Stockton, through the Davis Mountains, and up the Rio Grande's ancient river road to El Paso.

The Butterfield stage made the run to Fort Stockton by a direct route from Horsehead Crossing, and as far as the topography is involved, it could be easily done today. The region is quite flat, with few obstacles to a cross-country passage. Unfortunately, modern highways, trails and ownership boundaries force the traveler to use a mixed-media kind of road (paved, broken, gravel, then paved again) which led by the forgotten village of Buena Vista. It is as straight as a surveyor's instrument can make it.

Arriving at Fort Stockton, you find a very interesting old town southwest of the new one. The Butterfield stage swung in below the present town, touching the fort and passing the celebrated Comanche Spring (or Springs), then among the largest in the southwest. Alas, today the springs are bone dry, and what was once a huge outdoor swimming pool, fed by the springs, has been physically cut down to half size and filled by means of a municipal water supply. The dry springs outlet, still covered by a protective grill, is very sad to contemplate. In the summer of 1939 I spent some time in Fort Stockton with my uncle, Grady Cole, who owned a movie house

186

there. Every week there was some sort of water entertainment offered at the springs. The big grandstands are still maintained.

The fort itself, rebuilt after the Civil War, offers several restored buildings, with shops in one. Like Fort Concho in San Angelo, it is surrounded by the town. Adjoining the Fort Stockton ruins is a still lovely park, its many channels and canals once fed by the huge flow of the springs, a sad reminder of better days.

The courthouse square, across which the path of the Butterfield stage lay, has enough historical structures around it so that the area is more than worth spending an hour or so touring. The tree-shaded square is more like a plaza than the usual courthouse square. The courthouse sits to one side, not in the center. A "zero stone" denotes the official center point of the 1875 town of St. Gall. The Butterfield station, at the southwest corner across from the square, has been replaced by the courts building. The oldest structure in Fort Stockton is the adobe sutler's store of the original 1859 post. It sits only a block south of the square at Nelson and Sherer streets. Peter Gallagher, the man from whom the town of St. Gall got its name, had a store and post office which stood on the southeast corner of the square.

The Butterfield Trail picked up the old San Antonio-El Paso mail road at Comanche Springs and went directly west along U.S. I-20 (U.S. 290) passing Leon Springs waterhole. Turning off I-20 onto Kennedy Road, to follow the trail as closely as possible, you encounter a seven or eight mile section of open trail that is probably very much like it was when the stage passed over it going southwest. But beware. Although county maps show it continuing another five miles, the rough path encounters a locked gate, and you must let your imagination send the Butterfield stage continuing into the low hills that lie before you. The trail of the old mail road going west later intersects Hovey Road, which goes off I-20 to the south a few miles beyond Kennedy Road. But be warned again, unless you can obtain permission to use this part of the trail you are stopped by a locked ranch gate before you can even start.

Telling ourselves that the Butterfield road would have demolished our automobile, and that we certainly got the genuine feel of the

1859 stagecoach running in the few desolate miles we managed, we returned to I-20 and sped to Balmorhea, taking Highway 17 out of that pretty little village. One 1849 explorer said a Spanish outpost had been built here a century or more before, and another writer found fruit trees growing near here that had been planted during Spanish ownership of Texas and Mexico. Balmorhea's name sounds Spanish, but it is a contraction of the names of three land promoters who laid out the town in 1906: Balcom, Morrow and Rhea. So much for the romance of Texas names.[32]

The Balmorhea State Park, with its enormous spring-fed outdoor swimming pool, once advertised as the largest such in the world, is worth the short side trip. The San Solomon Springs here gush forth in quite an impressive flow. You might also, as you turn off I-20, get a glimpse of the locally owned Pecos Valley Southern Railroad ("Pea Vine Special"), a little thirty-four mile line for which disaster has been predicted for decades—but still running in the 1990s with modern equipment. Once, as a boy, I observed the spectacular motive power for the road, at that time a Model T Ford equipped with flanged wheels and a handmade wooden body to accommodate two or three passengers, some packages, and a mail bag or two.

Highway 17 goes straight south and quickly becomes a lovely piece of travel, heading toward the looming peaks, then squirming in between the Barilla Mountains to the east and Star Mountain to the west. As the highway makes a sharp right turn around Star Mountain, we found an unlocked gate for the trail alongside Limpia Creek which led to the site of Limpia Station. (Barilla Springs station was several miles back east on this trail.) This is one section of the Butterfield that will defeat anything short of a big pickup truck. When first entering this particular part, we encountered a friendly young cowboy, mounted on a four-wheel steed, and asked about the road. It is a private road, he said, but he didn't reckon anyone would object to our using it. However, the gate on the highway is usually locked, and might be locked again at any time, so nobody knowing we were traveling the road, we might find ourselves unable to resume our travels for a few, possibly several, hours. Rather nervously, Judy and I proceeded and reached the spot where the station had been, but the combination of fears about locked gates and rugged roads persuaded us to inch our vehicle around and go back to Highway 17 at a crawl.

By now our admiration for the Conklings in their 1930 Buick, using shovels to make a road where one no longer existed, reached proportions of awe. But though they drove in a day when there were no interstate highways, and scarcely any paved roads at all along the Butterfield Trail, they also had the advantage of a time when there were no strangers to the farmers and ranchers. Even the busiest farmer or rancher would stop whatever was underway to either lead the historical researchers to some site or allow them the freedom to roam around on his land until they found it. Today the interstate highways, the motor vehicles, television, changing industries, and game hunters work against that kind of knowledge. The small towns and villages that once formed some kind of nucleus for the area around them—furnishing a post office or a school at least—are now gone, the post office closed by a rural route and the schools consolidated so a fleet of yellow school buses can carry the students sixty, eighty, or a hundred miles a day. Also, most of the big ranches are now owned by inheritors or managed by corporations in cities hundreds or thousands of miles away. And thanks to television's view of American history, a West Texas landowner might believe in the historical importance of the Oregon Trail and not even know about the Butterfield Trail that passed over his own property.

At the foot of Star Mountain, Highway 17 enters Wild Rose Pass, or what is so described today. The actual pass has been circumvented by the modern road—a bulldozer can change more history in a week than a historian can record in a lifetime. Today's highway nonetheless makes an awesome passage along Limpia Creek. At the summit of the modern pass there are historical markers calling attention to the importance of this route, not just to the army troops, the emigrant wagons and mail coaches, but to the Native Americans who centuries earlier found this the way through the fastness of the wooded "Pah-cut" mountains, as the Apaches were said to have called them. Judy had a suggestion which I think has a great deal of artistic as well as historical merit. "Why not," she asked as we stood, looking up, breathing the high, cool, air, impressed by the rocky beauty of it all, "plant wild roses in profusion all along Wild Rose Pass?" Opinions differ as to when the wild roses disappeared, but if they grew here once they would grow here again.

Going through Limpia Canyon—named for the creek whose name means clear, or limpid—you by necessity pass along and pass over the tracks of the old mail road. There are places where the narrowing canyon scarcely admits, even to the bulldozer, room for a roadway. Pretty as it is today, how lovely it must have been in its fresh, vibrant naturalness, when the loudest sound was the striking of a horse hoof on the path. Even in modern times Limpia Canyon has been famous for the number of times the road crosses Limpia Creek. Today the number is down to something like eighteen; in an earlier day, when I came along here with my grandmother, she driving a 1935 Chevrolet sedan, we *forded* (not crossed), Limpia twenty-seven times. My grandmother, always alert for the possibility of disaster, could scarcely keep her eyes on the tortuous road, so sure she was that despite the bright sunlit day, a "wall of water" would, any moment, come roaring down out of the mountains to wash us and our Chevy tumbling down the canyon. (I don't mean to make fun of her; these walls of water happened many times on Limpia Creek.)

Just as you start into the town of Fort Davis, the highway comes in from McDonald Observatory, there is a Mexican food restaurant which, reputedly, has one exposed adobe wall that belonged to the stage station. I'm not told which of the stage stations this was; it could have been any one of several because the San Antonio to El Paso, Santa Fe and San Diego mail roads—in addition to the Butterfield—all came across this spot. The Conklings specify this as the

Butterfield station location but do not mention the adobe wall.

The mail road led straight in toward the town of Fort Davis and sliced through a lower portion of the fort itself. Walking on the parade grounds today—Fort Davis is now a federal historical site—you occasionally are electrified by the sharp notes of bugles blowing, but do not let your romanticism overcome your eyes; the fort, while partially reconstructed, is still abandoned—and the sound is off a tape being played from headquarters. In the summer, however, a cavalry troop, said to be the last such to be officially part of the U.S. Army, is stationed here and performs maneuvers on the parade grounds. Someday, undoubtedly long after the writer of this book is himself history, the nation will realize the historical value of the frontier forts and reconstruct or preserve them, much as Europe has done with its castles. Someday, too, the descendants of Native Americans will realize that these outposts, while most of them were built to guard against their ancestors, are, in fact, monuments to the daring and persistence of a brave foe, facing the ineluctable odds of numbers and a more advanced technology.

The Butterfield Trail, leaving the fort grounds, parallels the modern highway along a city street about one block to the north. The street can be followed westward out of town, passing several interesting structures, including a New Englandish Presbyterian Church which, when we passed, had sheep grazing in the front yard. The town of Fort Davis is unusual in that it not only lies almost a mile high among the mountains, but it also has a quaint kind of sophistication. As you walk around the old city square and along the courthouse sidewalks in this seat of Jeff Davis County, you see quite a few pickup drivers, male and female, whom you sense are not cowboys. And when you observe a vehicle with the name of a famed university on its door, you realize a number of scientific agencies as well as academic centers are located here because of McDonald Observatory atop Mount Locke. Also, Fort Davis is blessed with a number of well liked eating places, and the historic old Limpia Hotel whose upper gallery is the finest place in Texas for a late-afternoon preprandial drink. But book well in advance, especially in summer. Despite the difficulty of getting here, Fort Davis is crowded with tourists who are escaping the Texas heat.

From Fort Davis going southwest, the Butterfield Trail skirted the mountain closely, edging along the giant rocky extrusion and paralleling the modern road, although seldom by more than a few hundred yards. The modern pilgrim, turning west on Highway 166, sees pretty much the same sights as the nineteenth-century stagecoach passenger. Unfortunately, Jim Gillett's bronze plaque dedicated to the old stage drivers at Point of Rocks is now on private property, and the spring that created the stage stop there has long since gone dry. From approximately ten miles west of Fort Davis, the modern road begins to cross and sometimes follows the old mail road. It's down there, somewhere, under the asphalt and concrete, portions of it dipped in blood. You must try to feel some of this—not just the blood but the whole saga of desperate enterprise—if chasing the Butterfield is to make sense. Besides, the old road was used before the Butterfield and continued to be used, never safely, for over two decades after Butterfield's Overland Mail stopped running.

This was the mail road, and hundreds of persons at both ends of the run waited with all the intensity and emotion we today feel, waiting for the mail. It was, it is, a magic phrase: the United States Mail. What else could drive us over mountains, through snow, floods and drought—never mind the weather—over deserts and into danger zones where death was never very far off? The mail must go through. Sometimes historians forget that the Butterfield Overland stage line was created to carry mail, and that was its primary concern. The U.S. government spent hundreds of thousands of dollars, which it knew would not be recovered, to deliver the mail to the isolated West Coast—an average cost of $69 per letter was attached to some routes—but that was what was demanded by the people. Letters, especially in those days before the development of the telephone and the spread of the telegraph, could be worth lives, not just of those who delivered them, but of those sending and waiting for them. All the urgency and speed of the Butterfield Overland Mail was dedicated to this one end.

Although you may be prepared for it, the sight of Skillman's Grove, for the past century Bloys' Camp Meeting place, is stunning. The giant oaks sweep across the highway and continue for almost a mile toward the mountains. And even with modern development covering acres and acres around the grove—cabins and cantonment-type shelters, camp roads and direction signs—the place with its remote location, its beauty, its atmosphere that frees the emotions, is altogether fulfilling. Skillman's Grove, like some other points on the Butterfield Trail, is worth whatever it may take to get there.

The modern highway dodges around high rocks and points of rocks, and now and then cattle in the middle of the road. The Barrel Springs Butterfield station site is not on the modern road, but on Barrel Springs Ranch, once owned by the legendary Texas Ranger Jim Gillett. The ranch is still in business and has a sign out on Highway 505.

As Judy and I drove through the valleys and onto the plateaus near Valentine, we saw in the sky a blimp floating over the scene south of the Southern Pacific Railroad. Judy immediately guessed it was up there attempting to spot wrongdoers, probably drug runners. Suddenly, coming into the ken of this eye in the sky, we felt guilty—though neither of us had ever used the recreational drugs the balloon was attempting to intercept—and almost wished we could crouch down in the car so as to hide. Then, watching the silvery shape so silently sailing along, we began to admire the beauty of this modern stranger in our ancient landscape. It stayed in sight for miles and miles, turning slowly, finally passing behind us as we moved west along I-10. Later, a border guard at the Fort Hancock crossing of the Rio Grande vouched for our supposition that it was a government airship on drug patrol, equipped with instruments that could read a wristwatch on someone below it.

The old mail road passed almost straight across the open country north of Valentine, below El Muerto Peak, not joining U.S. 90 and the railroad until Chispa siding. Valentine, the smaller of the only two towns in the 2,265 square miles of Jeff Davis County, has truly romantic connections. It was named by a railroad construction gang which reached the spot on February 14, 1882. Once a division point on the Southern Pacific Railroad, it is quaintly listed as "inactive" on the official Jeff Davis County map of the State Department of Highways, but it comes to life once a year, in February, when letter writers from all over the world send their Valentine's Day love letters to this tiny Texas town to be hand stamped (by the one-woman staff) with a heart-shaped cachet: "Valentine, Texas, Valentine Station, February 14, 19— 79854." This has thrown the U.S. Postal Service into something of a quandary: keep the post office open, just so thousands of letters in that one month can be postmarked and dispatched with the unique loving geography inscribed? So far, lovers of the world have united in saying "Yes!"[33]

A year after Judy and I had first trailed the Butterfield, we took two other couples, Bob and Nancy Green and Fred and Jerrie Smith, on a revisit to the far western parts of the route. Bob, being a rancher with rancher friends all over Texas, got us invited to spend the night at the Reynolds Long X Ranch, far beyond the Pecos. Cliff Teinert, manager of the Long X, took us to have a chuck wagon dinner on the Means Moon Ranch, just across the mountains from the Long X. Both ranches are in the mountainous highlands south of Kent, a busy oasis of a store, filling station and post office (and nothing else) along the lonesomest stretch of Interstate 10.

Distance having little meaning to a Trans-Pecos rancher, Teinert drove us forty-five miles down to where Jon and Jackie Means had the chuck wagon cook busy. After a superb range meal—big grilled steaks, pinto beans, pan-fried potatoes, handmade biscuits, homemade pecan pie (from Jackie), coffee and ice tea, if you'd like to know what working cowboys eat—Jon mentioned that "a few miles" of the Butterfield Trail crossed the lower end of his ranch, going from

194

El Muerto (The Dead Man) station to Van Horn Wells. (You don't ask a Texas rancher how big his ranch is, but sizes of both the Moon Ranch and the Long X are more handily expressed in sections than in acres.)

We drove a few miles south, and there it was, the Butterfield Trail, easily discernible because of the difference in the vegetation of the trail and of the land alongside it. The trail is a long yellow pathway of grass, quite distinct from the other grasses. Larger rocks were pushed aside to shape a golden road that stretches west in a line across this wide, high valley, disappearing toward the Chispa Mountains. The Means family has been ranching in this region since the 1880s, and the Conklings, when they were here in the 1930s, said stumps of the poles of the 1876 military telegraph line could be found along part of the road. Jon said he thought it had been at least a century since the trail had been used. The Southern Pacific railroad from the south and the Texas & Pacific from the east built through in 1882, and that pretty well ended use of the stagecoach for intercity mail and passengers.

Standing under a high, autumnal sky, air fresh and bracing, the elevation at nearly a mile, the land rolling away in all directions, framed on all sides by mountains, I felt the Butterfield Trail take on a sudden emotional meaning, possibly the feeling those early passengers had as they reached this region, exclaiming to themselves that here was "the West," if a visual and emotional definition of that far country could be made. Fred Smith, a Maine native who has carefully preserved his Down East accent through nearly four decades of Texas residence, stood looking in awe, saying to Jon Means, "I can see why your family could never leave. I never would."

This is possibly the best preserved portion of any of the Butterfield roads; no asphalt, no gravel, no automobile tire tracks to dilute the sensation. We walked a mile of the trail, feeling, as we walked, the rumble of the stagecoaches, the hard cloppity-clop of the mules jarring the earth, hearing the jingle of harness and chains, as the coaches made good time across this wide level passage. Time had receded; you didn't have to close your eyes to be aboard the stage. What you saw was what the driver saw, what the riders saw, not even a fence or a utility pole to corrupt your gaze. In the peace, but the excitement, of the moment, it was hard to return to *now*.

The old mail road crossed U.S. 90 where a historical marker notes its passage heading for the station at Van Horn's Wells, a few hundred yards west of the highway. It can be walked, permission gained to do so. Trespassing on land is considered a major offense, especially in our day when hunting rights in some regions bring in millions of dollars per year. Non-paying hunters can expect severe consequences if apprehended. Since it is usually easy to obtain permission to visit historic sites, why take a chance?

The stage road followed slightly south of the Southern Pacific Railroad, to pick its way across the deserty foothills of the Van Horn Mountains. The historical traveler must continue to Van Horn, then take a rough gravel road leading southwest from town to visit the Butterfield traces at Eagle Flat Draw. Again, a private road stops further movement, so back to Van Horn we go. The landscape below Van Horn is almost surrealistic. You are surrounded on three sides by mountains that look like someone painted them there; a well done but artificial backdrop for a western movie.

Proceeding northwest on I-10 again at Van Horn, you reach the great Allamore talcum plant where the crusher has put a slight coat of white powder on all the buildings. The town was named for Alla, wife of W. S. Moore, one of its 1885 founders. Here another rocky gravel road leads south to Hot Wells on the Southern Pacific and past that about a mile to where the stage line crossed and traces of the mail road may be seen. But, having made it, we did not think it worth the jolting trip. We rejoined I-10, still marveling at our ignorance on the topic of talcum production, and drove to Sierra Blanca.

Sierra Blanca is famous for the fact that here, in 1882, the race between the Galveston, Houston & San Antonio Railway (later Southern Pacific), building toward El Paso from San Antonio, and the Texas & Pacific Railway, building furiously across West Texas from Weatherford toward the same goal, came to a tie. Thus, from Sierra Blanca the two roads (the T&P is now Union Pacific) share trackage to El Paso. And though we do not recommend spending the night there (let us tell you about 1930s motels in tiny towns), Sierra Blanca proved to be the gateway to what we consider the wildest, most picturesque miles on the entire Butterfield stage line through Texas: Quitman Canyon entered by Quitman Pass.

Throughout our journey along the old Butterfield Trail, we had sought spots or pieces of road where the drama of its history was powerful enough to be almost palpable. The pleasant roads among the green hills of back-country Wise and Montague counties certainly leave you with a "long ago" feeling, as does that unpaved section west of Jacksboro and the stretch crossing the West Fork of the Trinity River with its beautiful fording place unchanged. But in all these spots there is the hand of modern man: the Wise and Montague county roads are paved, utility poles and oil well pump-jacks dot the Jacksboro gravel section, and the Trinity ford is best seen from an iron bridge that is old fashioned, true, but dating from long after the Butterfield stage plunged into the river below.

Mountain Pass almost qualifies for "is-as-was," if you can overlook the barbed wire fences (they're mostly hidden by vines), and the view up Valley Creek comes close, save for a bridge. But Mountain Pass is a short trip, and Valley Creek but a single site. Even Horsehead Crossing, lonely and bleak on the Pecos, is historically exciting, but the river is nowhere near either the size or volume of its former day, and the place where wagon, ferry, or the thousands of cattle made their way to a far shore, only a sufficiently endowed historical imagination can create.

But going toward Quitman Pass and Quitman Canyon, the present disappears as you leave Highway 1111 at the base of 4,500-foot Devil Ridge and take the path leading southwest into the mountains. Judy and I departed Sierra Blanca early in the morning and drove along Highway 1111 in semi-darkness. The mountains that surround you make day late and night early. When we turned off the pavement we almost immediately found ourselves moving back in time. The oft-bloody history of Quitman Pass and Canyon seized us so that by the time we had reached the tightly twisting, turning, mountainous portions of the road, both of us were prepared to find our way blocked by horsemen, hide shields and spears warning us that this was their territory. Even the immediate flora is menacing: tall, thin cactus arms seem to be reaching toward you. At night I imagine this is absolutely frightening. Judy, Missouri born, gave serious thought to an Apache ambush, but her West Texas born husband, while assuring her the last Apache death on this trail had occurred in 1880, slyly flipped the automatic locks on our vehicle doors.

The road quickly degenerated into a trail which shortly becomes a trace, a mere footpath. At the numerous crossings where mountain torrents have torn away the approaches, you must ease your vehicle carefully over the washouts; moving so slowly the speedometer scarcely registers it—a speed no faster than the stagecoach made—you ease your way upward. Time after time we were forced to make an S-curve across a deep draw (which obviously washes out every time there is a rain), and immediately make a corkscrew turn just as we were negotiating a ten-inch drop-off. Apache ambush? Maybe not—but I'm certain that the spirits of those old Apache warriors must watch with glee the difficulties of modern motorized passage. This isn't Jeep or four-wheel-drive country: this is horse and foot country. This has to be the most dramatic road in Texas; at least as dramatic as any to which the public has access.

Judy remarks, with a touch of awe, "Nothing has ever given me more respect for the Butterfield Trail, for the stage drivers, for the people who came west—than going through Quitman canyon. This is exactly like it was." The sandy watercourse, which crisscrosses the trail and runs beside it so that you can't get away from it, sometimes looks like a smooth wide road, the underpinnings for a major highway—and yet, it's a dry river; and I can just imagine what a torrent it becomes in a downpour.

But here, amidst the gloom of a mountain morning, over roads so rocky and unkept that I vow my steel-belted radials are pushing aside a good many rocks last pushed aside by the iron tires of the stage-coaches, I feel totally immersed in the lure of "the trail": Henry Skillman's run, the U.S., Mexican, and Indian troops of the back-and-forth wars across and along the Rio Grande—it was all here for me, in these canyons, on this untended road that has neither fence nor pole nor pump jack; as it was, and as I hope it will always be.

As we reach Quitman Pass we find the sun gradually making its way over the mountains. Topping the pass, I sense the puffing of the mules, the rattle and jingle of harness, the pop of the whip, the cries of the driver—a triumphant moment for every run of the mail coach. Coming off the pass, moving down the canyon, we eventually reach a high, open ridge that can only be described, burnished by the morning light, as glorious. The car stopped, as though by its own decision, and both of us got out to look around and breathe and shout. It seemed to us we had been hours traversing these sixteen miles or so and that, like explorers of old, we had found a new country. I cannot explain this feeling other than to say we had been in another century, and now we were returning to our own. And having found what we were looking for, we will never go back.

Unfortunately for history, particularly for the history of the Butterfield Overland Mail and the other mail runs that came this way for so many years, the Rio Grande, lying at the southern mouth of Quitman Canyon, has been confined, its channel turned, straightened, and denied water. Once you descend from the thrilling heights of the Quitman Canyon area, it becomes an ugly, dusty country—with a redeeming backdrop. Beginning the drive toward El Paso, you see an impressive mountain range on your left, and at first you are not sure where the river is: does it flow among the mountains? But you realize these high mountains are in Mexico and do not touch the Rio Grande.

Much of the famed old River Road up to El Paso was demolished in the twentieth century by a river rectification project. What replaced it, Highway 192 and Highway 20, passes along paved and easy, but is historically neutral. This road along the river is mostly cotton fields, a little grain—and a lot of desert. You can quickly see the difference in what happens to this desert when you irrigate.

The ruins of Fort Quitman lie near the river on private grounds with a few adobe buildings remaining, although not "resembling marble in their several coats of whitewash" as Richardson found them in 1859.[34] The town that once lay around the fort bearing the same name has made a sad departure, leaving evidence, in one ruin, of some fairly heavy industry: two exceptionally heavy electrical towers, once used to feed power to some vanished gin or processing plant, now left lonely and disconnected in a barren area.

The cultivated region increases as you progress toward The Pass. Room-sized stacks of compressed seed cotton, covered with yellow, orange, or blue plastic wrappings, give a touch of color to the empty gray fields. At Fort Hancock, the town, we turned the short distance to the river and engaged the U.S. Customs agent—who happened, like Judy, to be Missouri born—in an enlightening conversation about the modern border. We advanced to the center of the modest bridge that passes over the modest Rio Grande, and by moving a few inches back and forth around the boundary monument (a childish game, I will admit), I visited, then departed, the Republic of Mexico dozens of times—in five minutes! The Rio Grande in the vicinity of El Paso, in fact, for a hundred miles below, is a most disappointing river, nothing to match the heroic original name, Rio Bravo del Norte: Wild River of the North.

At Fort Hancock we pick up Highway 20, which was part of the Camino Real of Spanish empire days. It passes by the site of old Fort Hancock, now a large cotton patch, marked by a historical tablet atop a wide platform made of red bricks salvaged from the fort itself. Camp Rice, the original 1884 name for Fort Hancock, is commemorated by a shattered dedication stone, set in concrete, said to have been found amidst the ruins when Fort Hancock was razed. There are small roads leading toward the river at many points, but there are no crossings other than the official ones. Down some of these roads you may observe the cultivation of chile peppers, an increasingly important crop as more and more of the nation seeks a taste of the fiery *salsas* and food known as Tex-Mex. In the season when we passed there were gangs out picking the red and green chiles. I had thought that jalapeños (my lovely ambrosia) would be harvested with a machine, but it was being done by hand; stoop labor. However, I explained to Judy, they can have all they can eat. (Judy, to whom plain black pepper is sufficiently warm, cringed.)

Much of this modern road was obviously laid over the old mail and military roads to El Paso. As at Wild Rose Pass, there's nowhere else for it to have gone as it follows the river. Rio Grande station was located near the western edge of Hudspeth County, but the station site now appears to be under either an irrigation canal or a field of cotton. In this part of the river it is almost hopeless to find old landmarks, because everything has been torn down and turned into crop lands.

Nearing the community of Alamo Alto, the roads and the railroad enter El Paso County and carry us into Mountain Time, thereby losing (or is it gaining?) an hour. Staying on Highway 20 (half a dozen different routes become available at this point), we go through Alamo Alto and Tornillo, both once on the river. We then reach Fabens, a more modern city than the little Mexican communities that outdate it by centuries. Ben Ficklin's El Toro station was located between present-day Fabens and Cuadrilla, on the old river bed. Highway 258 (as we drop off from Highway 20) continues to follow, in general, the mail trail. The character of the valley here is a little different from the lower, deserty section. You have some old and quite large trees bordering the canals, a large pecan orchard gives the impression of a wooded preserve, and the mountains of Mexico gain more color as you drive along the American side.[35]

On the road by the river, you see a lot of strange harvesting machinery, with cabs riding high upon one side, or up front, or in back. You don't know whether that's where the person rides who drives it or whether that's someone who just guides it behind other power.

The next Butterfield station was at the historic town of San Elizario, once located across the Rio Grande in Mexico and today retaining much of its Spanish-Mexican origin and the charm of a Mexican village. The plaza is tree shaded with a bandstand in the center and around it are historic buildings, including an adobe Roman Catholic church, containing the carved wooden statue of San Elzeario (the original spelling), patron saint of the town. A building across the south end called "Los Portales" (The Arcade or Porches) is noted as being the first site of any number of important developments in the community. The streets of San Elizario twist and turn in a manner perhaps considered haphazard, but how could square blocks work in a simpatico place like this? Too much history has taken place in this village to describe even the bulk of it, but on the plaza are several large detailed tablets relating the past. The station was located in a building, still standing, facing the wall of the old presidio, just off the plaza.

A few miles farther is Socorro, settled around 1683, even earlier than San Elizario. Socorro has San Miguel church in which resides another famed religious statue, the carved wooden likeness of that saint, brought from Mexico City more than 300 years ago. It is venerated throughout the valley. Although the town (now engulfed by El Paso) was not a Butterfield station, the stage did drop off and pick up passengers here. Continuing up the road, Ysleta is, like Socorro, now part of greater El Paso. Ysleta was on the route of the mail stages, but Butterfield did not have a station there.

Finding your way to downtown El Paso by way of the old road becomes a puzzle for the modern traveler, and sticking parallel to the Southern Pacific Railroad may be as near as you can get without a local guide to interpret older street directions. The Butterfield company's elaborate Franklin station was in what is now downtown El Paso, covering most of the area from Overland Street (named for the stage line when it opened in 1859) on the north, Oregon Street (not then opened) to the east and El Paso Street to the west. The station building, with a twelve-arch arcade, fronted 112 feet on El Paso

Street. The station and corral extended back 141 feet on Overland, where a gate to the corral opened. The installation covered two acres. Razed in 1900, the station was replaced by commercial buildings, including *la esquina descuentos*, or The Discount Corner, at Overland and El Paso.

Other than the name of the street and historical markers, there is no trace of the Butterfield installations and it is difficult to bring back the memory of the imposing station as seen in old pictures. However, a short walk northward brings you to the historic heart of the city, around the plaza, and the atmosphere is pleasant for strolling or using a park bench.

We arrived on a Friday afternoon and the crowds were thick but jovial; there was an air of festival with families out together, street vendors selling their wares, sidewalks crowded. We asked if there was some local holiday or an event of note taking place, but were told it was just Friday afternoon in El Paso and in Juarez across the river.

The old road going north and northwest from modern El Paso is impossible even to track. For one thing, the channel of the Rio Grande is now a mile east of where it was in the middle of the nineteenth century, as you may see by noting the sawtooth edges of the boundary line between Texas and New Mexico, now landlocked, although based on the river as it was in the 1850s. As for the pass for which the city and the region is named (El Paso del Norte), as you drive on I-10 or U.S. 85, the historic significance of the name and the difficulties of the pass are hard to discern. Going along the Rio Grande, you are more impressed by the mammoth smelter works than by river or road. But centuries of travelers found this the gateway to both *Nuevo Mejico* and the Spanish province of *Tejas*. Its use predates either, going back, probably, to Cabeza de Vaca, Dorantes and Estabanico in 1536.

Once I-10 is crossed by Highway 20 heading north and west, the latter follows the mail road more closely. The first station out of El

Paso was called Cottonwoods. The Conklings located it as having been some 350 feet northwest of the Santa Fe Railroad station at LaTuna. Highway 20 follows the Santa Fe closely through this region. The railroad still runs, but LaTuna is a federal correctional institution, although having the look, from afar, of an inviting white walled city.

Although Mesilla is not in Texas, it was the logical ending place for the Texas section, since none of the Texas station sites above El Paso can be discerned; secondly, we were curious to see the old Butterfield station now a Mexican food restaurant named La Posta. Besides, the drive up to Mesilla, staying on Highway 20 and its New Mexico extension, follows the mail road pretty well, and the 8,000-foot Organ Mountains to the east are a beautiful accompaniment. The morning after our stay in Mesilla they were suddenly white crowned, after a light snowfall in the upper region.

The Butterfield stage line paused at Fort Fillmore, the ruins of which can be found wedged between I-10 and New Mexico Highway 478 about six miles south of Las Cruces. The Butterfield company installed a ferry over the Rio Grande a short distance from the fort, halfway between there and Mesilla, which then lay west of the river. The huge flood of 1865 shifted the river channel so far west that Mesilla was left a few miles to the east of it, where it is today. In 1858, Ormsby found the river, which the stage forded, "an insignificant puddle, being very low." But the Reverend Tallack, in 1860, reported it to be four hundred feet wide, twelve feet deep "and very rapid."[36]

Ormsby, while admiring the crops and the irrigation system around Mesilla, found the people "squalid, dirty . . . and indolent" remarking on the town itself, "I never saw such a miserable set of people in my life." A few "speculating yankees," he observed, who were making fortunes keeping stores, "get what prices they please for what goods they please."[37]

Today, we were pleased to find the little town a charming, Mexican-influenced place; the plaza, where the Confederate flag was once raised, is lined with many old buildings and many varied out-lets. The reconstructed Butterfield station is itself a sort of arcade, allowing visitors to come and go without having to partake of food or other wares if they just want to look around. As for the Mesilla merchants of today getting "what prices they please for what goods they please," that, happily, is not the case. My wife, for instance, found herself possessed of a beautiful silver concha belt at some-thing like half the ticketed price.

In Mesilla—after following the Butterfield Trail into, across, and out of Texas—Judy and I became concerned that in the name of his-torical fulfillment we should continue on to Apache Pass in Arizona to see the only spot where a Butterfield stagecoach was ever at-tacked. About 150 miles from Mesilla, it is a short distance by the standards of West Texas, which we had just finished crisscrossing. But time, that decider of destinations, ruled we shouldn't, so the Apache Pass had to wait a year and become part of a motor trip to California.

On that later trip, we didn't try to visit all the numerous Butter-field stations west through New Mexico, although they lie on one side or another of Interstate 10, the highway we traveled. Our one disappointment was that Soldier's Farewell—the station which shares status with Phantom Hill as the Butterfield Trail's most un-usual name—failed to show up as we hurried over the Continental Divide, in the Burro Mountains between Silver City and Lordsburg. Legend has it that in 1856 a U.S. dragoon camped there with Major Enoch Steen[38] on the way to take over Tucson, suddenly went mad, dashed from his tent, cried, "Farewell, everybody!" and before he could be restrained, shot himself through the head. J. M. Farwell, the *Alta California* correspondent of San Francisco, put a bit more romance in his report of October, 1858:

The romantic and somewhat musical name arose from the cir-cumstances that one becoming weary of a "soldier's couch, and a soldier's fare," bade farewell to "the plumed troop and the big wars," etc., and shortened his life by suicide. The Spanish name is not quite so musical or romantic. It is "Ojo de los Burros."[39]

Having missed that New Mexico site, it was doubly consoling to arrive in Arizona and find that Apache Pass—the station, the road, the geography of the pass itself, and even the weather—exceeded our expectations, which were high to begin with.

The road to Apache Pass leads south out of Bowie, Arizona, which lies only a few miles from the New Mexico line. (The Conklings went southwest from San Simon, Arizona, on a road no longer in public use.) The town of Bowie is named for old Fort Bowie, built in 1862, which lies about twelve miles to the south. A Department of the Interior publication points out that Fort Bowie National Historic Site "[is] dedicated to preserving the Butterfield Mail Route, the Apache Pass Stage Station, Apache Spring, and the Fort Bowie complex"[40] even though the fort was not built until a year after Butterfield coaches had stopped running.

The first two miles of the road out of the town of Bowie lead through a commercial grove of thousands and thousands of pistachio nut trees. After that the pavement becomes gravel, then the road goes to gravel and dirt. As you start climbing toward Apache Pass the 8,300-foot Dos Cabezas (Two Heads) peak on the north, and the 8,100-foot peak called Cochise Head on the Chiricahua Mountains to the south frame what looks to be a solid frontier, but gradually the slight nick in the center becomes an opening. You are on the Butterfield Trail by this time. The old mail road did not follow the present county road all the way through the mountains, but branched off to the left just as you reach the eastern entrance to the pass.

Once the auto road has climbed into the mountains you find that Fort Bowie National Historic Site lies a mile and a half to the south and is reached solely by a rough path. The National Park Service has wisely kept auto traffic from the fort itself. There is an adequate parking area at the head of this Park Service trail, and in order to inspect the ruins of the Apache Pass Butterfield station and the fort, you foot it up the path that, as the entry sign assures you, is an easy hike—with one or two exceptions.

The Butterfield Trail, which is crossed on the way to the fort, is easily identified, and easily followed. For much of its climb to the old station it used what is now a wide, sandy wash, winding smoothly uphill, under oak and walnut trees that grow along the ravines. The Park Service has traced the Trail with a line of modest wooden posts. Walking it, you can easily imagine that you are sharing the ride with the old stage travelers: there is little to remind you that time has progressed and the world has changed.

The ruins of the Butterfield station are outlined in rock, with a large stone corral where coach and team were able to enter and be protected—as proved to be the case in the Apache attacks of February, 1861. (The Conklings, in a rare error, reported the station was of adobe, but John C. Cremony, who was an officer with the California Column when it fought the Apaches at the pass, reported, "The [station] house was built of stone, and afforded ample shelter. . . .")[41]

Gazing around at the splendor of the mountains, drinking in the refreshing mile-high air, it is hard to accept the idea that within looking distance so many lives were lost. Tragedy and death overtook not just Butterfield drivers and stationkeepers but freighters and all kinds of travelers in addition to soldiers and Apache tribesmen. Less than a mile on the trail eastward from the station, a detachment from the California Column (the Union force marching toward Texas to take El Paso) saved itself from a deadly ambush by firing mountain howitzers into the group of astonished Apache ambushers hidden on the hillsides of the valley that leads to Apache Spring (which still flows). Major Cremony said he afterwards learned "from a prominent Apache who was present in the engagement," that while only three warriors died from musketry fired, 63 were killed by the shelling. The next day another ambush was attempted in an even narrower valley, but again the howitzers, after one cannon team had a stupid mishap, finally felled the ambushers. The Apache chief told Cremony, "We would have done well enough if you had not fired wagons at us." Cremony adds, "The howitzers being on wheels, were deemed a species of wagon by the Apaches, wholly inexperienced in that sort of warfare."[42]

Apache Spring was the reason the Butterfield engineers sent the trail this way, why the station was located where it was, and later, why Fort Bowie was established here. You are able to walk to the spring today, now walled in and flowing only a trickle, but enough to create a pleasant little rivulet through the site of two bloody battles.

The path to the ruins of Fort Bowie passes the post cemetery, although most of those still interred are not soldiers. By the time it was deactivated in 1894, the fort had become a relatively modern outpost. It had an electrical system, a piped-in water supply from a reservoir on a hillside above it, and, wonder of wonders, it had indoor flush toilets! There are about a dozen adobe ruins along the wide parade ground and, with the aid of maps and old photos, the layout is easily visualized as you stand on the elevated porch of the ranger station. On your return walk to the auto park you may take a much steeper path over a 5,000-foot mountain. It is not recommended for the frail, but the summit gives a glorious view not only of the fort layout but of the windings of the Butterfield Trail. [43]

It is possible to walk the historic trail up to the old station site, but private property is fenced at this point. However, the spot where the Apaches tried to stop one stage with burning grass, the site of the same-day attack on another Butterfield stage, the place where two of the American freighters were captured (later murdered) and eight Mexican freighters killed, and the spot where Lieutenant Bascom hanged six followers of Cochise for revenge, are all easily reached a few hundred yards along the Trail beyond the fenced property. The summit of Apache Pass lies at 5,115 feet, and driving the road through is reasonably scary. (The Butterfield Trail went through the pass a few yards below and to the south of today's road.)

Ten days after the howitzer battles between the Mangas Colorados Apaches and the California Column took place, the arrow-and-bullet-filled bodies of thirteen slain Americans were found two miles below the eastern entrance to the pass. The victims (who lost $55,000 worth of gold dust), had been successful gold miners and were well armed and cautious, but lacking intense knowledge of the local geography, they were trapped in an ambush and killed. This event also took place on the Butterfield Trail.

Driving along the Apache Pass road and eventually reaching the flat lands at the western end, you are inclined to believe this twenty miles or so is worth a 150-mile detour, even if you are not on the way to California. The air in the mountains is bracing, the scenery is gorgeous, and the various historic sites are marked—but if you know a little additional Butterfield history, every yard of the pass through the mountains is memorable. Afoot, you hate to have to stop walking the old depression that was the road, you hate to come down off that high mountain which holds the optional return path, and as you drive away you hate to emerge from the pass.

The dust of the Trail has settled for the modern Butterfield travelers, the noises of the swaying, crowded coach are hushed. The overland mail now makes its way silently overhead with a chalk line of white against a sky of blue. But for us, old John B's Overland Mail coaches, their mules, drivers and riders will forever continue to roll.

Notes

1. A later reminder of this type of western optimism may be found in the number of nineteenth-century railroads carrying the name "Pacific" which never got out of Texas, or Kansas or Missouri. Even the name Butterfield was

appropriated. A western writer noted, "David A. Butterfield, unrelated to John Butterfield . . . was one of Denver's most successful and best liked business-men of the early 1860s. In December, 1864, he established a 'fast freightline' between Atchison [Kansas] and the West. . . . In 1865 a joint stock company was formed [named] 'Butterfield's Overland Despatch.'" Ralph Moody, *Stage-coach West* (New York: Thomas Y. Crowell Co., 1967), 280. He may have been well liked in Denver, but elsewhere there were accusations of nefarious deal-ings. In October, 1867, a Texas editor (probably quoting another newspaper) wrote: "D. A. Butterfield sold Apaches at Fort Larned infantry coats which cost him one dollar and 12 1/2 cents for eleven dollars; blankets costing thirteen for twenty-three." More serious was the claim in the Galveston *Daily Bulletin* that D. A. Butterfield made an agreement with the Kiowa to rob his wagon train "in order that he might put in a claim against the government for losses, and that the agreement was carried out." C. C. Rister, "The Significance of the Jacks-boro Indian Affair of 1871," *Southwestern Historical Quarterly* XXIX (January 1926): 183.

2. Walter B. Lang, *The First Overland Mail: Butterfield Trail* (Washington, D. C.: n.p., 1940), 156.

3. Displayed in Wells, Fargo Bank history room in San Francisco.

4. Named for T. V. Munson, who was awarded the Legion of Honor after he helped save the French vineyards from a disastrous infestation of grape phyl-loxera with Texas root stock immune to the plant lice.

5. A conflagration in 1875 wiped out the entire south side of the courthouse square where the Butterfield station and the post office stood.

6. Much has been written about the colorful Waggoner family, particularly the founders, father Dan Waggoner and son W. T. (Tom) Waggoner, as well as Electra, once considered the richest woman in Texas. The Waggoners and the Three D Ranch (the D branded backward) have become legend. For the history of the ranch, see Lawrence Clayton, *Historic Ranches of Texas* (Austin: University of Texas Press, 1993). For information on Waggoner history see *Handbook of Texas*, Texas State Historical Association, 1952 edition. For infor-mation on Electra see Frank X. Tolbert, "Glamour Girl Called Electra," *Leg-endary Ladies of Texas*, ed. Francis Edward Abernethy (Denton: University of North Texas Press, 1994), 173–74.

7. Ida Huckabay, *Ninety-four Years in Jack County* (Austin: Steck Company, 1950), 169–70.

8. Llerna Friend, ed., *M. K. Kellogg's Texas Journal, 1872* (Austin: Univer-sity of Texas Press, 1967), 150–51. The Butterfield imprint remained strong. Kel-logg noted: "Encamped at Butterfield Ranch near good water hole in rocks. Sketch abandoned Ranch of Butterfield from ledge of sandstone rocks over

water hole. It lies in a bowl surrounded by rugged oaks, the road running through centre. . . . The ranch an old stage station [probably Murphy's]."

9. Friend, 149.

10. Texas has nearly forty "Elm Creeks" plus a number of "Elm Forks," many the scene of interesting events, which can lead to a certain amount of historical confusion.

11. Carrie J. Crouch, *A History of Young County, Texas* (Austin: Texas State Historical Association, 1956), 91.

12. Roscoe P. and Margaret B. Conkling, *The Butterfield Overland Mail 1857–1869*, Vol. I (Glendale, CA: Arthur H. Clark, Co., 1947), 16–17. Dr. J. C. Tucker tells of a crowded Butterfield stage where the chivalrous acts of a handsome young Texan drew the romantic attention of a male gambler's consort, arousing his jealousy. He challenged the Texan to a duel, on reaching Fort Chadbourne. The Texan, though badly wounded, killed the challenger. The tale has earmarks of a dime western, but if you want to read it, you may find it on p. 185 of David Nevin, *The Expressmen* (Alexandria: Time–Life Books, 1974), and more fully in Captain William Banning and George Hugh Banning, *Six Horses* (New York: The Century Co., 1930), 157–68. The original story, "A Wild Ride," in "The San Francisco Argonaut," (September 1890) is so full of inaccuracies that even a lapse of 31 years (Dr. Tucker said he rode the Butterfield stage in 1859) cannot excuse them.

13. J. Evetts Haley, *Fort Concho and the Texas Frontier* (San Angelo: Standard Times, 1952), 156.

14. The remoteness of this station site remains today. A participant in the 1993 archaeological project at Head of Concho station site wrote: "[The] Butterfield Overland Mail Route stop . . . on the Rocker B Ranch [is] on a portion of the ranch known as the 'Head of the River Pasture.' There remained on the site only rocks . . . a set of walls remained, though not too high and somewhat in disarray. A refreshing, though lonely place, with a view of the world I had not had before—trying to recall what I thought it might have been like to be stationed at such a remote, isolated, dry, barren spot. All sorts of pictures came to mind." Don R. Franks, "Concho Valley Archaeology Society News," Spring 1994.

15. Paul Patterson, *Pecos Tales* (Austin: Encino Press, 1967), 30.

16. Patterson, 67–68.

17. Martin W. Schettmann, *Santa Rita, the University of Texas Oil Discovery* (Austin: Texas State Historical Association, 1943), tells the story of how this legendary well was brought in, and how the University of Texas came to own the land.

18. John Salmon Ford, *Rip Ford's Texas*, Stephen B. Oates, ed. (Austin:

University of Texas Press, 1963), 500.

19. Patrick Dearen, *Castle Gap and the Pecos Frontier* (Fort Worth: Texas Christian University Press, 1988), 13.

20. Conkling, Vol. I, 372.

21. "Pecos Bill," the bodacious cowboy, often treated as a Texas legend, was a modern creation, dating back only to the 1920s, inspired perhaps by Paul Bunyun. "Pecos Bill" was the product of someone who hoped to add to the Texas mythos. The real Pecos riders never heard the name.

22. Oliver Loving, the famed Texas cattleman who blazed the Goodnight-Loving cattle trail to New Mexico, was mortally wounded on that trail in 1867 when he and One-Arm Billy Wilson, who had gone on ahead of the herd, were attacked by Comanches at Loving Bend on the New Mexico part of the Pecos River. True to his promise to the dying man to bury him back in Texas, Charles Goodnight, the younger man in the partnership, together with W.D. Reynolds and one of Loving's sons, devised a hearse made of flattened square five-gallon kerosene cans soldered together and fitted around a wooden box, filled with charcoal, which contained Loving's body. This big tin-clad box was mounted on the running gear of a wagon, and Loving's body was brought back through nearly a thousand dangerous miles, to be buried in Weatherford. J. Evetts Haley, *Charles Goodnight, Cowman & Plainsman* (Boston: Houghton Mifflin, 1936), 195 passim. Joseph C. McConnell, *The West Texas Frontier* (Vol. 1, Jacksboro, 1933; Vol. 2, Palo Pinto, 1939) 194–98.

23. Alton Hughes, *Pecos, A History of the Pioneer West* (Seagraves, TX: Pioneer Book Publishers, 1978), 7.

24. Kenneth Neighbours, "The Expedition of Major Robert Neighbors to El Paso in 1849," *Southwestern Historical Quarterly* LVIII (July 1954): 48.

25. Waterman L. Ormsby, Jr., *The Butterfield Overland Mail*, ed. Lyle H. Wright and Josephine M. Bynum (San Marino: The Huntington Library, 1955), 75.

26. Conkling, Vol. I, 124.

27. Be careful of the spelling. "Cornudo" is Spanish for "cuckold," i.e., "A man with horns."

28. Conkling, Vol. I, 405.

29. John Sherman, Mike Head, James Crump and Dave Head, *Hueco Tanks: A Climber's and Boulderer's Guide* (Evergreen, CO: Chockstone Press, Inc., 1991), 24, 25, 161.

30. Sam Woolford, ed. "The Burr Duval Diary," *Southwestern Historical Quarterly* LXV (April 1962): 498.

31. C. L. Sonnichsen, *Pass of the North: Four Centuries on the Rio Grande* (El Paso: Texas Western Press, 1968), 142.

32. *Handbook of Texas*, Vol. 1, 104.

33. Harvey Bourland to A. C. and Judy Greene, 14 February 1993.

34. A. Richardson, 236.

35. On a prehistoric dig in Israel many years ago, a young Israeli archeologist reproached me for saying "American" when I meant the U.S. exclusively. There were other American nations. I assured him I was not disregarding the other North American countries, but pointed out that the name of my nation was "The United States of America" and the name of the Mexican Republic (which he used as his example) was "The United States of Mexico" . . . and thus.

36. Lang, 148. Fort Fillmore was taken by Confederate forces from Texas in 1861 but was retaken by Union troops a few months later. The Texan invasion of New Mexico, while temporarily successful—Albuquerque and Santa Fe were taken—resulted in disaster and was one of the most wasteful, needless efforts in the Confederate war west of the Mississippi. (See Martin Hardwick Hall, "The Formation of Sibley's Brigade and the March to New Mexico," *Southwestern Historical Quarterly* LXI (January 1958): 383.

37. Ormsby, 81.

38. Both Ormsby and the Conklings spell the name "Stein," but "Steen" is correct. A New Mexico mountain is also named Stein's Peak, probably also for Major Steen.

39. Lang, 120.

40. "Fort Bowie National Historic Site, Arizona," National Park Service, Department of the Interior, n.p., n.d. Texans needn't feel a stir of pride at the name Bowie; the fort honored Colonel George Washington Bowie, who was not only not from Texas but was an officer of the California Column of Union Troops and became commandant of El Paso when the California Column took over trans-Pecos Texas.

41. John C. Cremony, *Life Among the Apaches* (New York: Time-Life Books, 1981), 162.

42. Cremony, 162–67.

43. The mountainous area is not always so delightful. A Dr. Jones reported in the *Missouri Republican* (St. Louis, December 18, 1858) that one Butterfield passenger had his feet frozen while walking twelve miles through the snow in Apache Canyon, after the stage was forced to stop because of snow drifts. Rupert Richardson, "Some Details of the Overland Mail Company," *Southwestern Historical Quarterly* XXIX (July, 1925): 13.

PART FIVE

Crossroads

An Inspector's Report

IN 1858 Goddard Bailey, Special Agent for Postmaster General Aaron V. Brown, inspected the transcontinental mail systems, including the route across the Isthmus of Panama. After that, he was on the first Butterfield stage going from San Francisco to St. Louis, and his report on the line is of interest.[1]

"The establishment of a regular and permanent line of communication, overland, between the Atlantic States and California being a matter of general interest, some desire may naturally be felt to know how far the enterprise recently inaugurated under the auspices of your department has succeeded," Bailey wrote. "I am induced, therefore, to reproduce somewhat in detail, the notes I took while accompanying the first mail sent from the Pacific under the contract with the Overland Mail Company."

Pointing out that the stage, in San Francisco, started from the Plaza shortly after midnight on September 14, he says he arrived at Tipton, the Missouri terminus of the Pacific railroad, at 9:05 A.M., October 9:

Service, then, has been performed within the contract time, and as this pioneer trip was attended with many difficulties and embarrassments, which each successive trip will gradually remove, there is no reason to apprehend that a longer period will be required in future. On the contrary, I feel safe in expressing the opinion that a continued exertion of the energy and perseverance which have thus far characterized the operations of the Overland Mail Company, will enable the contractors to reduce the time to twenty days.[2]

The actual distances greatly exceed those specified in the mail contract, he notes, but says this is accounted for by the fact of "the double necessity of keeping within reach of water, and beyond the usual range of hostile tribes of Indians." The most material variance from the contract route, Bailey remarks, occurs in Texas. He explains a saving of nearly one hundred miles might be made by running directly east from Pope's Camp on the Pecos to Fort Belknap, "along the route followed by Lieutenant Garrard and Captain Pope in 1854." But he adds that the company, "with reason," alleges that unless the government should "interpose for their protection" by building a line of military posts along that northern frontier of Texas, "it would be impossible for them to maintain the necessary stations." (This was also the route laid out by Captain Randolph Marcy in 1849, called "The California Trail" or the "Emigrants' Trail.")

"From Fort Belknap," Bailey continued, "the road follows Captain Marcy's trail, portions of which the company have greatly improved at their own cost . . . and crosses Red River at Colbert's Ferry." He concludes,

. . . the company have faithfully complied with all the conditions of the contract. The road is stocked with substantially-built Concord spring wagons, capable of carrying conveniently four passengers with their baggage, and from five to six hundred pounds of mail matter. Permanent stations have been, or are being established at all the places mentioned [in an attached schedule], and where, in consequence of the scarcity of water, these are placed far apart, relays of horses and spare drivers are sent forward with the stage to insure its prompt arrival.

The various difficulties of the route, the scant supply of water, the long sand deserts, the inconvenience of keeping up stations hundreds of miles from the points from which their supplies are furnished; all these, and the many minor obstacles, naturally presented to the successful management of so long a line of stage communication, have been met and overcome by the energy, the enterprise, and the determination of

218

the contractors. Thus far the experiment has proved successful [but] whether this great artery between the Atlantic and
Pacific states is to pulsate regularly and uninterruptedly, does
not, however, depend entirely upon the Overland Mail Company. They have conquered the natural difficulties of the route,
but they have yet to encounter an enemy with whom they cannot successfully cope unaided. I refer, of course, to the tribes
of hostile Indians through whose territory they necessarily
pass. Their stations in Arizona are at the mercy of the Apache,
and the Comanche may, at his pleasure, bar their passage
through Texas.

Bailey adds his testimony " . . . to the necessity . . . for a prompt and
effectual intervention on the part of the government for the protection of the route. He notes that in the Fifth Division of the Overland Mail route from Franklin (El Paso) to Fort Chadbourne, a total
of 458 miles, "There is no water on the route between Franklin and
Pope's Camp, and between Horse Head Crossing and the Mustang
Ponds (near the head of Concho) except at the stations." He also
notes that there is two hours and nine minutes "difference of time
between San Francisco and St. Louis." Today the difference is two
hours with no minutes added to the time zones; the present standard time zones of the United States were not instituted until 1883.

The Great Gainesville Hanging of 1862

Until recent years, little had been written about that stygian chapter in the Lone Star story known as the Great Gainesville Hanging
of 1862, one of the most ruthless, pointless episodes in Texas history.
Thirty-nine Cooke County citizens were hanged after either con-
fessing to membership or being accused of having membership in

something given the hazy designation of the "Order." Two others were shot allegedly trying to escape after being found guilty. Three Confederate soldiers were hanged by a semi-military group for the same "crime"—membership in the Order. There were two nearly opposite accounts written a few years after the events took place: one by Thomas Barrett, a Disciples of Christ minister who was a fearful and unwilling participant as a member of Gainesville's "citizens court" jury, the other by George Washington Diamond, which purports to be the court records of the mock trials and defends the actions of the perpetrators.

The reason a section on the event is included in this book is that the Butterfield Overland Mail Company and its employees were assigned an unfair burden of blame by G. W. Diamond for their alleged part in helping cause the gruesome proceedings. This involvement of Butterfield employees has not been mentioned in other books and articles about the Butterfield Overland Mail operation in Texas, because the Diamond account did not become available until 1963. Diamond wrote his version sometime before 1876 (he was not in Gainesville at the time of the hangings), but the discovered manuscript was not published until the 1960s. Barrett's account was published in 1885, but the pamphlet was suppressed, becoming a bibliographic rarity so that at the time it was republished by the Texas State Historical Association in 1961, only three battered copies were known to exist.

No historical comparison has been made of the two surviving texts, thus the following attempts to reach some reasonable estimate of the true events. Barrett's writing, while self-justifying to a degree, faces the reality of the horrible crime. Barrett wrote in his Introduction, "The universal idea almost is that these men were hung because they were union men, which is not the fact, which the following pages will abundantly show. Do not be startled, reader, at this statement, for facts are stubborn things and never yield to opinions formed from uncertain rumor."[3]

Barrett was apparently a good man, but like so many good men in Texas under the Confederacy, he was forced to be a coward or a *dead* man. It is understandable, I suppose, that a majority of Southern men, even non-slaveholders, were initially motivated to take up arms in defense of what they interpreted as their rights. Robert E. Lee, though disapproving of slavery and of the coming war, refused to draw his sword against his native state of Virginia. My great-great-grandfather Sam Dockray, who never owned a slave or wanted one, ran off to join the Confederate army to "fight for his rights," leaving a pregnant wife and two children on the San Saba County frontier of Texas.

Wrong though history may show them to be, these were men inspired by a conviction which became a cause. They saw death, they caused death, but they were honest in their bloody dealings: kill or be killed, defeat or be defeated. And the enemy was equipped equally for the battle. But reading the account by George W. Diamond, brother of John R. Diamond, the Butterfield stationkeeper, brings a shudder of horror to even the most ardent defender of the southern cause in Texas. It is without even a taint of nobility or purpose. The accused, and those executed, are revealed as hapless victims of panic and hatred. The prevalence of confessions, two or three to the point of thanking the jury that sentenced them to die, can be taken as reasonable proof that threats against wives, children and other family members were used to extort this self-incrimination.

This part of Texas history is distressing to many who have tried to whitewash the actions of the murderers by alluding to "a threatened invasion from Kansas," or by accepting the imaginary plot by Union sympathizers, or—prior to the start of hostilities—crediting the fear of a mythic Negro insurrection. The passage of time has proved all these fanciful "dangers" to be ridiculous. Today, the kindest interpretation possible of the Gainesville hangings is mass hysteria deliberately incited by a handful of sadistic leaders. It is difficult to believe that these vicious men acted out of any concern either for their own safety or that of their fellow citizens. Their motives were tyranny, malice, and a taste for cruelty. Their allowing some wives

and children of the condemned to witness the public hangings—
many of which took place within minutes of "conviction"—leaves
little room for belief otherwise.

All a modern reader needs to do to accept these unhappy con-
clusions is compare the two surviving accounts, Barrett's and Diamond's. Diamond's account is self-contradicting, full of fantasy—"if"
becomes "thus" time after time—and so glossed over are the actions
of those who hired him that his account doesn't support even minor
points of fact. Barrett's account defends his own actions, and lack
of action in some cases, but it is convincing in that it admits his own
weaknesses and fear. Even as a historical narrative, Barrett's account
is more informative and readable.

Also, it is hard to forgive modern historians who have remained
silent, or paid historical deference to the defenses offered for the
Gainesville hangings. It does not take a revisionist to acknowledge
the guilt. History blames no one, but historians must not retreat behind that fact.

The oldest of the six Diamond brothers was James J., a fanatical
spokesman for slavery and "southern rights." As soon as Abraham
Lincoln won the 1860 presidential election, a meeting of wealthy
slaveholders and planters was called at Whitesboro, Cooke County,
by James and brother John R. (a Butterfield stationkeeper), another
firebrand secessionist. John R. presided at the incendiary meeting.
The gathering demanded that Governor Sam Houston call a secession vote, and publicly demanded that Texas sever ties with the federal Union—even though the region they assumed to speak for,
Cooke and Grayson counties, had few slaves and was mainly populated by people of loyalist sentiments.[4]

When the Texas secession vote was held in February, 1861, secession carried by a three-to-one margin, but the North Texas area
voted overwhelmingly against leaving the Union. This undoubtedly
inflamed the secessionists and aroused their fervor to make any opposition a matter of treason rather than mere political disagreement.

At first those opposed to secession tried to co-exist with the new regime, joining local militia or frontier defense units. But the Confederate Conscription Act of April 16, 1862, the first such draft in American history, was bitterly resisted. It provided for compulsory military service for all southern males between the ages of 18 and 35—but slaveholders who owned more than ten slaves were exempted from conscription, and slaves, of course, were not drafted. This was the beginning of open resentment of the Confederacy by farmers who "owned no slaves and didn't want to fight for someone else's." (The ill will caused by the Conscription Act was not confined to Texas; it spread across the entire Confederacy.)

But the enormity of the Gainesville hangings was brought on by Colonel James Bourland, who took over Cooke County after General William Hudson (Confederate commander of the First Brigade of Texas, headquartered in Gainesville), declared martial law following Bourland's inflamed reports of invasion and insurrection. Bourland, once the hysteria took hold, seemed determined to arrest, try, and hang every man in Cooke County who might have voted against secession, dragging out anyone even suspected of sheltering Unionist thoughts. Bourland was described as "a typical South Carolina gentleman and an unmistakable Southern aristocrat . . . [who] had always championed States Rights and had vigorously defended the slavocracy of the cotton kingdom."[5]

James J. Diamond who had, by October, 1862, become a stay-at-home colonel, was primary architect of a self-appointed, extra-legal "committee of public safety." He was the organizer and manager of the forcibly drafted "Citizens Court" assembled in Gainesville, the county seat of Cooke County, to try those unfortunates Bourland dragged in. There, after threats of death to dissenting members, the court approved the executions, following trials reminiscent of the infamous Soviet Purge show trials of the 1930s, wherein everyone confessed guilt before being executed.

The actions in Cooke County led the way for adjacent counties to resort to lynch law. Five men were hanged in Wise County, and one each executed in Grayson and Denton counties. All three counties had voted heavily against secession.

George W. Diamond, not present for the hangings and not a Cooke County resident until years later, wrote his account at the obvious coaching of his brothers. His book opens with these paragraphs, which blame the Butterfield employees and passengers for being Union sympathizers who formed the mythical "Order":

Early in the year 1858, after the organization and establishment of the Overland Mail through Texas, people of every shade of opinion and men guilty of every species of crime began to pour into the State from all quarters of the globe.

With St. Louis as the great north-western depot, immigration teamed into Northern Texas by this line to an extent hitherto unknown. So rapid was this influx of a heterogeneous population that in a short time the character of the citizenship in Cooke and Grayson counties was materially changed. Until that time this section was thinly settled, with a quiet, hardy, industrious population which had not been excited and disturbed by political divisions and discussions. This sudden and rushing tide caused alarm among the older inhabitants . . . because the actions and conduct of so many strangers in their midst created suspicions and fears that the interests of the old class would not harmonize with the new. . . . And finally, upon the suspension of the Overland, and the withdrawal of the coaches and stock belonging to the Company, many of those who had come to Texas under its auspices returned to the North, taking with them their property and families. But many of those who remained seemed to be restless and adventurous in their dispositions, manifesting an unfriendly spirit toward the older settlers. . . . [I]n a short time mutual distrust and dislike, criminations and recriminations characterized the intercourse between the two parties. And it may be truly said also that many who had resided for several years in this section of the state, from the South as well as the North, espoused the

224

cause of theft, rapine and murder, and became leaders and helpers in their wicked crusade against the peace, the property and the lives of good citizens. . . . The bold denunciation of the act of secession by the Northern immigrants, also by a small class of the Southern people, was the foundation upon which unscrupulous men bent on ruin and plunder based their criminal conduct [and] began a regular system of robbery, rapine and murder unparalleled in the history of this country.[6]

What is seldom understood about the political climate of Texas immediately preceding and during the Civil War is that moderation in human, social, or religious ideas simply was not tolerated by certain political opportunists who—with no restraints from law, religion or government—had made themselves the dictators of Texas. These were not the old heroes of the 1836 revolution or those few high-minded persons who guided Republic of Texas affairs. Neither, once fighting began, were they the foot soldiers and officers of the Confederate States Army. No, this was a more recent set, historic examples that power corrupts. Some, but not all, were adventurers, some were shameless opportunists; all were arrogant in hot-headed belief, brutal and unprincipled. Some were possibly mad, insane with larceny and the opportunities of power.

Initially, the enemy was the illusory Abolitionist, and the slavery lovers were capable of lying, fabricating evidence, cheating, or killing if, in their perception, the holy institution of slavery was endangered. In modern terms, they were Hitler's predecessors, using Big Lie techniques so pervasively that even natural disasters were blamed on the Abolitionists, despite the fact that Texas, if it had any by 1860, could have had no more than a dozen real Abolitionists. As soon as the Civil War started and the Abolitionist scare was reduced to the phantasm it had always been, members of this group turned their zeal for power to areas they declared were endangered by Union sympathizers and secret plotters. Although found throughout the state, the most oppressive regimes operated in the areas that had voted heavily against secession: German-settled Texas Hill Country and

225

that block of North Texas counties on or near the Red River—Cooke, Grayson, Collin, Wise, and Denton.

High-level cabals of home guard military officers, wealthy slave-owners, slave dealers and sycophants, demagogic lawyers and conniving judges were formed, not just to take over local control but to carry out vengeance on local enemies. Fearful editors and timid commentators, rabble-rousing preachers, firebrand "patriots" and self-seeking adventurers, all fell in line. Remember, in the early months of the Civil War, any wealthy man—whether a professional army officer or not—could form his own unit, usually taking for himself the title of colonel.

With the election of Abraham Lincoln to the national presidency in November of 1860, southern society's popular panic lent this despotic segment growing authority, appealing to the fears and prejudices of the citizenry—or when that didn't work, using physical threats, economic blackmail, and command of the courts. By the time the Civil War was actually begun, even those Texans merely desirous of escaping the coming disaster, not to mention those wanting to enlist in the Federal forces, were hunted down and, if caught, usually murdered. Even Governor Sam Houston, deposed by an extra-legal secessionist rabble, was threatened with death because of his scorning to take the oath of allegiance to, as he rightly predicted, the doomed and bloody Southern Confederacy.

Court records of the time are worthless because in many parts of Texas the lawyers and judges—in fact, most elected officials—were under the control of this ruthless element. But with the war taking away thousands of sound civic and political leaders, as well as troops, the unofficial power of the militia gained absolute status—so a mythic Abolitionist conspiracy was replaced by a frenzied ardor for wholesale Confederate devotion.

The amazing thing about the fire-eating leaders was not their ability to disregard moral and human rights—after all, hundreds of southern ministers fervently preached slavery as a divine ordinance—no, the thing most surprising is the attachment of such calculating opportunists to something which so early manifested certain failure as the Confederacy.

After the heinousness of their crimes began to sink into the horrified conscience of even a credulous wartime Texas, the perpetrators of the Great Gainesville Massacre desperately tried to give a color of legal, if not human, decency to their barbarism. To this end, in about 1869 newspaperman G. W. Diamond was employed by the executioners and given the "court" records to, as he wrote, "offer to the public as a just vindication of the conduct of those whose acts have been the subject of unjust criticism from one end of this broad land to the other."[7]

In his Introduction, Diamond says the court records "are now offered to the public," but the reader is told that "a complete transcript from the record of the Court would have been unnecessary to vindicate the course pursued [by] the trial."[8] In other words, the only court actions in a large number of such "trials" was the verdict: hanging. Diamond also assigns a portion of blame for the hangings to imagined Unionist threats to create another state if Texas voted to secede. In actuality, there had been no real threat, only the short-lived suggestion of an Austin anti-secession group dated January 15, 1861, worded thus:

> . . . should the state [secession] Convention so far disregard the wishes of the Conservative Union men of the State of Texas . . . as to declare the State of Texas out of the Union without submitting their action to the people of Texas for ratification at the ballot box . . . we resolve, as a Dernier Resort, to make an effort to unite a sufficient number of northern counties of Texas into a state, and make application at the proper time for admission into the Union.[9]

The *ad hoc* secession convention's action was submitted to Texas voters who ratified secession, and that should have been the end of it.

The alleged fear of the idea—creation of a separate state such as had happened in Virginia when West Virginia separated—was used as excuse for more crime. Diamond's *apologia* stated, somewhat incorrectly, "The paper in which this proposition had its practical origin was published by one Capt. Foster [of Sherman]."[10] Editor E. Junius Foster, a strong anti-secessionist, had apparently reprinted the piece concerning a new state from the Austin source. As soon as secession was voted and the Civil War began, the proposal disappeared.[11] But the memory of his act helped seal Foster's doom. By 1862 even a hint of Union sentiment became a death warrant.

In October, 1862, during the turmoil of the Great Gainesville Massacre, the Sherman editor was shotgunned to death by an "unknown assailant." Later, Captain James D. Young proudly admitted the murder. His father, Colonel William C. Young, largest single slaveowner in Cooke County and a fomenter of the Gainesville hangings, had recently been slain from ambush by an unknown bushwacker. After having his slaves hang the two men accused of the killing, Captain Young rode the short distance east to Sherman and assassinated Editor Foster who, Jim Young said, refused to retract a comment the son interpreted as approval of his father's death. In truth, Foster's demise awaited only some tiny provocation. If Jim Young hadn't killed him, someone else would have, as long as the Sherman editor was known to have anti-secession views. He should be counted among the Gainesville victims. Jim Young, in fury at his father's death, personally supervised the hanging of the final nineteen Gainesville prisoners; all summarily executed although all were seemingly acquitted by the court the previous week. One of Jim Young's victims, 70-year-old Barnabas Birch, charged with "insurrection," was too feeble to walk to the gallows without some assistance.

Another chapter of Diamond's account of the Gainesville hangings adds a further Butterfield sidelight. Two women, a mother and daughter of a Butterfield company family, narrowly escaped hanging. Fortunately for the women, they were beauties, and Diamond's tale of their unsuccessful attempt to flee the massacre leers with sexual innuendo. In his book, Diamond has the rather curt notice that A. N. Johnson and John Cottrell, "accused of disloyalty and treason," were court martialed and hanged. Both men were unfortunate enough to have been members of the same Jim Young's company of Partisan Rangers, and it was Young, their commanding officer, who hanged them. The women, "the beautiful Mrs. Hawley and her pretty daughter," as Diamond repeatedly calls them, were accompanying the two soldiers (Johnson was the new husband of the pretty daughter) when, without the women realizing it, the men were arrested, hustled off to prison, and hanged by Jim Young. "The lovely Mrs. Hawley" was believed to have been left in Texas as a spy when Mr. Hawley allegedly "went North" earlier in the conflict.

But Diamond has more to say about the case, and, as previously noted, his report contains obvious sexual overtones as regards the females reportedly involved, who almost lost their own lives to the hemp:

> The history of Cottrell is not a little diversified with adventure and romance. When the "Over Land Mail Route" was established in 1858, one of the employees, Mr. Hawley, a genuine down-Easter, moved his family to Gainesville. His family consisted of Mrs. Hawley and *her* daughter. These ladies were received in Society, and attracted no small degree of attention. They were evidently accomplished. Doubtless they were handsome, for both herself and daughter were distinguished by the enviable sobriquet, "the beautiful Mrs. Hawley and her pretty daughter." Soon after the breaking out of the war, Mr. Hawley fled the Country, going, no doubt, to his native home in the North. The lovely Mrs. Hawley was left with no consolation but her wit, and no dowry but her beauty. It was afterwards ascertained that she was left as a spy, and at the proper time she was to go to Missouri and, *perhaps* rejoin her husband. In the month of July 1862, (the pretty Miss Hawley having united her destiny with a Mr. Johnson in the holy bonds of wedlock)

Cottrell, Mrs. Hawley, Johnson and his adored Armarylis [sic] set out for Missouri. The citizens, thinking it unproper to give them a passport at that particular time, arrested their movements and lodged Cottrell and Johnson in prison. Thus was spent the first night after marriage—the bridegroom in prison and the bride (only such, by virtue of the ceremony) weeping and blushing and wasting much sweetness on the desert air.

Again, just before the [later] arrest of the prisoners on the 1st of Oct., Mrs. Hawley attempted to escape north, taking the said Cottrell for her guide and help . . . sending out the information that she was going to Shreveport, La.[12]

Diamond then uses a letter from one John T. Gilmore, of Gainesville, who swore to the County Clerk as follows:

[A]n old friend of mine recently in Grayson County asked if I knew Dr. Cottrell of Gainesville. I told her that I knew a Mr. Cottrell, who was before the Provost Marshal when I saw him last. She then asked if I knew Mrs. Cottrell, the widow of Mr. Hawley, late of Gainesville. I told her that I knew Mrs. Hawley, but that she was not a widow, her husband having left our town on account of his Northern sentiments. . . . She then told me that not long since Cottrell called at her house and asked to stay several days with his family . . . he had some business in the Indian Nation and wished them to stay until he returned. That night they demeaned themselves as man and wife, occupying the same room.

Mrs. Hawley [said that] the Doctor was not the father of the children; that she was a widow, and the Doctor a widower; that her husband died in California and the Doctor's wife died in Missouri . . . and they were married about three months. All the children called Cottrell their good Papa. The Doctor did not return.

Diamond appends this conclusion:

> The story of Cottrell and his wayward paramour was an ingenious fabrication, a lie from beginning to end. Cottrell had a wife in Cook [sic] County and Mrs. Hawley a husband in the North. Cottrell only went to Red River to take observations and ascertain, if possible, the most eligible point for crossing the river and escaping detection. In this undertaking he was discovered and arrested; and consequently never had an opportunity to return to his family.[13]

The only "Hawley" shown on surviving Butterfield records was Giles Hawley, one of the original directors. After the line began operating he was in charge of the section from Fort Yuma to Los Angeles. Later Hawley and William M. Buckley had charge of the Sixth Division from El Paso to Tucson. Whether he had any connection with the "Mrs. Hawley" of the above is not known.

There have been several studies and investigations of the Great Gainesville Hanging, none of them wholly adequate. Claude Elliott's "Union Sentiment in Texas 1861-1865"[14] attempts to give a fair estimate of some of the outrages practiced against Texas Unionists but, strangely, falters when it comes to the Great Gainesville Hanging, using contemporary Texas newspaper reports as basis for its interpretation—and Texas newspaper accounts of that day are worse than useless, they are wholly biased and misleading. The modern editors of the George Washington Diamond account seem hesitant to reveal the sadistic brutality of the Cooke County leadership, possibly to protect the feelings of the family that supplied the long-lost manuscript. Several more recent stories and novels based on the tragedy have acknowledged the horror of it all but some have sacrificed reality for "balance." Ray Cowan's talk before the East Texas State Historical Association annual meeting in September, 1992, did a good job of presenting the background of the outrageous murders and assassinations across North Texas, and added needed analysis

231

of motives and movements. Michael Collins's, *Cooke County, Texas: Where the South and the West Meet*, faces the situation there forthrightly and, under the circumstances of its publication, bravely. However, most Gainesville citizens have long ago given up holding the prejudices and defending the sins of their forefathers, if such there were—even those whose forefathers were thick with blame.

Other Mail Lines

The first mail contract from San Antonio to Santa Fe, by way of Paso del Norte, Mexico, was issued in 1851 to Henry Skillman. The contract called for a trip per month, with thirty days to complete the trip. Service started November 1, 1851, reportedly with a Concord coach drawn by six mules and guarded by eighteen mounted men, led by William "Bigfoot" Wallace. (For a time the mail went by horseback, with Wallace as one of the riders.) When the line started there were no stage stations, and teams were herded along for replacement. The stage coach stopped every night to rest. Passengers were carried to El Paso for $100 and food and were not required to stand guard. When Skillman's contract expired in 1854, he asked for an increase in the annual subsidy from $12,500 to $50,000. The contract was subsequently awarded to a low bidder, David Wasson, who contracted to run the mail for $16,760 per annum. It is not clear just how long Wasson actually ran the line, although we find references to his coaches in early accounts. He didn't retain the contract very long and on March 13, 1855, sold it to George H. Giddings. This time the contract called for monthly service to Santa Fe by way of Franklin (on the U.S. side of the Rio Grande) in twenty-five days. Giddings continued to operate the San Antonio-Santa Fe mail line until 1861, eventually having the compensation increased to $35,000. By 1858 service had been changed to weekly, with a $55,000 annual payment.

In 1858 the line to Santa Fe became a branch of the San Antonio-San Diego line, and from 1860 to 1861 was operated by the Butterfield company.

The San Antonio-San Diego mail line was famed as the "Jackass Mail" because donkeys were originally used to haul passengers as well as mail on the 100-mile Yuma to San Diego segment. The 1,476-mile line was to offer semi-monthly service. It was derisively described as "From no place through nothing to nowhere." Out of San Antonio it went by way of Fort Clark, then to Fort Stockton and over the Davis Mountain route and along the Rio Grande to El Paso, thence westward to Yuma and southwest to San Diego. For the first several months, the stages stopped and passengers camped out each night because no stations had been built. The contract was originally let to N. P. Cook, who transferred it to James Birch and Birch's general agent, I. C. Woods, in June, 1857. Birch, a California stager, was among the 400 who drowned on September 12, 1857, when the steamship "Central America" foundered off the coast of South Carolina. George Giddings, who had been a mail contractor since 1846, then took over the San Antonio-San Diego operation, which became known as "The Giddings Line."

The mail for San Diego entered Texas at Indianola, then went to San Antonio. The entire run from San Antonio to San Diego took from fifty to sixty days. The line, as described in the original contract, only operated for one year and made only $601 that entire year. The first coach was driven part of the way by "Bigfoot" Wallace, and Henry Skillman was also an initial driver. In 1858 the Butterfield mail line took over the segment from El Paso to Yuma and in 1860, after the Butterfield had switched to the Davis Mountain route, the San Antonio-San Diego line ended at Fort Stockton. Even after the firing on Fort Sumter in mid-April, 1861—and a month after the Butterfield stages ceased to run in Texas—the U.S. Post Office Department renewed a contract for mail from San Antonio to San Diego, and the order to discontinue service was not issued until August 2, 1861, when all service to seceding states was ended.

Following the Civil War, new mail lines throughout western Texas were begun under contract to Ben Ficklin and others, most following the older stage routes. W. S. Mabry, joining a survey team out of San Antonio in 1873, reported, "At that time there was a line of stages running from San Antonio to El Paso, via Fredericksburg, Fort McKavett, Fort Concho, Fort Stockton, and Fort Davis to El Paso. Ben Ficklin and F. C. Taylor were the owners of this stage line."[15] There was also a well-known mail route bearing the title "Fort Worth to Yuma," although it did not traverse that distance via one continuous ownership or road as did the Butterfield. The coming of the Texas & Pacific Railway across West Texas in 1881–1882 and the Southern Pacific to El Paso and eastward at the same time ended the major mail line stages through those areas.

I know of no better way to get the authentic "feel" of a stagecoach journey across Texas than by means of a small, hard-to-find book of fiction: *Stagecoach 22 San Antonio-El Paso Stage Line, 1869*, by Big Bend rancher Rudolph Mellard (Anson Jones Press, Salado, 1977). The book is accurate in its details of stage line activities on the part of driver, conductor, stationkeepers (husband and wife), and passengers. There is much information about several Texas forts and camps and the soldiers stationed there as well. I would recommend this book for research use before several nonfiction books on the subject. And the narrative is good, completely in keeping with the manners, mores and events of the period. And yes, there is a pretty girl on Stagecoach 22 in its return trip from El Paso to San Antonio.

Later Tragedies along the Butterfield Trail

Warren Wagon Train Massacre – Elm Creek Raid – Turtle Hole

In 1867 the army built Fort Richardson on the southwest side of Jacksboro and the town grew not only in size but in importance. It was the site of the nationally publicized trial of Satanta and Big Tree in 1871. They were the surviving pair of the three Kiowa chiefs (the other, Satank, was shot on the way to the trial) charged with leading the Warren wagon train massacre of May 18, 1871. The attack took place along the old Butterfield Trail in Throckmorton County just west of where Dennis Murphy's station had been located. During the onslaught, seven freighters were slaughtered (one seemingly burned alive) by a band of one hundred fifty Kiowa raiders from the Fort Sill, Oklahoma, reservation. Although called the "Warren wagon train massacre," Henry Warren, the contractor, was not with the train. Nathan S. Long, the wagonmaster in charge, was one of the victims.

The ten-wagon train was westbound, taking corn from Weatherford to Fort Griffin and using that blood-drenched portion of the old mail road between Fort Belknap and Fort Richardson at Jacksboro. (W. S. Nye said the wagons "were hauling supplies from the railhead at Weatherford,"[16] but Weatherford didn't get rails until 1880. In 1871 the West Texas region was without railroads; even Dallas had no rail service until 1872.)

In 1871 General William Tecumseh Sherman, Commanding General of the U.S. Army, was making a tour of Texas forts, accompanied by the great southwest explorer, Colonel Randolph Marcy, now Inspector General of the Army and a brevet major general. Sherman, reportedly "inclined to doubt Texan representations" of frontier depredations, had questioned the dangers claimed by the settlers, appearing to believe Texans exaggerated conditions in order to have federal troops sent from Reconstruction duties to the frontier.[17]

The Sherman party, with a military escort of only fifteen soldiers, had passed over the same section of the mail road, eastbound, only a few hours before the onslaught on the wagon train. The raiders had been watching the road from behind two hills, and had this powerful tribal force chosen to attack the lightly guarded Sherman party, it is most likely that most, if not all, of the members would have been killed. Sherman got the news of the wagon train massacre from a

235

survivor named Thomas Brazeal, who limped into Fort Richardson about midnight following the attack. The general immediately ordered Colonel Ranald S. Mackenzie to pursue the raiders, but a blinding deluge made pursuit impossible. The bodies of the seven teamsters were buried in a wagon box by the troops who found them.

As historian Robert Utley noted, "Sherman's doubts about frontier conditions vanished."[18]

Several of the raiding party later said a medicine chief—known to white authorities as Maman-ti (Sky-Walker), but to his tribal associates as Do-ha-te, the Owl Prophet—had been in charge. The night before, he had informed the tribesmen that two parties would travel the road the next day. The first party would be small, easily overcome, but should not be attacked. The medicine forbade it. But the second party over the Butterfield road was theirs to assault and they would be successful. This, apparently, saved the life of General Sherman.

Back at the Fort Sill reservation following the massacre, the Kiowa leaders freely admitted their part in the raid. Satanta, proud of the raiding party's success, bragged to General Sherman about his role in the bloody affair—although he later claimed he only blew a bugle and observed the young men doing the killing. It was demanded that the leaders be sent back to Texas for a state trial, and Satank, after singing his death song, attempted to kill a wagon guard in a plainly suicidal effort and was shot as the prisoners were leaving Fort Sill. Today no one is sure just why three other Kiowa leaders, Eagle Heart, Big Bow, and Fast Bear, were not charged, even though their roles in the killings were admitted.

Satanta and Big Tree were brought to trial July 5 in Jacksboro, were convicted of murder and sentenced to be hanged, but Washington intervened and Texas Governor E. J. Davis commuted their sentences to life in the Texas penitentiary at Huntsville. Two years later both were paroled at the behest of a strong Quaker group within the Indian Bureau. Both chiefs immediately began marauding again, leading and inciting warriors in killing and stealing raids. Satanta, who seems to have been the most influential (and the most devious) among the paroled leaders, was sent back to Huntsville along with Big Tree, where he committed suicide October 10, 1878, by leaping off a balcony to the prison courtyard. Big Tree was later released, eventually becoming a respected Baptist deacon and dying at age 84 in 1929.

The story of the massacre and its subsequent developments is told by several historians and writers, the best account being that of Colonel W. S. Nye in *Carbine and Lance*. He began writing this book, a history of Fort Sill, in 1933 when he was stationed there in advanced Field Artillery School. He did oral interviews with old men and women and visited many sites of the Kiowa battles and raids of the old war days. The Nye account of the massacre accurately relates the official story but also gives the Indian side, which is valuable as it comes from actual participants, none of whom seeks to excuse or defend the actions of himself or his fellow raiders. An account by Brigadier General R. H. Pratt, who was at Fort Sill at the time of the massacre, gets details of the event backward, but footnotes by the editor, Robert Utley, correct these. Pratt's account of the subsequent arrest and delivery of the guilty chiefs is valuable. Pratt went on to found Carlisle Indian School, through support of Carl Schurtz, then Secretary of the Interior.

The Warren wagon train massacre, as related in Carrie Crouch's *A History of Young County, Texas*, is too full of errors to be useful. Carl Coke Rister's *Border Command* is based on official Army and government reports and is a reliable account of the event from the white and military point of view. It has been used as basis for accounts by several succeeding historians. Mildred Mayhall's *Indian Wars of Texas* (1965) seems to have mostly accurate accounts of the Warren wagon train massacre (based on *Carbine and Lance*) and additional information on the Elm Creek raid of 1864.

Another tragedy along that same piece of Butterfield Trail occurred January 24, 1871, when four freighters were killed, including Britton

(Brit) Johnson, already famed for his heroic role in rescuing his wife, two of their children, and three others kidnapped in the Elm Creek raid of October 13, 1864. That raid took place west of Newcastle in Young County near the present day community of Proffitt. With nearly one thousand warriors involved—one settler, using a spyglass, said he counted 375 during one separate attack— it was the largest such raid in Texas history. The killing and capture swept along a line of cabins and makeshift "forts" to claim fourteen lives.[19]

Brit Johnson was a free Negro, and, as one writer put it, "allowed the enlarged liberty which belongs to the frontier."[20] At the time of the Elm Creek raid, he and his family lived on the ranch of Dr. Moses Johnson, whose son Allen had been raised with Brit. Brit had not taken part in the 1864 raid because he had been sent to Parker County for supplies. On arriving back at the Johnson ranch, Brit discovered his little son Jim had been killed and his wife and three daughters kidnapped by the raiders.

Johnson then volunteered to undertake the dangerous mission of trying to ransom the captives or take them by stealth. Through ingratiating himself with the Comanche and Kiowa tribes that held the captives—especially through his marksmanship—Brit Johnson saved one woman whose family was wealthy enough to meet the Comanche's first ransom demands. Making many trips with ransom goods, and becoming a welcome visitor in the tribes, he managed to get two additional white children ransomed. But his own family was held by the Kiowas, who at first would not parley with him. Only after four or five trips into the Texas Panhandle region was he allowed to meet with his wife and children and eventually, through cunning and the aid of Milky Way, a Comanche chief, to obtain not just his family members but three more white captives. Only Millie Jane Durgan, an 18-month-old girl whose mother had been killed, was kept by the tribe, later becoming an "Indian" wife and mother. Not until three years before her death in 1934 did Sain-toh-oodie Goombie (her Indian name) supposedly learn her true identity— many still doubt that this woman was Millie Durgan.

In the 1871 tragedy, Brit Johnson, Dennis Cureton and Paint Crawford (both ex-slaves) were engaged in hauling supplies from Weatherford to Fort Griffin and were camped near a small body of water called Turtle Hole. They were attacked at daybreak by twenty-five Comanche and Kiowa raiders under the Kiowa chief Sky-Walker. Brit Johnson's companions were killed early in the action, but he put up a desperate fight, using their weapons and reloading during lulls in the attack. After his death, his attackers mutilated his body with unusual ferocity as though in vengeance for his earlier success over them, cutting off his ears and an arm, then disemboweling him and thrusting into the cavity the carcass of a little dog that always accompanied him on the wagon, and which had shared its master's fate. U.S. cavalrymen who found and buried the bodies counted 173 brass shell cases where Brit fell.[21]

Faithful Old Dog "Shep" at Crow Springs

Texas Ranger Jim Gillett in his book, *Six Years with the Texas Rangers*, tells an unusual story about Crow Springs on the Butterfield Trail. In January, 1880, two mining engineers, seeking to purchase a hundred pack-train burros, asked the Ranger lieutenant at Ysleta about the best route to follow to the upper Pecos valley. They were advised to take the longer stage road through Fort Davis, thence up the Pecos River, but they decided to take the old abandoned Butterfield route east out of El Paso, even though the lieutenant warned that this was a very dangerous way, "without a living white man from Ysleta to the Pecos River, more than one hundred fifty miles distance, and through Indian country all the way."[22]

The two men, well equipped with a new ambulance, weapons and Shep, a big black shepherd dog which Gillett called, "the finest I had ever seen," decided to take the shorter road anyway and the third day out reached the abandoned stage station at Crow Flat. A cold north wind was blowing so the two men drove their ambulance inside the old station walls, unhitched and hobbled their horses and pony and were soon busy preparing and then wolfing down a meal. The horses had wandered off a few hundred feet when a dozen Apaches suddenly appeared—it was open country and one could see for miles—and drove off the stock. After fruitless pursuit on foot, the engineers decided to stay in the old stage stand until night, rigging up two dummy "sentinels" and setting them on guard. Shep, the dog, was left with a sack of corn and a side of bacon under the ambulance and made to understand he was to stand guard.

The men headed east for the Pecos, using the old Butterfield trail, and at daybreak they had made twenty-five miles to the foot of Guadalupe Peak. Deciding to take an old Indian trail, the worn out men walked until late in the day when, in a sudden bend in the trail, they came in full view of an entire Indian village coming toward them. They were discovered immediately, and knowing they could not outrun the mounted warriors, took refuge on a small peak and threw up a breastworks of rock. After an exchange of fire, the besieged men discovered the Indians were crawling up toward them, pushing boulders in front for protection. It was getting dark quickly, but one of the two men saw the top of a head over a rock and fired. The head disappeared as the warrior fell wounded, and, with the two white men running right behind it, the boulder went thundering down the hill. Before the Indians could realize what had happened, the white men were gone—back to the Crow Springs station, where good dog Shep and the two dummies were still on guard.

This time the men decided to return west to Ysleta, and after several days, "dragged their weary bodies . . . into the ranger camp." Eight rangers and two mules were dispatched to return to Crow Springs and bring back the ambulance. After a long, monotonous tramp, the party arrived in the night and were promptly challenged by the faithful sentinel, old Shep. "Recognizing them as friends, Shep went wild with joy, barking and rolling over and over."

Gillett said the faithful animal had been there alone for fifteen days. The dog had finished the bacon, was half way through the sack of corn, and had worn the top of the adobe wall smooth, keeping off coyotes. "But with the assistance of the dummy sentinels," Gillett wrote, "Shep had held the fort just as the owners had left it. The rangers were as much delighted as if they had rescued a human being," he added.

Bloys Camp Meeting

According to a 1972 magazine article, the idea of the annual Bloys Camp Meeting at Skillman Grove originated in 1889 when the Reverend William B. Bloys, a Presbyterian circuit rider, met with some ranchers and their families for two days of religious services.[23] John Zack Means, the rancher who had proposed that first meeting, declared, "I want to tell you, the word of God sank deep."[24] The ranchers decided to buy the grove for a permanent camp meeting site, and at two dollars an acre, collected the $1,280 cost of a section (640 acres) at a later meeting. The next year it became an annual interdenominational coming together, continuing as a growing, but still private, gathering until 1900, when it was formally organized and incorporated with four major Protestant denominations represented by specific "ranch camps." The purely religious tone changed also to allow musical and cultural presentations. From the beginning, no collection plates were passed and nothing was sold, all food being supplied by ranch chuckwagons and local residents— which practice continues. Virtually everyone who grew up in the Big Bend or Davis Mountain areas attended the Bloys Camp Meeting, no matter the denomination. It was a social as well as a religious occasion. Mrs. Herbert (Thelma) Fletcher, who, with her husband, created the Anson Jones Historical Press, was reared on the ranch of her father, Deputy Sheriff Fletcher Rawls, deep in Presidio County near Casa Piedra. In 1912, when Thelma was a girl of seven, her family, including her uncle Tom Rawls, went by wagon the one hundred miles or more to the Bloys meeting site, camping out on the way. A buggy or buckboard wouldn't do; it took a big wagon because tents and bedrolls had to be carried as well as pots and pans and dutch ovens to prepare food during the journey. At the campground, services were held in a big tabernacle. While meat was supplied to each family to cook at their camp, some other food was prepared in huge amounts and eaten by the crowd picnic style.[25]

Ora Jane Pruett, age twelve at the time, was among the forty-six who attended that 1890 gathering where Bloys used an Arbuckle's coffee box as a pulpit. Ora later married John Prude, an area rancher (the Prude and the Means ranches are still operating), and she eventually attended eighty-eight consecutive Bloys camp meetings, becoming famous as a "Firster." Her final meeting came in August, 1977, when she was ninety-nine years old. She died the next year at age one hundred, the last charter member of the Bloys camp meeting.

A monument in the grove, where they are buried, pays tribute to the Reverend Mr. Bloys and his wife.[26]

John Russell Bartlett

John Russell Bartlett, U.S. Boundary Commissioner on the international commission surveying the U.S.-Mexico boundary following the Mexican-American War, had nothing to do with the Butterfield Overland Mail Company. He left the Southwest five years before the Butterfield stage line was projected through Texas. But his two volume set, *Personal Narrative of Explorations and Incidents in Texas, New Mexico, California, Sonora and Chihuahua 1850–1853*, is among the great descriptive works on the west and undoubtedly had a lot to do with many of the routing and station location decisions made by the Butterfield engineers from west of the Pecos River.

A New York bookseller and ethnologist, Bartlett found it difficult to support his wife and four children, so in 1849 he tried to use his friendship with Albert Gallatin, plus his Whig associations (the Whigs had won the presidency in 1848), to gain an appointment as Danish ambassador. Despite the backing of several senators, including John C. Calhoun, Jefferson Davis, and Thomas Hart Benton, he failed to get the post. However, he was offered appointment, at $3,000 annually (a handsome salary for the time), as U.S. Commissioner on the commission surveying the U.S.-Mexico border according to the 1848 Treaty of Guadalupe Hidalgo that ended the Mexican-American War. Politically, it was a perilous appointment. The job had already seen one Commissioner removed and a second appointee back out.

During the course of determining the boundary, the U.S. Commissioner was also "to collect information on the possible route of a road, canal or railway through the area, to seek knowledge of quicksilver, precious metals, ores and other substances; to look for a more practicable route to California for immigrants; and to keep full records and make a map of the country traversed."[27]

Despite his ignorance of international diplomacy and his lack of qualification to lead a surveying party—or any other kind of expedition—through the uncharted and wild border country, Bartlett took the job. It paid too well to turn down. As an ethnologist, he thought the job would give him a chance to study firsthand the American Indian. He said he accepted it, also, because he had led a sedentary life and wanted to travel for a change.

From the beginning Bartlett showed his inexperience in hiring and controlling men. For his surveying party he accepted useless favorites and out-and-out criminals. Even his good men were constantly running off after California gold when they had worked long enough to get a stake. In fact, his entire time as Commissioner was a disaster. His major mistake was caused by his reliance on, and stubborn defense of, the infamous and erroneous [John] Disturnell map. Bartlett and Mexican Commissioner Garcia Conde agreed on an Initial Line at 32 degrees 22' going west from Doña Ana, New Mexico, based on Disturnell's faulty marking—a mistake that would have cost the United States thousands of square miles of territory.[28] Army surveyors refused to sign any of Bartlett's boundary agreements with the Mexican commissioners (Conde having died), and in 1853, after two Texas members of congress made it impossible for the Bartlett-led Boundary Commission to draw any money, Bartlett returned home to Providence, out of a job. A new Boundary Commissioner, General Robert B. Campbell, and Major William H. Emory, the surveyor, aided by the Gadsden Purchase, finished the job Bartlett had left in tatters. (Emory, too, wrote a basic western book, *Report on the U.S. and Mexican Boundary Survey 1858–1859.*)

Bartlett was so discredited with the administration that, unlike the treatment given reports by Emory and Andrew B. Gray (of Texas), the final surveyors, the government refused to publish Bartlett's *Personal Narrative* report, so he had it put into print by D. Appleton and Company. Bartlett was a better writer and observer than he was a leader, and as historian Odie B. Faulk noted, in his introduction to a modern reprinting of *Personal Narrative,* "The publication of the work in 1854 marks a high point in Southwestern literature. [It] has been footnoted so many times its value to scientists and historians is well known [and] for many years it was the standard guide for travelers . . . passing through the area. It was reliable, factual, clear."[29]

Bartlett despised the harsh West Texas country he crossed, country the Butterfield Mail coaches would have to traverse a few years later. His description of the region in 1852, while causing us to smile, was still altogether true in 1858 when the Overland Mail service began. Bartlett wrote: "At the headwaters of the Concho, therefore, begins that great desert region, which, with no interruption save a limited valley or bottom land along the Rio Grande . . . extends over a district embracing sixteen degrees of longitude, or about a thousand miles, and is wholly unfit for agriculture. It is a desolate barren waste, which can never be rendered useful for man or beast save for a public highway."[30]

Bartlett and his party found woeful evidence that hundreds of emigrants, striving for California, had crossed the Pecos at Horsehead Crossing and used the west bank despite the dangers and lack of water. In his *Personal Narrative*, he tells that his group was constantly finding costly wagons that had broken down, and other valuable paraphernalia of passing emigrants, or dying horses or oxen, that had been left along the roadside. Bartlett was saved in one desperate situation by finding an abandoned wagon with a large steel pin in place which replaced the one that broke on the tongue of his own vehicle.[31]

Paragraphs in Bartlett's book, written as the Commission expedition neared Delaware Creek, are examples of the toll the country took on those who crossed it:

Passed the carcasses of five oxen lying about the road. . . . Their lank bodies were dried up with the skins still adhering to them, showing that even wolves do not attempt to find subsistence on this desolate plain. The remains of wagons were also seen along the road, and furnished our cook with firewood, an article which he had much difficulty in procuring since leaving the Concho River, and particularly since we struck the region near the Pecos. . . . Passed the carcasses of four cattle by the road side; and in another place, where . . . water had at sometime accumulated, there lay the carcasses of five more, which had doubtless mired in endeavoring to satiate their thirst. Portions of wagons, boxes, and barrels were also noticed along the road. . . . Many carcasses and skeletons of oxen, and several skeletons of mules, marked our route today, as well as the remains of broken wagons. As the prairie did not furnish us fuel to make our fires, we gathered up the fragments of the wagons and carried them with us for the purpose . . . but for the broken wagons that were providentially left in our way, we could not have procured wood enough to cook our food.

Reached Delaware Creek and pitched our tents on a spot where there appeared to have been a very large encampment a few months before. Besides the fragments, there was one large Pennsylvania wagon nearly complete, numerous ox-yokes, boxes, barrels, etc., etc. These were collected and carried to our camp for firewood.[32]

Despite a lack of food and recently having suffered the effects of a "Norther" and snow storm, Bartlett was awed by his first sight of Guadalupe Peak:

No sunrise at sea or from the mountain's summit could equal in grandeur that which we now beheld, when the first rays struck the snow-clad mountain, which reared its lofty head before us. The projecting cliffs of white and orange stood out in bold relief against the azure sky, while the crevices and gorges, filled with snow, showed their inequalities with a wonderful distinctness. At the same time the beams of the sun playing on the snow produced the most brilliant and ever changing iris hues. No painter's art could reproduce, or colors imitate, these gorgeous prismatic tints.

After six hours of rugged passage over Guadalupe Pass, he added, "I regretted that we were not able to spend more time in this interesting Pass, the grandeur of which would, under any other circumstances, have induced us to linger; but we had too much at stake to waste a single hour."[33]

As he was leaving Texas and entering New Mexico, Bartlett opined:

Both the Spanish and the aborigines display a much better taste in the appellations given by them to mountains, and other

objects of natural scenery, than is usually exhibited by our people. Their names are significant of the appearance which the
mountain assumes, while ours are christened after some military officer or politician, who may have made a little noise in
his day, but may have never been near the locality which bears
his name.[34]

After his tenure as Boundary Commissioner, Bartlett became
Rhode Island Secretary of State, performing enormous jobs of clas-
sifying and arranging the two hundred years of documents of the
state. After that he performed a similar service for Brown University's John Carter Brown collection. Bartlett died of "paralysis of the
heart" on May 28, 1886.

Death at Quitman Pass

In 1854 raids on Eagle Springs became so bad a colonel in New Mexico wrote that despite the Springs not being within the limits of his
department, "I felt it my duty to detach one of the companies from
Fort Bliss to take post there until other arrangements could be made
for the safe transportation of mail, and also for the protection of emigrants en route to California."[35] (The mail line in question was David
Wasson's 1850 line from San Antonio to Santa Fe.)

The passage of years failed to lessen the dangers along that part
of the mail road. In 1880 a surveyor wrote in a letter,

The Indians have crossed over again into Texas and have already commenced their fiendish atrocities. They killed the
stage driver and one passenger Saturday night, between Ft.
Quitman and Eagle Springs, last week they killed in all eight
Mexican soldiers—a few days before I passed thro' Bass's

247

Canon, they killed a woman (Mrs. Sherman) and two men between Eagle Springs and Van Horns Wells,—About two months ago, they killed and mutilated twenty-nine, men, women and children, near Corizal, in the Canddaria [Candalaria] Mountains, the very place that I am going to work.[36]

In 1880 the stage station at Eagle Springs was rebuilt and a detachment of cavalry was sent there to guard against the great Apache commander, Victorio. But despite the preparedness of the army and the Texas Rangers along that border, for a hectic two weeks, July 28 to August 12, Victorio and his warriors harassed Texas.[37] Crossing the Rio Grande below Eagle Springs, they attacked the San Antonio stage in Quitman Canyon, killing the passenger, General James J. Byrne.[38] Although Victorio was known to be raiding Texas, the stage driver and the general had only one gun between them and only one cartridge for it. When the driver met the Indians, he somehow whirled his stage around, regained the narrow road, and set out full-speed to return to Fort Quitman with the raiders in pursuit. When the fort was reached, it was found that General Byrne had received a fatal wound in the thigh, noted (by Texas Ranger Captain George Baylor) as being "within an inch of a wound he received at Gettysburg."[39]

Gillett gives a more graphic account of this tragedy:

On August 9, 1880, Ed Walde, stage driver, started out (from the mail station near Fort Quitman to Fort Davis) on his drive with General Byrne, retired army officer, occupying the rear seat of the coach. The stage entered the box-like pass [Quitman]—an ideal place for an Indian ambuscade. Walde had driven partly through this pass when, at a short bend in the road, he came suddenly upon old Victorio and his band of one hundred warriors. The Indian advance-guard fired on the coach immediately, and at the first volley General Byrne was fatally wounded, one bullet striking him in the breast and a second passing through his thigh. Walde turned his team as quickly as he could and made a lightning run back to the stage stand with the general's body hanging partly out of the stage. The Apaches followed the stage for four or five miles trying to get ahead, but the two mules [going downhill] made time and beat them to the shelter of the station's adobe walls. It was a miracle that Walde, sitting on the front seat, escaped death without a scratch and that both of the mules were unharmed. At old Fort Quitman I examined the little canvas-topped stage and found it literally shot to pieces.[40]

Gillett said it was from Walde he obtained the particulars of the fight that resulted in the general's death.

Although General Byrne had been a Union officer in the Civil War, he was well known and well liked all over western Texas. He and his much younger wife lived at Fort Worth, and he was frequently at such localities as Weatherford, Phantom Hill, Fort Griffin and along the projected T&P railroad route, having been head of the T&P surveyors since 1873. At Fort Quitman, Captain George Baylor reported, "We (a mixed crowd of Confederates, local citizens, Rangers and U.S. troops) buried Gen. Byrne and fired a couple of volleys over his grave."[41] A few weeks later, Pat Dolan, a loyal associate of Byrne, exhumed the body and carried it by wagon back to Fort Worth for permanent burial.

General Byrne foresaw his immediate death and wrote out a prophetic love letter to his wife Lilly Loving Byrne. The letter, carefully setting out what he owned, what he owed, and who owed him, was also a last will and testament, and was later used as such. He ended his letter with, "My own, my beloved, my darling wife: Sweet companion of my happiest hours on earth, my hope of everlasting joy in [the] great hereafter, these last few parting words: the offering of a love that's more than earthly . . . if the spirits of the dead can hover round and protect the loved ones left behind, mine will always be with you." He told Lilly he wished to be buried beside their only child, who had died in Fort Worth, and assured her, "If my estate is honestly administered you will have enough for all your earthly wants." He insists, "I do not expect you to devote your days to grieving after me. Your years, temperament and perfection of head and heart [she was young and beautiful] will crave a kindred companionship . . . I only ask and dying pray that you will counsel your best judgment, to enable you to make a choice, in all things worthy of you. . . . I'll pray and invoke Gods choicest blessings on your union. I could also ask that my remains, if they can be found, should be buried beside our darling child the offspring of our love, and that you will be buried next to my heart. . . . Goodbye, My darling—my wife—my heart is breaking with the thought that I may see you no more." The letter was signed "Usleta [Ysleta] Aug 4/80." Gen. Byrne was killed five days later.[42]

A day or two after the death of General Byrne, Victorio's Apaches tore down the military telegraph lines, dragged the poles two or three miles, and knocked off the insulators, causing Baylor, the Ranger leader, to remark, "Vic is becoming scientific!"

Colonel Benjamin H. Grierson drove the Victorio Apaches back across the river, but U.S. troops were not part of Victorio's final defeat. Victorio and his band were wiped out by Mexican General Juaquin Terrazas and his soldiers at the battle of Tres Castillos, in the northern Mexican state of Chihuahua, early on October 15.[43] But a band of twelve warriors, four women and four children had left Victorio before his death, making their way into Texas in a series of deadly hit-and-run raids on small detachments of soldiers, isolated herders, and travelers. Early in January, 1881, this band attacked the mail stage in Quitman Canyon and the driver and a passenger were killed. They were finally tracked down and four warriors were killed in a short daybreak battle atop a mountain in the Sierra Diablos. After the fight, the rangers made their breakfast on horse meat, venison, and roasted mescal taken from the Indians. Baylor wrote, in his report of the affair, "We had almost a boundless view from our breakfast table . . . The beauty of the scenery only marred by man's inhumanity to man, the ghostly forms of the Indians lying around."[44] Walter Prescott Webb, in *The Texas Rangers*, called this "doubtless the last real Indian fight on Texas soil."[45]

Tragedy at Apache Pass

The tragedy at Apache Pass, Arizona (called Puerto del Dado, or "Pass of the Dice," i.e., chancy), began early in February, 1861, only four weeks before the end of the Butterfield stage run through the southwest. An eager West Pointer, Lieutenant George N. Bascom, determined to make the Apaches return allegedly stolen stock, and certain he knew "how to handle" the Indians, lured Chief Cochise and his family into a trap, unjustly holding the rest of the family hostage after Cochise had sliced his way out of a tent and escaped. From then on it was war, although Cochise had been relatively peaceful. The chief, mistakenly believing a friendly Butterfield driver named James Wallace had a hand in the deception, appeared with a party at the Apache Pass Butterfield station and called for Wallace to come out—some say Cochise carried a white flag. Not knowing what Lieutenant Bascom had done, Wallace, Charles Culver, the station agent, and a hostler named Walsh went out to meet them. Grabbed in an ambush, Culver and Walsh broke free and tried to return to the station. Culver was killed by the Apaches, and Walsh was unintentionally shot and killed by a soldier in the station who thought Walsh was an Indian. Wallace was taken captive. Later the same day, Cochise and his band waylaid a wagon train on the trail west of the station, and captured two Americans and eight Mexican drovers. The Americans were made prisoners and the eight Mexican freighters tied to wagon wheels and (it is believed) burned alive.

Following the escape of Cochise, Lieutenant Bascom and his men moved to the Butterfield station at Apache Pass. A day later

Cochise again approached within shouting distance of the station, and Wallace, a rawhide lariat around his neck, acted as his interpreter. Cochise offered to trade his captives—Wallace and the two freighters—for the family members held by Bascom. Wallace, knowing he and the two captive Americans would be tortured and killed otherwise, pleaded with Bascom to release the relatives of Cochise, but even with First Sergeant Reuben Bernard arguing the dreadful finality of refusal, Bascom adamantly refused, putting Sergeant Bernard under technical arrest and insisting Cochise return cattle his tribe was accused of stealing and a boy they allegedly kidnapped. (Both charges were apparently baseless.) Recognizing he would not make the trade, Cochise spurred his horse around and galloped off, dragging Wallace to his death. A few days later, all three of the captives' bodies were found, also on the trail, almost unrecognizable save for Wallace's gold teeth. Bascom promptly hanged a brother of Cochise and two nephews, as well as three other Chiricahua Apaches, near the spot where the bodies were found, then released Cochise's wife and young son to carry the news back to the chief.

On February 16, the eastbound stage was ambushed by Cochise and his warriors at Apache Pass. Two mules were downed and the driver wounded, but the stage's nine passengers (one was Butterfield's sectional Superintendent William Buckley; another was A. B. Culver, brother of the slain stationkeeper) fought off the ambush while Culver and a helper cut the dead animals out of harness. All reached the station safely.

Bascom, by then a captain, was killed a year later at the Battle of Valverde, New Mexico.

Rights and Wrongs of the Butterfield Trail

The Southern Overland route through Texas continued to have critics well after the Overland Mail line had been changed to the Central route. In *The Overland Stage to California*, by Frank A. Root (an old Central route stager) and William Elsey Connelly,[46] we find the following bits of hyperbole:

> Now that more than forty years have gone by since the Southern or Butterfield line was equipped and in operation, it will not be out of place to state that a goodly portion of that route . . . was almost impracticable for staging. But for the mild winter climate it would have been entirely so. . . . Passengers traveling it became almost crazed by the long and tedious twenty-three days' journey day and night, much of the way without any rest and comparatively little break in the monotony.[47]

One of the first studies on the Overland Mail operation that went beyond a travel memoir—"Some Details of the Southern Overland Mail"[48]—was by Texas historian Rupert N. Richardson. While recognizing that the Overland Mail had been "treated briefly by several historians, and the romance and adventure . . . not overlooked by the writers of more popular works," he felt the significance of "this great pioneer enterprise" should be examined more closely.[49] A native of West Texas and lifelong resident (born in 1891, he lived to be 95), he was capable of finding soft spots in the operation of the Southern Overland Mail through that area. Having spent most of his life observing the often fickle climate of the place, Rupert Richardson knew that a wet spring in West Texas (such as Captain Randolph C. Marcy obviously encountered in some of his explorations—describing running creeks, gushing springs and holes of sweet water) could create a deadly illusion of an abundance which would not be repeated for years, even decades. In his opinion, this led the Butterfield company, particularly in its lengthy stretch from Fort Chadbourne westward, to overestimate the assets of the route.[50]

Richardson criticizes the path chosen for the Butterfield stage: "In Texas some two hundred miles more of frontier settlement could have been served with little additional mileage if the line had been run more to the south after leaving Sherman." This route would have led to Dallas, Fort Worth, or as far south as Waco.[51] Perhaps Richardson was right. However, two facts intrude: passenger travel was not the main reason for the Butterfield stage line, and Texas was not the goal of the Overland Mail, merely an intermediate consideration in the routing of the Butterfield stage. California was the Golden Goal; anything in between was merely a problem to be solved the easiest way. As the need was speed, it is not likely much financial advantage would have been gained with a switch of routes, and more time would certainly have been lost.

Some of the interesting sources used in Dr. Richardson's article are the contemporary news accounts taken from passengers of the Butterfield mail stages by such newspapers as the *Missouri Republican* of St. Louis, the St. Louis *Democrat*, the San Francisco *Herald*, and the San Francisco *National*. Dr. Richardson reported,

> For the first year there are unusually complete accounts as to the passengers that arrived in St. Louis. . . . [I]nquiring newspaper reporters generally met them and proceeded to gather from them all the information possible about their journey, the number of persons who left San Francisco, the number who joined the party or left it at the different way stations, the number that left the St. Louis route at Fort Smith bound for Memphis, the destination of all parties, and their names and occupations.

As is usually the case with "eyewitness" accounts, the facts seem to expand with every mile distant from the alleged scene. For instance one story, repeated by later writers, quotes a Mr. Hough, who tells of a passenger who was forced to remain at a way station because he had gotten off "to rest" and, "although he offered a liberal bonus," had been marooned for a month, unable to secure a seat on any following stage.[52] Errors and rumors swept the frontier and were customarily believed in toto, as any historian knows who attempts to use such reports. The inaccuracy came from informants who, like the modern-day tellers of "urban myths," swore they either saw something "with their own eyes" or "knew" it happened to a kinsman or a neighbor of said kinsman. Texas historians have wasted many an hour researching Indian raids and bank holdups, attested to by great-granddaddy, that never took place.

A great deal more material has come to light on the Butterfield line since 1925, and as good a historian as Rupert Richardson was—and he was without peer in West Texas—some of his statistics and details have been altered by later findings, such as those of the Conklings, the accounts of the Reverend William Tallack, and Albert Richardson's *Beyond the Mississippi*. Rupert Richardson seems not to have had access to the latter two works, and the Conkling trilogy had not been written.

Unfortunately, in setting up a great many of the state historical markers along the Butterfield Trail, Richardson's 1925 article has been the only source utilized, and not always wisely or well. This has produced, in a number of locations, not just the repetition of errors, but a mindless copying of orotund phraseology, i.e., "a pioneer enterprise of unusual magnitude . . . worthy of consideration among the annals of our national achievement." Amusingly enough, Rupert Richardson, from whom these phrases were lifted, was implying the opposite of that grand declaration. His preceding sentence reads, "the southern Overland Mail never accomplished what its promoters and friends hoped for. While it was not without its influence on national development, it cannot be said that it was an achievement of great national significance."[53]

Regarding historical markers along the Butterfield Trail: the historical accuracy of the Butterfield Overland Mail markers throughout the Texas route is so-so. The best seem to be the ones found in the Sherman area and in far West Texas. A great many important Butterfield locations are not marked, especially in the Trans-Pecos region between Fort Stockton and the city of El Paso. Vandalism may account for certain noticeable gaps.

The Butterfield Stations in Los Angeles

Although the first transcontinental trips of the Southern Overland Mail Company began in mid-September of 1858, the Overland Mail Company had instituted service between San Francisco and Los Angeles in August. Waterman Ormsby, on October 8, 1858, noted: ". . . the Overland Mail Company, through the energy of Mr. [Marcus L.] Kinyon, have been running a tri-weekly stage between San Francisco and Los Angeles for two months, using the Concord coach to San Jose and the canvas-covered thoroughfare wagons [celerity wagons] the rest of the distance."[54]

The Conklings wrote: "Los Angeles was not included on the original itinerary of the Overland Mail [because] the route proposed by the Post Office department was to run from Fort Yuma to San Bernardino and then through Cajon canyon to Fort Tejon. . . . The abandonment of the plan and routing the line over [Col. Philip St. George] Cooke's old road to Warner's Ranch and then on to Los Angeles was not a concession to appease any public demand, but was made compulsory when the contractors found the San Bernardino route impracticable."[55]

The Butterfield station in Los Angeles was located on the west side of Spring Street, 119 feet south of the southwest corner of First Street. The large brick building erected there (1860) was the second largest and best equipped company-owned station after that in El Paso.[56] At the time of the Conklings' writing, the site was occupied by the then-new building of the *Los Angeles Times*, one block south of the Los Angeles Civic Center. A second Butterfield station in what is now Los Angeles was called Cahuenga, twelve miles northwest of the downtown station site. It was located on the west side of Lankershim Boulevard, "almost directly opposite the entrance gate to the Universal City Studios."[57]

Notes

1. Three years later, in 1861, Bailey, by then with the Interior Department, was indicted for extracting $870,000 in bonds from the Indian Trust Fund and turning them over to William H. Russell, founder of the Pony Express, on orders of Secretary of War John B. Floyd, who had been unable to pay Russell for Pony Express expenses because the government was broke. It became a major political scandal and all three men were indicted. The indictments were lifted as the Civil War began and Floyd (who apparently did nothing illegal) joined the Confederate States Army. Walter B. Lang, *The First Overland Mail: Butterfield Trail* (Washington, D.C.: n.p., 1940), 105–10.

2. Lang, 105–10.

3. Thomas Barrett, *The Great Hanging at Gainesville, Cooke County, Texas, October, A.D. 1862* (Austin: Texas State Historical Association, 1961), 2.

4. "According to the 1860 census . . . of the 3,760 individuals listed on the federal population schedule, only sixty-six owned slaves, and two men [Colonel James] Bourland and [Colonel William C.] Young, held almost one-quarter of the bondsmen." Michael Collins, *Cooke County, Texas: Where the South and the West Meet* (n.p.: Cooke County Heritage Society, 1981), 10.

5. "The Unionists in Cooke County could not have had a more formidable foe. Bourland bore a commanding presence, his steel blue eyes reflecting a stern and uncompromising nature. A quick-tempered man, 'hot-headed' . . . a strict disciplinarian. One observer remembered him as 'a good fighter and a good hater.' Another characterized him as being 'as great a tyrant as ever reigned since Nero.'" Collins, 11.

6. George Washington Diamond, *Diamond's Account of the Great Hanging at Gainesville,* ed. Sam Acheson and Julie Ann Hudson O'Connell (Austin: Texas State Historical Association, 1963), 2.

7. Diamond, 2.

8. Diamond, 9.

9. *Southern Intelligencer,* Austin, January 1861.

10. Diamond, 9.

11. Diamond, 8. Sam Acheson and Julie Ann Hudson O'Connell, editors, in a 1963 note to the Diamond account state "No copy of any detailed 'proposition' to organize a separate state in North Texas is extant," 8. However, historian Terry Cowan, speaking to the East Texas State Historical Association in Nacogdoches in September, 1992, is quoted as saying that the *Sherman Patriot,* Foster's paper, proposed boundaries for a new state that would have encom-

passed ten northern Texas counties and, across the Red River, the Chickasaw and Choctaw Nations. Kent Biffle, "No Quarter for Unionists in North Texas," *The Dallas Morning News*, 27 September 1992, 47A.

12. Diamond, 87.

13. Diamond, 88.

14. Claude Elliot, "Union Sentiment in Texas 1861–1865," *Southwestern Historical Quarterly*, L (April 1947): 449.

15. Sue Watkins, ed., *One League to Each Wind* (Austin: Texas Surveyors Association, 1964), 68.

16. Colonel W. S. Nye, *Carbine & Lance* (Norman: University of Oklahoma Press, 1962), 125.

17. Brigadier General Richard Henry Pratt, *Battlefield and Classroom: Four Decades with the American Indian, 1867–1907*, ed. Robert Utley (New Haven: Yale University Press, 1964), 42n.

18. Ibid.

19. Some claim as many as nineteen ultimately died.

20. J. W. Wilbarger, *Indian Depredations in Texas* (Austin: Pemberton Press, 1967), 580.

21. Brit Johnson's story and the story of the Elm Creek raid have been written about extensively but few of the accounts agree. The most detailed story of his death is in Wilbarger's *Indian Depredations in Texas*, which, romanticized as always, nevertheless holds up well considering what has come out since its publication. Carrie Crouch's *A History of Young County, Texas* adds some local information, although errors and contradictions make the book unreliable. This was one of a series of county histories published in the 1950s by the Texas State Historical Association. Most are unworthy of the imprint. Colonel Nye, in *Carbine and Lance*, gives a brief note of Brit Johnson's death fight but adds a few Indian details gleaned from the mouths of elderly participants. Buck Barry, in his classic work *A Texas Ranger and Frontiersman*, edited by James K. Greer, gives a brief account of Brit Johnson's death but adds quite a lot (some of it conflicting with other accounts) on the Elm Creek raid where his father-in-law David Peveler and brother-in-law Franz were among the besieged settlers. Barbara A. Neal Ledbetter's *Fort Belknap Saga* gives much family data for Brit Johnson and other Belknap citizens, particularly some important black and mulatto families. The section of Kenneth Porter's "Negroes and Indians on the Texas Frontier," *Southwestern Historical Quarterly* LIII (October 1949): 155, about Brit Johnson's death, is a compilation of earlier sources.

22. James B. Gillett, *Six Years with the Texas Rangers 1875–1881* (New Haven: Yale Univerity Press, 1925), 171–76.

23. Janet Edwards, "Gospel West of the Pecos," *The Texas Historian*, January, 1972 n.p.

24. Edwards, n.p.

25. Thelma Fletcher to A. C. Greene, October 14, 1992, at Salado, Texas.

26. Edwards, n.p.

27. John Russell Bartlett, introduction to *Personal Narrative of Explorations and Incidents in Texas, New Mexico, California, Sonora and Chihuahua 1850–1853,* (Chicago: Rio Grande Press, 1965), n.p.

28. The Disturnell map, for example, located El Paso at 32 degrees 15', which is many miles too far north from its true location at 31 degrees 45'.

29. Bartlett, Introduction.

30. Bartlett, 104.

31. William Goetzmann gives more data on the political goings-on that took place in and around Bartlett's attempt to run the boundary and the eventual actions which led to the Gadsden Purchase that made the western extension of the Butterfield mail route feasible. William Goetzmann, *Exploration and Empire* (New York: Alfred A. Knopf, 1966), 261–63.

32. Bartlett was also a more than adequate artist and his *Personal Narrative* is illustrated by woodcuts made from his drawings. His dramatic watercolor of an incident which occurred when the Commission group was fording the Pecos at Horsehead Crossing (Bartlett was almost drowned) is historically accurate and more exciting than a photograph. It is now at Brown University. For a black and white reproduction see Sam D. Ratliffe, *Painting Texas History to 1900* (Austin: University of Texas Press, 1992), 72.

33. Bartlett, 119.

34. Bartlett, 195.

35. Roscoe P. and Margaret B. Conkling, *The Butterfield Overland Mail 1857–1869,* Vol. II (Glendale: Arthur H. Clark, Co., 1947), 37–38.

36. Watkins, 185.

37. Gillett, 180–89.

38. Walter Prescott Webb, in *The Texas Rangers: A Century of Frontier Defense* (Austin: University of Texas Press, 1965), uses the name "Bynum" but notes the discrepancy in the spelling of proper names between Ranger Captain George Baylor and Gillett who spells it properly. J. J. Byrne was a retired Union general and former U.S. Marshal for Galveston. He was Chief Engineer of the surveyors of the Texas & Pacific Railway, a project he did not live to see completed.

39. G. A. Holland, in his history of Weatherford and Parker County, quotes a Weatherford man who knew the general as saying Byrne was wounded at Chickamauga.

40. Gillett, 181.

41. Gillett, 182.

42. Watkins, 184–87.

43. Frank D. Reeve, "The Apache Indians in Texas," *Southwestern Historical Quarterly* L (October, 1946): 212–13 .

44. Gillett, 209.

45. Webb, 430. A diorama of the final fight is displayed at the Fort Davis National Historic Site.

46. Frank A. Root and William Elsey Connelly, *Overland Stage to California: Personal Reminiscences* (Topeka: n.p., 1901), 483.

47. Ibid.

48. Rupert N. Richardson, "Some Details of the Overland Mail Company," *Southwestern Historical Quarterly* XXIX (July 1925): 1.

49. R. Richardson, 2.

50. R. Richardson, 5.

51. R. Richardson, 17.

52. R. Richardson, 8n.

53. R. Richardson, 18.

54. Ormsby, 127.

55. Conkling, Vol. II, 260.

56. Ibid.

57. Conkling, Vol. II, 263.

PART SIX

Epilogue –

Dreams End But Legends Abide

John Butterfield

John Butterfield had a sad finale to his Overland vision. His problems started in 1859 when Congress, because of internal political conflicts, failed to pass the annual Post Office Appropriation Bill. President James Buchanan refused to call a special session to authorize payments on mail contracts, and the Overland Mail Company, in order to continue, had to make repeated new loans with Wells Fargo and Adams Express Company. The Adams Express loans were covered by the contract payments owed from the Post Office Department; thus, Wells Fargo remained the major risk-taker.[1]

As a result of the increasing debt load of the Overland Mail Company and policy differences with John Butterfield, Wells Fargo management grew annoyed. Several Wells Fargo directors "expressed concern" about the management and "excessive expenditures" of the OMC. The climax came on March 19, 1860, at the board's New York meeting. Danford N. Barney, a Wells Fargo director and an original director of the Overland Mail Company, earlier had demanded the OMC "take steps to secure [Wells Fargo] for advances made" to the amount of $162,400. On that Monday morning, Barney threatened to foreclose on and take over "all [Overland Mail Company] Horses, Mules, Harnesses, stage Coaches, Waggons, and other property effects now owned by it."[2] Since they could not pay the enormous sum, and the Wells Fargo representatives knew it, Butterfield, the president, felt the threat was unfair and unjustified—and he left the chair in protest. Minutes later, Barney, who had taken over the chair, offered to withdraw the foreclosure petition on one condition: John Butterfield must be removed as president. In the ensuing election by the Overland Mail Company directors, William B. Dinsmore was voted new president. More than a month passed before Butterfield, now a mere token director, attended another board meeting. Thus, Wells Fargo succeeded in ousting the father of the Butterfield Overland Mail Company from the presidency of his company. He was not allowed to resign. The Conklings, relying on earlier data, stated Butterfield had suffered a breakdown and was unable to carry on the job. This, we know today—thanks to Wells Fargo/Overland Mail board minutes—was not the case.[3]

A San Francisco newspaper report of April 30, 1860, commenting on the abrupt changes in the Overland Mail Company—the General Superintendent of the Mails had also been replaced and a new director put on the board—made mention of a plan by Butterfield of which little or nothing has been reported by later historians. This was his proposal to establish a pony express run through Texas and the southwest. The newspaper noted,

> The precise cause of the recent difficulties in the Company is not ascertained; but it is supposed to have grown out of opposition to Mr. Butterfield's earnest desire to start a horse express over the [southern] road in competition with Russell & Majors [who had started the mid-route Pony Express in March, 1860]. His associates did not consider such an enterprise desirable, as the distance is so much greater on the Southern route, that it would be impossible to compete with the Salt Lake route, in good weather.[4]

What Wells Fargo decided became fact, because Wells Fargo was the banker. And as historian Roy S. Bloss noted, the financial fabric of the Overland Mail Company "was largely woven with skeins of Wells Fargo yarn."[5]

The standards of discipline and efficiency instituted and maintained under Butterfield's regime, were, unfortunately, allowed to relax after he dropped the reins of control in April, 1860. From that time there was a noticeable decline in the general morale of the operating force. . . . Fort Smith agent Hiram Rumfield denounced these later employees as "a set of ignorant and brutish road-agents."[6]

A few months after his ouster as president of the Overland Mail Company, Butterfield did suffer a physical breakdown and went into seclusion in Utica, New York, for two years. Some historians believe it was brought on, in great part, by the action of Wells Fargo and the ending of his "grand stage adventure." Butterfield returned to business, heading at least one railroad, the Utica and Waterville Rail Road Company. He was Mayor of Utica in 1865, but suffered a paralytic stroke in October, 1867, and died November 14, 1869. His funeral was the biggest in Utica history. New York Governor Horatio Seymour led the list of those attending—but none of the directors of the Overland Mail Company was named a pallbearer.

Waterman Ormsby, Jr.

On the successful completion of the first transcontinental mail run by coach, Waterman Ormsby was feted in San Francisco, but was caught in the net of newspaper competition. The *San Francisco Bulletin*, jealous of the *Herald* reporter's reception, sneered, "it is known that said correspondent was specially employed [by] the company to go over the route and write it up!"[7]

After returning to New York, Waterman Ormsby for the next twelve years worked for three other New York papers, the *Times*, *World*, and *Sun*. Unfortunately, we have very few of his further writings. By 1870 he had joined the Continental Bank Note Company, holding a position there for fourteen years. He reportedly was the de facto president of the New York Liberal Club during the years when Horace Greeley (who died in 1872) was supposed to be the presiding officer. In 1885 Ormsby became official stenographer of the magistrates' court of New York City, in which capacity he continued until his death on April 29, 1908. He was survived by his wife, a daughter, and two of the three sons born to the couple—both sons stenographers of the New York supreme court.

Waterman III, the young "Butterfield" baby, if you will, had a career similar to his father's. After graduating from College of the City of New York in 1876, he was a newspaper reporter, private secretary, and amanuensis. In 1882 he was appointed secretary to the senate of the State of Pennsylvania and two years later became official stenographer to the supreme court of New York, a position he held until his death in 1914.[8]

The Butterfield Trail

It has long been assumed that the reason the Butterfield Overland Mail line abandoned the southern route was because of the Civil War and the dangers inherent in the U.S. Mail traveling through enemy territory. In reality, its days were over regardless of war. From the beginning it had been bedeviled by criticism, not of the service but of the route. Efforts were made, time and again, to get the contract canceled or the line moved farther north,[9] so the southern route was already in the process of being changed to a more northerly route before the war began. On March 2, 1861, Congress passed a law which allowed the Postmaster General to discontinue service on the Southern Overland Mail route and provide for a daily overland mail stage on the Central Route from Atchison, Kansas to Placerville, California. The Overland Mail Company (then minus John Butterfield) became the only bidder, and as soon as the contract for the entire route was signed, began farming out various branches and segments of the required service.[10]

On March 16, 1861, the last movement over the southern route was made and the operating schedule immediately shifted to the central line. The company began transfer of stock and manpower to the new route about April 1, 1861.[11]

Despite the rigors and dangers of the route through Texas, New Mexico, and Arizona, the Butterfield mail line had grown in favor so that by 1860 a California newspaper reported that more letters were being sent by the Butterfield route than by the ocean steamers. "So regular is its arrival that the inhabitants know almost the hour and the minute when the welcome sound of the post horn will reach them. The Overland is the most popular institution of the Far West." Leroy Hafen wrote, "Even in England sealed letter-bags were made up regularly for San Francisco and the English Pacific Coast possessions to go overland during the intervening period between the dates of departure of the Panama steamers."[12] (Is it too romantic for us to imagine the flow of dainty English letters, perfumed perhaps, written on topics so foreign to their environment of the moment, passing routinely through the primitive villages, lonely stations and outposts of West Texas?)

After the Civil War there were voices belatedly asking that the Overland Mail be reinstituted. A Decatur correspondent writing to the old Dallas *Herald* in the spring of 1867 said, "The town of Decatur is the point where the Overland Mail touched as it passed through Wise County [and] now that peace has been established, the people of North Texas desire the re-establishment of the Overland Mail."[13] A historian, writing afterward, complained, " . . . the mail route was discontinued. The effect was immediately felt and was one of the evidences of the ruthlessness of war."[14]

On October 10, 1958, to celebrate the hundredth anniversary of the beginning of the Butterfield Overland Mail line over the southern route, a four-cent commemorative stamp was placed on sale at San Francisco. The center feature shows a coach under attack—the coach, a firing rifleman and dramatically rearing horses superimposed on a map of the southwest with the Butterfield route lined in.

It may sound like quibbling to note that the scene is erroneous; as noted, an attack on a Butterfield mail coach took place only once, and the rearing horses should be mules, because horses were not used at Apache Pass in Arizona where the attack took place. And the Concord-type coach depicted on the stamp should be a "celerity wagon," as the heavier coaches were in use only after reaching California. The design was the work of William H. Buckley, a member of the Citizens' Stamp Advice Committee (was he kin to the William Buckley who was aboard the Apache Pass coach which was attacked?) and the art work was prepared by Charles R. Chickering of the Bureau of Engraving and Printing. Alas, if someone on the Citizens' Stamp Advisory Committee could only have been a historian.

An earlier proposed Butterfield Overland Mail stamp would have commemorated "a century of progress in the transportation of the United States Mail" with a map depicting the routes of both the Butterfield Overland Mail line and the San Antonio-San Diego line. The design would have been centered around the Butterfield's Pinery station. A jet airplane was shown flying high above the Guadalupes and the station.[15] A letter to the *Southwestern Historical Quarterly* in 1947 from a stamp and cover collector said that in thirty years of collecting he had never seen an Overland Mail cover with a Texas cancellation.

Philatelic celebration wasn't the only form of honor for the Butterfield mail centennial. Albert H. Oechsle of Jefferson City, Missouri, announced he had produced a memento of the Butterfield Overland Stage in the form of two editions of sterling silver enameled spoons, one called "moccha" the other "demi-tasse." The limited editions sold for $5.50 and $5.25 respectively: the demi-tasse spoon being fractionally smaller than the moccha.

The most extensive celebration was the 1958 Overland Mail Caravan which actually carried U.S. mail, following the line from Tipton, Missouri, to San Francisco, keeping as close as possible to the old route and observing the Butterfield timetable. The Caravan left Tipton, Missouri, on September 16, 1958, and entered Texas on September 21 at Denison after crossing the Red River on the U.S Highway 75 bridge. Included in the Overland Mail Caravan was a reconditioned Concord coach (formerly property of Pawnee Bill's Wild West Show) owned and driven by John D. Frizzell of Oklahoma City, and his son, John, Jr. The motorized version of the Overland Mail coach was the refurbished U.S. Highway Post Office No. 1. It was a specially equipped red, white and blue Model 788 White bus which had introduced U.S.H.P.P. service on February 10, 1941.[16]

The other vehicles in the Caravan included the Centennial Highway Chapel, with Chaplain Charles F. Arnold in charge; the Anvil Unit, with Al Ferris as farrier (horseshoer); a California State Unit, with a collection of Overland Mail historical books; and a wagon for Hugh Park, editor of the *Press-Argue* of Van Buren, Arkansas, who printed a daily Caravan newspaper, *The Stagehorn*, on his early American hand press.

The idea for the centennial celebration came from American Airlines senior pilot Captain Vernon H. Brown of Tulsa, Oklahoma. He said the Butterfield Trail first caught his interest when he saw the fading traces of the old stage road below him while flying the same route the Butterfield stage had followed. Captain Brown began planning the celebration several years before the actual centennial year. A note in the January, 1955, *Southwestern Historical Quarterly* reports his activities as chairman of the Oklahoma committee for the centennial and says "present plans include the restoration of the 'Pinery.'" A year later the *Quarterly* noted that Captain Brown and H. William Moore, of Hollywood, were working on a project to film the Butterfield Trail. Moore wrote, "We expect to cover this route in a series of 13, 12 1/2-minute color and sound [16 mm] films . . . for television. A folk ballad singer will carry the story and the continuity." Moore adds, "By 1958 color television will be a reality in all or at least many homes."[17]

The Centennial Caravan successfully made it to San Francisco as was scheduled, with much interest along the route, but the Texas portion, as should have been expected, was reportedly the most responsive to the celebration.

The Butterfield mail, the Butterfield stage, the Butterfield line— however you term that compelling page in history's book of the west—was over with the demise of the southern route of the Over- land Mail. The Overland Mail name continued, using the Central route from Missouri to California, its coaches still emblazoned "OMC"—but the man on whose shoulders the legend reposes was no longer in charge of his Great Adventure. The Butterfield stage had ended its run.

Notes

1. W. Turrentine Jackson, "A New Look at Wells Fargo, Stagecoaches and the Pony Express," *California Historical Society Quarterly* (December 1966): 298–301.
2. Jackson, 300.
3. Ibid.
4. Jackson, 301.
5. Roy S. Bloss, *Pony Express–The Great Gamble* (Berkeley: Howell-North, 1959), quoted by W. Turrentine Jackson in a speech before the Western His- tory Association in El Paso, October 14, 1966.
6. Roscoe P. and Margaret B. Conkling, *The Butterfield Overland Mail 1857- 1869*, vol I (Glendale: Arthur H. Clark Co., 1947), 148.
7. Ormsby, x.
8. Data on Waterman Ormsby, his son, and quotes from the San Francisco Bulletin are all from Waterman Lily Ormsby, Jr., *The Butterfield Overland Mail*, ed. Lyle H. Wright and Josephine M. Bynum (San Marino: The Huntington Library, 1955), ix–xi.
9. Leroy Hafen, *The Overland Mail* (Glendale: Arthur Clark Co., 1926), 99.
10. The famed Pony Express had begun on April 3, 1860, undertaken by William H. Russell, of Russell, Majors and Waddell, another western stage op- eration. It lasted until October 24, 1861 and was ruinous financially. Russell

was indicted for accepting $870,000 of Indian Trust Fund Bonds in a huge financial scandal. The indictment was dropped in the excitement of the Civil War, but Russell was a ruined man. (See also: Note #1 in Part V.)

11. Rumfield, Butterfield agent in Fort Smith, reportedly made an unusual trip across Texas after the Butterfield stages ceased running. The Conklings wrote: "Before Rumfield abandoned his post at the outbreak of the Civil War (the Confederate flag was raised over Fort Smith on April 23, 1861), he made a trip over the route as far west as Fort Fillmore, New Mexico, with the object of closing accounts at the various agencies, establishing claims for losses incurred, and arranging for the transfer of such livestock and equipment as could be collected and moved. Except in Texas where it was either confiscated or stolen, the greater part of the company's livestock and equipment on other sections of the route was salvaged. Rumfield managed to make his way back over the route and arrived in Springfield [Mo.] on August 8, 1861. Shortly after this he entered upon his new duties in the Overland Mail Company office at Salt Lake City, Utah." Conkling, Vol. II, 338.

12. Hafen, 99.

13. Cliff D. Cates, *A Pioneer History of Wise County* (Decatur: Wise County Historical Society, 1971), 143.

14. Ibid.

15. H. Bailey Carroll, ed., "Texas Collection," *Southwestern Historical Quarterly* LXII (January 1959): 395; LX (April 1957): 553.

16. The first letter this Highway Post Office No. 1 carried had been mailed by President Franklin D. Roosevelt on his birthday, January 31. President Roosevelt was a noted philatelist.

17. Despite Moore's prescient view of television's future, these interesting visual projects apparently did not reach the public eye.

Bibliography

Abernethy, Francis Edward, ed. *Legendary Ladies of Texas*. Denton: University of North Texas Press, 1994.

Banning, Captain William and George Hugh Banning. *Six Horses*. New York: The Century Co., 1930.

Barrett, Thomas. *The Great Hanging at Gainesville, Cooke County, Texas, October, A.D. 1862*. Austin: Texas State Historical Association, 1961.

Barry, Buck. *A Texas Ranger and Frontiersman: The Days of Buck Barry in Texas, 1845–1906*. Ed. James K. Greer. Dallas: Southwest Press, 1932.

Bartlett, John Russell. *Personal Narratives of Explorations and Incidents in Texas, New Mexico, California, Sonora and Chihuahua Connected with the United States and Mexico 1850–1853*. Chicago: Rio Grande Press, 1965.

Bierschwale, Margaret. "Mason County, Texas, 1845–1870." *Southwestern Historical Quarterly* LII (April 1949): 379–97.

Biffle, Kent. "No Quarter for Unionists in North Texas." *The Dallas Morning News*, 27 September 1992, 47A.

Biggers, Don Hampton. *History That Will Never Be Repeated*. Ennis, Texas: Hi-Grade Printing Office, 1902.

Bloss, Roy S. *Pony Express—The Great Gamble*. Berkeley: Howell–North, 1959.

"Butterfield Overland Mail Centennial." Tulsa, OK. August 1958. Unpaged timetable for Overland Mail Centennial Caravan.

Carroll, H. Bailey, ed. "Texas Collection." *Southwestern Historical Quarterly* LIX (July 1955): 91–121.

_____. "Texas Collection." *Southwestern Historical Quarterly* LX (April 1957): 548–67.

_____. "Texas Collection." *Southwestern Historical Quarterly* LXII (April 1959): 542–59.

_____. "Texas Collection." *Southwestern Historical Quarterly* LXII (January 1959): 386–400.

Cates, Cliff D. *Pioneer History of Wise County*. Decatur: Wise County Historical Society, 1971.

Chrisman, Brutus Clay. *Early Days in Callahan County*. Abilene: n.p., 1972.

Clayton, Lawrence. *Historic Ranches of Texas*. Austin: University of Texas Press, 1993.

Collins, Michael. *Cooke County, Texas: Where the South and the West Meet*. n.p.: Cooke County Heritage Society, 1981.

Conkling, Roscoe P. and Margaret B. *The Butterfield Overland Mail 1857–1869*. 3 Volumes. Glendale: Arthur H. Clark Company, 1947.

Connor, Seymour V. *The Peters Colony of Texas*. Austin: Texas State Historical Association, 1959.

Cox, Mike. *Red Rooster County*. Hereford, Texas: Pioneer Book Publishers, Inc., 1970.

Crawford, Leta. *A History of Irion County, Texas*. Waco: Texian Press, 1966.

Cremony, John C. *Life Among the Apaches*. New York: Time-Life Books, 1981.

Crimmins, Colonel Martin, ed. "Colonel J. K. F. Mansfield's Inspection Report of Texas." *Southwestern Historical Quarterly* XLII (October 1938): 351–87; (April 1939): 122–48; (January 1939): 215–57.

Crouch, Carrie J. *A History of Young County, Texas*. Austin: Texas State Historical Association, 1956.

Dary, David. *Entrepreneurs of the Old West*. New York: Alfred A. Knopf, 1986.

Dearen, Patrick. *Castle Gap and the Pecos Frontier*. Fort Worth: Texas Christian University Press, 1988.

Diamond, George Washington. *George Washington Diamond's Account of the Great Hanging at Gainesville, 1862*. Ed. Sam Acheson and Julie Ann Hudson O'Connell. Austin: Texas State Historical Association, 1963.

Dooley, Claude and Betty. *Why Stop?: A Guide to Texas Historical Roadside Markers*. Houston: Gulf Publishing Co., 1985.

Eagleton, N. Ethie. *On the Last Frontier: A History of Upton County, Texas*. El Paso: Texas Western Press, 1971.

Edwards, Janet. "Gospel West of the Pecos." *The Texas Historian*, January 1972.

Elkins, Captain John M. and Frank W. McCarty. *Indian Fighting on the Texas Frontier*. Amarillo: Russell & Cockrell, 1929.

Elliot, Claude. "Union Sentiment in Texas 1861–1865." *Southwestern Historical Quarterly*, L (April 1947): 449–77.

274

Emory, William H. *Report of the Survey and the Territory Acquired Under the Treaty of December 30, 1853.* House Exec. Docs., 34th Congress; August, 1856.

_____. *Report on the U. S. and Mexican Boundary Survey 1858–1859.* 34th Congress, 1st Session, Senate Ex. Doc. 108, 1859.

Faulk, Odie B. *Too Far North, Too Far South.* Los Angeles: Westernlore Press, 1967.

Ford, John Salmon. *Rip Ford's Texas.* Ed. Stephen B. Oates. Austin: University of Texas Press, 1963.

"Fort Bowie National Historic Site, Arizona." National Park Service, Department of the Interior. n.p., n.d.

Foster-Harris. *The Look of the Old West.* New York: Viking Press, 1955.

Franks, Don R. "Concho Valley Archeology Society News." San Angelo, Texas. Spring 1994.

Frazer, Robert W. *Forts of the West.* Norman: University of Oklahoma Press, 1965.

French, Captain S. G., T.E. 1849, 31st Congress, 1st Session, U. S. Senate. No. 64.

Friend, Llerena, ed. *M. K. Kellogg's Texas Journal 1872.* Austin: University of Texas Press, 1967.

Gillett, James B. *Six Years With the Texas Rangers 1875–1881.* New Haven: Yale University Press, 1925.

Goetzmann, William. *Exploration and Empire.* New York: Alfred A. Knopf, 1966.

Good, Marilyn J., ed. *Three Dollars Per Mile.* Austin: Texas Surveyors Association, 1981.

Grant, Bruce. *American Forts Yesterday and Today.* New York: E. P. Dutton & Co., 1965.

Greene, A. C. *The Last Captive.* Austin: Encino Press, 1972.

_____. "Fort Davis Became Necessity." *Abilene Reporter-News,* 20 August 1959, 1B.

Greer, James K. *Colonel Jack Hays, Texas Frontier Leader and California Builder.* College Station: Texas A&M University Press, 1987.

Hafen, Leroy. *The Overland Mail, 1849–1869.* Glendale: Arthur Clark Co., 1926.

275

Haley, J. Evetts. *Fort Concho and The Texas Frontier*. San Angelo: *Standard Times*, 1952.

_____. *Charles Goodnight, Cowman & Plainsman*. Boston: Houghton Mifflin, 1936.

Halff, M. H. (Hal). *My Memoirs*. Ed. Barbara Steele Hendricks. Austin: For China Pond, Elliot Ranch, 1987.

Hall, Martin Hardwick. "The Formation of Sibley's Brigade and the March to New Mexico." *Southwestern Historical Quarterly* LXI (January 1958): 383–405.

Heitman, Francis B. *Historical Register and Dictionary of the United States Army, From Its Organization, September 29, 1789, to March 2, 1903*. 2 vols. Published under Act of Congress, 1903.

Holden, Frances Mayhugh. *Lambshead Before Interwoven*. College Station: Texas A&M University Press, 1982.

Hopkins, Joseph G. E. *Concise Dictionary of American Biography*. New York: Charles Scribners' Sons, 1964.

Huckabay, Ida. *Ninety-Four Years in Jack County*. Austin: Steck Company, 1950.

Hughes, Alton. *Pecos, A History of the Pioneer West*. Seagraves, TX: Pioneer Book Publishers, 1978.

Hughes, Anne E. *The Beginnings of Spanish Settlement in the El Paso District*. Berkeley: University of California Press, 1914.

Hunter, J. Marvin, ed. *Trail Drivers of Texas*. Austin: University of Texas Press, 1985.

Jackson, W. Turrentine. "A New Look at Wells Fargo, Stagecoaches and the Pony Express." *California Historical Society Quarterly*, December 1966, 295–301.

_____. *Wagon Road West*. Nebraska: First Bison Book, 1979.

Johnson, Allen and Dumas Malone, ed. *Dictionary of American Biography*. New York: Scribner's Sons, 1946.

Lammons, Frank B. "Operation Camel." *Southwestern Historical Quarterly* LXI (July 1957): 20–50.

Lang, Walter B. *The First Overland Mail: Butterfield Trail*. Washington, D.C.: n.p., 1940.

Ledbetter, Barbara A. Neal. Fort Belknap Frontier Saga. n.p., 1982.

Lomax, John A. *Cowboy Songs and Other Frontier Ballads*. New York: Macmillan Co., 1936.

Lucas, Mattie Davis and Mita Holsapple Hall. *A History of Grayson County, Texas*. Sherman: Scruggs Printing Co., 1936.

McConnell, Joseph Carroll. *The West Texas Frontier*. 2 vols. (Vol. 1, Gazette Print, Jacksboro, 1933; Vol. 2, Texas Legal Bank & Book Co., Palo Pinto, 1939.)

Marcy, Randolph B. *Thirty Years of Army Life on the Border*. Philadelphia: J. B. Lippincott Co., 1963.

Mayhall, Mildred P. *Indian Wars of Texas*. Waco: Texian Press, 1965.

Mecham, J. Lloyd. "Antonio de Espejo and His Journey to New Mexico." *Southwestern Historical Quarterly* XXX (October 1926): 114–38.

Mellard, Rudolph. *Stagecoach 22, San Antonio-El Paso, 1869*. Salado, TX: Anson Jones Press, 1977.

Mills, Anson. *My Story*. Washington, D.C. n.p., 1918.

Moody, Ralph. *Stagecoach West*. New York: Thomas Y. Crowell, Co., 1967.

Morris, John W. and Edwin C. McReynolds. *Historical Atlas of Oklahoma*. Norman: University of Oklahoma Press, 1965.

Neighbors, Major Robert to General William S. Harney. 4 June 1849. Army Headquarters. Letters Received. Olds Records Sec. Washington, D.C.

Neighbours, Kenneth. "The Expedition of Major Robert S. Neighbors to El Paso in 1849." *Southwestern Historical Quarterly* LVIII (July 1954): 36–59.

_____. "Indian Exodus Out of Texas in 1859." *West Texas Historical Association Year Book*, XXXVI (October 1960): 80–97.

Nevin, David. *The Expressmen*. Alexandria, VA: Time-Life Books., 1974.

Nye, Colonel W. S. *Carbine & Lance*. Norman: University of Oklahoma Press, 1962.

Ormsby, Waterman L., Jr. *The Butterfield Overland Mail*. Ed. Lyle H. Wright and Josephine M. Bynum. San Marino, California: The Huntington Library, 1955.

Parker, William B. *Notes Taken . . . Through Unexplored Texas in the Summer and Fall of 1854*. Austin: Texas State Historical Association, 1990.

Patterson, Paul. *Pecos Tales*. Austin: Encino Press, 1967.

Pecos Enterprise, 1936.

Porter, Kenneth. "Negroes and Indians on the Texas Frontier." *Southwestern Historical Quarterly* LIII (October 1949): 151–63.

Pratt, Richard Henry. *Battlefield and Classroom: Four Decades with the American Indian, 1867–1907.* Ed. Robert M. Utley. New Haven: Yale University Press, 1964.

Protection of the Frontier of Texas. 35th Congress, 2nd Session, 1859. U. S. House. Ex. Doc. No. 27, 62.

Ratliffe, Sam D. *Painting Texas History to 1900.* Austin: University of Texas Press, 1992.

Reed, S. P. *A History of the Texas Railroads.* Houston: The St. Clair Publishing Co., 1941.

Reeve, Frank D. "The Apache Indians in Texas." *Southwestern Historical Quarterly* L (October 1946): 189–219.

Richardson, Albert Deane. *Beyond the Mississippi: From the Great River to the Great Ocean.* New York: Bliss, 1867.

Richardson, Rupert N. *The Comanche Barrier to South Plains Settlement.* Glendale: Arthur H. Clark Co., 1933.

_____. "Some Details of the Southern Overland Mail Company." *Southwestern Historical Quarterly* XXIX (July 1925): 1–18.

Rister, Carl Coke. *Border Captives.* Norman: University of Oklahoma Press, 1940.

_____. *Oil! Titan of the Southwest.* Norman: University of Oklahoma Press, 1949.

_____. "The Significance of the Jacksboro Indian Affair of 1871." *Southwestern Historical Quarterly* XXIX (January 1926): 181–200.

Root, Frank A. and W. E. Connelly. *The Overland Stage to California: Personal Reminiscences.* Topeka: n.p., 1901.

Santleben, August. *A Texas Pioneer, Early Staging and Overland Freighting Days on the Frontiers of Texas and Mexico.* Waco: W. M. Morrison, 1967.

Scannell, Jack C. "A Survey of the Stagecoach Mail in the Trans Pecos, 1850–1861." *West Texas Historical Association Year Book.* Vol. XLVII, 1971, 115–26.

Schwettmann, Martin W. *Santa Rita, the University of Texas Oil Discovery.* Austin: Texas State Historical Association, 1943.

Scobee, Barry. *Old Fort Davis*. San Antonio: Naylor Company, 1947.

Shelton, Hoope and Homer Hutto. *First 100 Years of Jones County, Texas*. Stamford: Shelton Press, 1978.

Sherman, John, Mike Head, James Crump, and Dave Head. *Hueco Tanks: A Climber's and Boulderer's Guide*. Evergreen, CO: Chockstone Press, Inc., 1991.

Sibley, Marilyn McAdams. *Travelers in Texas 1761–1860*. Austin: University of Texas Press, 1967.

Smith, William F. and William H. C. Whiting, T.E. 31st Congress, 1st Session, 1849, U. S. Senate. Ex. Doc. No. 64.

Smith, William G. and J. H. Agee. *Soil Survey of Eastland County, Texas*. Washington, D.C.: Government Printing Office, 1917.

Smithers, W. D. *Circuit Riders of the Big Bend*. El Paso: Texas Western Press, 1981.

Smithwick, Noah. *The Evolution of a State*. Austin: Steck-Vaughn Co., 1968.

Smythe, H. *Historical Sketch of Parker County and Weatherford, Texas*. Waco: W. M. Morrison, 1973.

Sonnichsen, C. L. *Pass of the North: Four Centuries on the Rio Grande*. El Paso: Texas Western Press, 1968.

Southern Intelligencer. Austin, January 1861.

Swint, Ocie Lea and Howard Hudnall. *The History of Sherman and Grayson County, Texas (1846–1987)*. Sherman: Sherman Public Library, 1983.

Texas Almanac. Dallas: *Dallas Morning News*, 1941–42.

Texas DAR Bulletin. Fall, 1993.

Tharp, B. C. and Chester V. Kielman, ed. "Mary S. Young's Journal of Botanical Explorations in Trans-Pecos Texas, August–September, 1914." *Southwestern Historical Quarterly* LXV (January 1962): 366–93; (April 1962): 512–38.

Thomas, Clayton L. *Taber's Cyclopedic Medical Dictionary*. 16th Ed. Philadelphia: F. A. Davis Co., 1989.

Tompkins, G. C. (Tom). *A Compendium of the Overland Mail Company on the South Route 1858–1861 and the Period Surrounding It*. El Paso: G. T. Co., 1985.

Watkins, Sue, ed. *One League to Each Wind*. Austin: Texas Surveyors Association, 1964.

Webb, Walter Prescott. *The Texas Rangers: A Century of Frontier Defense*. Austin: University of Texas Press, 1965.

Webb, Walter Prescott and H. Bailey Carroll, ed. *Handbook of Texas*. Three Vols. Austin: Texas State Historical Association, 1952.

_____."Texas Collection." *Southwestern Historical Quarterly* XLVIII (July 1944): 107–108.

West, S. H. "Life and Times of S. H. West." Sherman Public Library. Unpublished Manuscript.

"Wide Awake." *Grolier Encyclopedia*, Vol. 10. 1951.

Wilbarger, J. W. *Indian Depredations in Texas*. Austin: Pemberton Press, 1967.

Williams, J. W. "The Butterfield Overland Mail Road Across Texas." *Southwestern Historical Quarterly*, LXI (July 1957): 1–19.

_____. "Journey of the Leach Wagon Train Across Texas." *West Texas Historical Quarterly* XXIX (1957): 115–77.

Winkler, Ernest William, ed. *Journal of the Secession Convention of Texas 1861*. Austin: Texas Library and Historical Commission, 1912.

Woolford, Sam, ed. "The Burr Duval Diary." *Southwestern Historical Quarterly* LXV (April 1962): 487–511.

Wright, Muriel H. "The Butterfield Overland Mail One Hundred Years Ago." *The Chronicles of Oklahoma* 25 (1957): 1–12.

Wright, Muriel H., George H. Shirk, and Kenny A. Franks. *Mark of Heritage*. Oklahoma City: Oklahoma Historical Society, 1976.

Index

Big Rocky Creek, 163–64
Big Sandy Creek, 144
Big Spring, Texas, 37
Big Tree (Indian chief), 147, 235–37
Birch, Barnabas, 228
Birch, Dr., 47, 49
Birch, James E., 112, 233
Birchville, 112, 201
Bishop, Absalom, 95
Blackburn, Casper, 36
Blackburn's station (Brush Settlement, Indian Territory), 36
Blair, Montgomery, 100
blimp, 193
Bloss, Roy S., 264
Bloys Camp Meeting, 108, 193, 241–42
Bloys, William B., 241–42
Blue River, 37
Bluff Creek, 153
Border Command, 237
Bourland, James, 223
Bowie, Arizona, 206
Bowie, George Washington, 213n
Bradley, W., 136
Brandon, J. B., 95
Brandon's station, 95. *See also* stations
Brazeal, Thomas, 236
Brazos River, 45, 150; Clear Fork of, 47, 50, 148–49, 151, 153, 155
Bridgeport, Texas, 46, 95, 96, 132, 142, 144, 178
bridges, 95, 96, 134, 141, 142, 145, 146, 150, 155, 174, 197
Bronte, Texas, 132, 162
Brown, Aaron Venable, 14, 15, 217
Brown, Vernon H., 269
Bryan, F. T., 61, 75
Bryan, John Neely, 28n
Buckley, William, 252
Buckley, William H., 268
Buckley, William M., 231
Buddmatthews, 153
Buena Vista, Texas, 186

Buffalo soldiers, 62
bugle call, 19
Bump-Gate, Texas, 159
Burlington, Mr. and Mrs., 49
Burnet County, Texas, 61
Burro Mountains, 205
Burrows, H. D., 23
Butterfield, Charles, E., 27n
Butterfield, Daniel, 27–28n
Butterfield, David A., 210n
Butterfield Gap, 153, 162
Butterfield, John, 2, 9, 11, 12–13, 16, 21–22, 26, 35, 36, 39, 111, 263–65
Butterfield, John Jay, 27n, 36
Butterfield Overland Mail, The, 1
Butterfield Overland Mail, The, 1857–1869, 2
Butts, George N., 79n
Bynum, Josephine M., 1
Byrne, James J., 248–50
Byrne, Lilly Loving, 249–50

California, 10, 13, 15
California Overland Express, 15
"California Stage Company, The" (ballad), 24–25
Call, Oscar, 61
camel experiment, 106, 107, 115
Camp Charlotte, 60, 62, 166
Camp Cooper, 47, 156, 159
Camp Johnston station, 98. *See also* stations
Camp Joseph E. Johnston, 59, 164
Camp Melbourne Crossing, 121n
Camp Rice. *See* Fort Hancock
Camp Stockton. *See* Fort Stockton
Campbell, Robert B., 244
Cape Horn, 10
Carbine and Lance, 237
Cardis, Luis, 114
Carlsbad, Texas, 163
Carriage Point (Fisher's) station, 37. *See also* stations

Franz's station, 46, 151, 152. *See also* stations
French, Albert, 88n
French, S. G., 109, 126n
Fresnell, August (driver), 107
Frizzell, John D., 269
Frizzell, John D., Jr., 269
Fronteras, 118
Frontier Hotel, 116–17

Gainesville, Texas, 42, 80n, 96, 132, 138; station, 41, 137. *See also* stations
Gallagher, Barney, 69
Gallagher, Peter, 121n, 187
Gallatin, Albert, 243
Gardner, James V. P., 27
Garrard, Lieutenant, 218
Gaston, William H., 84n
Geary, A. W., 37
Geary's station, 37. *See also* stations
Gholson, Sam, 51
Giddings, George, 233
Giddings, William H., 232
Gildea, A. M. (Gus), 62, 69
Gillett, James B., 75, 107, 109, 192, 193, 239
Gilmore, John T., 230
Girvin, Texas, 173
Glover, James, 66, 69, 73
gold, 10, 122n
gold mines, 39
Goodnight, Charles, 101
Goodnight-Loving Trail, 101, 164, 174
Goold, James, 17, 18
Graham, Texas, 145
Grand Falls, Texas, 68, 99
Grape Creek station, 58, 59, 97, 163. *See also* stations
Gray, Andrew B., 244
Grayson County, Texas, 39, 135, 224, 225. *See also* Sherman, Texas
Great Gainesville Hanging, The, 41, 219–32

"Great Overland Mail Contract," 11
"Great Southern Overland, The," 14–15
Greeley, Horace, 30n, 55, 85n
Green, J. R. (Bob), 97, 152–54, 194
Green, Nancy, 194
Greene, A. C., 3, 131–209
Greene, Judy, 3, 131–209
Greenwood, Texas, 141
Grierson, Benjamin H., 250
Guadalupe Mountains, 54, 68, 70, 73, 100, 176, 182
Guadalupe National Park, 90n, 177, 178
Guadalupe Peak, 70, 178–79
Gwin, W. M., 11

Hackberry Pond, 103
Hafen, Leroy, 267
Hague, J. P., 117
Halff, Mayer, 170
Happy Valley, Texas, 159
Harney, William S., 100
Harper's Weekly, 106
Hawley, Giles, 231
Hawley, Mrs., 229–31
Hays, John Coffee, 122n
hazards, 10; attacks, 9, 45, 51, 58, 72, 98, 104–105, 106, 110; floods, 97; weather, 67, 111, 177–78
Head of Concho station, 61, 62, 63, 99, 166. *See also* stations
Helms, Elijah, 58–59
Herald (Dallas newspaper), 267
Herald (New York newspaper), 37, 41, 72
Highsmith, Samuel, 122n
Hill, James B. & Sons, 17
historical markers, 41, 64, 74, 102, 110, 136, 137, 140, 142–43, 145, 146–47, 150, 153, 157, 160, 163, 173, 175, 189–90, 200, 203, 255
History of Young County, Texas, A, 237
Hog Eye Prairie region, 43
Holland, Alexander, 27n
Holloway, William, 36

Leon Water Hole station (*Agua Delgada*), 102–103, 187. *See also* stations
Leslie, Frank, 106
lighting. *See* vehicles
Limpia Creek, 189, 190, 191
Limpia Hotel, 191
Limpia Station, 104, 105, 188
Little Rock, Arkansas, 16
Livingston & Fargo. *See* American Express Company
Llano Estacado, 52, 59, 61, 66, 98
Llano Estacado station, 170. *See also* stations
Lobo, Texas, 110
Long, Nathan S., 147, 235
Longstreet, James, 71
Lordsburg, New Mexico, 205
Los Angeles, California, 132, 256
Los Tres Hermanos ranch. *See* ranches
Lost Creek, 145
Lost Creek station. *See also* stations
Lost Love, 30n
Loving County, Texas, 99, 174
Loving, Oliver, 101
Lyndon B. Johnson National Grasslands, 140

Mabry, W. S., 234
McCamey, Texas, 132, 172
McCullough, Henry E., 55
McDonald Observatory, Mount Locke, 190, 191
McHenry, Mr. (freighter), 67
MacKenzie, Ranald S., 236
McKinney, Bobby, 87n
McKinney, Texas, 96
McKittrick Canyon, 177
Magoffinville, Texas, 185
mail service, 16–17, 20, 22, 35, 60, 66, 67, 96, 109, 115, 192–93, 217–19, 232–34, 247, 254; Eastbound mail, 45, 53, 66; foreign mail, 26; rates, 26, 192; Westbound mail, 36, 39, 55, 66. *See also*

timetable stations
Major Peak, 106
Maman-ti (Sky-Walker, medicine chief), 236, 239
Marcy, Randolph, 48, 50, 70, 75, 97, 122n, 176, 218, 235, 253
Marcy trail, 137, 218
markers. *See* historical markers
Maryetta, Texas, 144
Mather, Mr. (rider), 56
Matthews, J. A., 153
Matthews, Joe B., 97
Matthews, Watt, 97, 152–53
Matthews-Lambshead Ranch. *See* ranches, Lambshead Ranch
Matthews-Reynolds ranches. *See* ranches
Maximilian's treasure, 65, 172
Mayhall, Mildred, 237
Means, Jackie, 194
Means, John Zack, 241
Means, Jon, 194, 195
Means Moon Ranch. *See* ranches
Mellard, Rudolph, 234
Memphis, Tennessee, 11, 12, 13, 14, 16
Mentone, Texas, 174
Merkel, Texas, 132
Mesilla, New Mexico, 119, 204, 205
Mesilla *Times*, 116
Mexican-U. S. War, 114, 118, 122n
Mexico, 101, 111, 199
Michler, Nathaniel, 122n
Middle Concho station, 60. *See also* stations
Middle Kings Creek, 151
Milky Way (Commanche Chief), 238
Mills, Anson, 54–55, 96, 101, 115–16
Mills, William W., 88n
mines. *See* coal mines; gold mines
Mississippi River, 11, 13
Missouri, 11, 13, 15, 21
Missouri, Kansas and Texas Railroad. *See* railroads

101, 166, 172–74, 197
Pecos Valley Southern Railroad. *See* rail-
roads
Pecos, Texas, 174
Pennington, Joel, 58–59
*Personal Narrative of Explorations and
Incidents in Texas, New Mexico,
California, Sonora and Chihuahua
1850–1853,* 242
personnel. *See* employees
Peters Colony, 52, 184
petroglyphs, 76–77, 184
Phelps, John S., 11
Pierpont Ranch station, 112. *See also* sta-
tions
Pilot Point, Texas, 95, 96, 132
Pine Springs, 177
Pinery station, 70–71, 77, 177, 178–79.
See also stations
Point of Rocks, 107, 192
Polancio, Jose Maria, 71
Pontoon Crossing of the Pecos. *See*
Camp Melbourne Crossing
Pool, Billy, 171
Pope, John, 53, 66, 68, 89n, 99, 218
Pope's Camp, 66, 68, 69, 70, 99, 175, 218,
219
Porterville, Texas, 99
Post at El Paso. *See* Fort Bliss
Post on the Clear Fork of the Brazos. *See*
Fort Phantom Hill
postal rates. *See* mail service
Poteau River, 36
Pratt, R. H., 237
Press-Argue (Van Buren, Arkansas,
newspaper), 269
Preston, Texas, 14, 28n, 37, 79n
Proffitt Cemetery. *See* cemeteries
Proffitt, Texas, 233
Prude, John, 242
Prude, Ora Jane Pruett, 242
Pumpelly, Raphael, 30–31n
Pusley, Silas, 36
Pusley's station, 36. *See also* stations

Quien Sabe ranch. *See* ranches
Quitman Pass, 110, 197–99

railroads, Cisco & Northeastern, 151,
152; Houston & Texas Central, 80n;
Missouri, Kansas & Texas, 80n, 135,
153; Pacific, 35; Panama, 10; Pecos
Valley Southern, 188; Rio Grande
Northern, 110; Rio Grande Valley
Traction Company, 113; Rock Island,
96, 144, 145; Santa Fe, 118, 167, 204;
Southern Pacific, 109–110, 111, 136,
193, 194, 195, 196, 234; Texas & Pacif-
ic, 137, 195, 196, 234; Texas Export,
144; Union Pacific, 111
Ramstein, Henry, 70
ranches, Barrel Springs, 109, 193; Buck
Nail, 155; Circle Dot, 170; Concor-
dia, 116, 185; Davis, 154; Frank Con-
rad, 154; Hunter, 179; J. L. Nail, 47,
153; Lambshead, 47, 152–53; Los Tres
Hermanos, 119; Matthews-Reynolds
ranches, 97; Means Moon, 194;
Quien Sabe, 170; Reynolds Long X,
194; Rocker B, 194; South Spring, 69;
Spencer's, 88n
Rankin, Texas, 65, 132, 170
Rawls, Fletcher, 242
Rawls, Tom, 242
Red Bluff Lake, 175
Red River, 36, 37, 40, 134, 135, 138, 218
Reeves County, 104
Reynolds Long X Ranch. *See* ranches
Richardson, Addy Sage (McFarland),
30n
Richardson, Albert D., 2, 4–5, 20–21,
30n, 37, 43–44, 46, 49, 55, 64, 66, 97,
100, 101, 106, 108, 111, 115, 117, 145,
162, 255
Richardson, Mary Louise (Pearce), 30n
Richardson, Rupert N., 253–54, 255
Riddle, John, 36
Riddle's station, 36

Cross Creek
Visalia
Packwood
Tule River
(Las Vegas)
Fountain Spring
Mountain House (Woody)
Miguel
Paso Robles
Poso Creek
Kern River
(Bakersfield)
Gordon's Ferry
San Luis Obispo
Kern River Slough
⑨ Sink of Tejon
Beale's Ranch
Rose's
Tehachapi Pass
Tejon Pass
FT. TEJON Est. 1854
Reed's
Mud Spring
(Barstow)
French Jonn's
Widow Smith's
Santa Barbara
King's
Hart's
San Buena Ventura
San Fernando
Cahuenga
El Monte
San Jose
Cajon Pass
Los Angeles
San Bernardino
Pomona
Chino Ranch
Temescal
⑧ Laguna Grande
Willows
Temecula
Tehunga
SALTON SEA
248 ft. below sea level
Oak Grove
Warners
Palm Sprg
San Felipe
Vallecito
Carrizo Creek
(El Centro)
Sand Hills
Old Town
Hall's Wells
Indian Wells
(Calexico)
Monument
San Diego
Alamo Mocho
Gardeners Wells
Cooke's Wells
BAJA CALIFORNIA
Old Courier Route to Mexico